Gender Roles and Sexuality in Victorian Literature

edited by

CHRISTOPHER PARKER

SCOLAR PRESS

Published by
SCOLAR PRESS
Gower House
Croft Road
Aldershot
Hants GU11 3HR
England

Ashgate Publishing Company
Old Post Road
Brookfield
Vermont 05036
USA

British Library Cataloguing in Publication Data

Gender Roles and Sexuality in Victorian Literature
I. Parker, Christopher
820.9008

ISBN 1–85928–146–X

Library of Congress Cataloging-in-Publication Data

Gender roles and sexuality in Victorian literature / edited by
  Christopher Parker.
      p.   m.
    ISBN 1–85928–146–X
    1. English literature—19th century—History and criticism.
2. Sex in literature. 3. Women and literature—Great Britain—History—19th
century. 4. Gender identity in literature. 5. Sex role in literature. I. Parker,
Christopher, Principal Lecturer and Head of History.
PR468. S48G46 1995
820.9'3538'09034—dc20   94–42738
                                    CIP

ISBN 1 85928 146 X

Typeset in Sabon by Raven Typesetters, Chester and printed in Great Britain by
Biddles Ltd, Guildford.

Gender Roles and Sexuality in Victorian Literature

Contents

The Nineteenth Century

General Editors' Preface

The aim of this series is to reflect, develop and extend the great burgeoning of interest in the nineteenth century that has been an inevitable feature of recent decades, as that former epoch has come more sharply into focus as a locus for our understanding, not only for the past but of the contours of our modernity. Though it is dedicated principally to the publication of original monographs and symposia in literature, history, cultural analysis, and associated fields, there will be a salient role for reprints of significant texts from, or about, the period. Our overarching policy is to address the spectrum of nineteenth-century studies without exception, achieving the widest scope in chronology, approach and range of concern. This, we believe, distinguishes our project from comparable ones, and means, for example, that in the relevant areas of scholarship we both recognize and cut innovatively across such parameters as those suggested by the designations 'Romantic' and 'Victorian'. We welcome new ideas, while valuing tradition. It is hoped that the world which predates yet so forcibly predicts and engages our own will emerge in parts, as a whole, and in the lively currents of debate and change that are so manifest an aspect of its intellectual, artistic and social landscape.

Vincent Newey
Joanne Shattock

University of Leicester

List of Illustrations

Notes on Contributors

Brian Maidment is Professor and Dean of Modular Programmes at Edge Hill College of Higher Education. He is the author of *The Poorhouse Fugitives: Self-taught Poets and Poetry in Victorian Britain* and *The Discourses of Popular Prints 1790–1860* (forthcoming). He was the editor of the *Tennyson Research Bulletin* (1977–81) and co-editor of *Human Passions Delineated*; he is editing a new edition of Edward Jenkins's *Ginx's Baby*. He has published a number of articles on Ruskin, Joseph Jacobs, working-class Victorian literature, popular culture and many other themes.

Cynthia Dereli is a lecturer in Modern European Cultural Studies at Edge Hill College of Higher Education. She has just completed a PhD thesis on the literature of the Crimean War.

Christopher Parker is Head of History at Edge Hill College of Higher Education. He is the author of *The English Historical Tradition since 1850*, and several articles and essays on the history and philosophy of history, liberalism, and racialism and literature.

Murray Steele is Head of Afro-Asian Studies at Edge Hill College of Higher Education. He has published on a range of subjects relating to Southern Africa, including articles and essays on Olive Schreiner, Doris Lessing and Arthur Shearly Cripps.

John Simons is Head of Humanities and Arts at Edge Hill College of Higher Education. He is the co-editor of *The Two Angry Women of Abington, The Poems of Lawrence Minot, New York: City as Text*, editor of *From Medieval to Medievalism*, author of *Cricket in Hampshire 1760–1914* and *Six Chapbook Romances* (forthcoming). He has also written numerous articles on English and American literature and popular culture.

Lyn Pykett is Senior Lecturer in English at the University of Wales, Aberystwyth. She has published widely on various aspects of nineteenth-century writing, and contemporary fiction. She is the author of *Emily Brontë*, and *The 'Improper' Feminine: the Women's Sensation Novel and the New Woman Fiction* (Routledge, 1992). A book on turn-of-the-century discourses of the feminine and the origins of Modernism will be published shortly.

Jeffrey Richards is Professor of Cultural History at Lancaster University. He is the author of *Visions of Yesterday, Britain Can Take It* and *Happiest Days: the Public Schools in English Fiction*, and editor of *Imperialism and Juvenile Literature*.

Fiona Montgomery is Head of Women's Studies at Edge Hill College of Higher Education. She is the author of several articles on a variety of themes including women's education, popular radicalism and culture, the Unstamped Press and gender and suffrage.

Acknowledgements

I would like to thank all the contributors. In particular, I thank Jeffrey Richards for helping me to a clearer perception of the theme of our book, and Fiona Montgomery for her most valuable suggestions regarding the Introduction, the faults of which remain stubbornly my own. I would also like to thank my College and Tina Hadlow for assistance in preparing the book.

Introduction

Christopher Parker

The Victorian debates about gender roles and sexuality owe most of their origin to the 'Woman Question'. The role of women in society was an issue that produced, in the words of some modern writers, 'prescriptive pronouncements, protests, and imaginative literature'. We shall be mainly concerned with imaginative literature, but it is important to note the wider dimensions of the debates, and we can start by sampling the protest and prescriptive pronouncement forms though not necessarily as typical of their genres, for it has also been acknowledged that there was an enormous variety of opinion on the subject and that not all voices spoke consistently or predictably.[1] It has been said that Victorian novelists, in particular, 'reflected in a peculiarly vivid and urgent way the social anxieties of their time',[2] but we shall see that a host of campaigners, educationists, philosophers and historians also were drawn to the debate.

It could be argued that any introduction to the conceptualization of gender roles in the modern period, and especially to the 'Woman Question' in Britain, has to start with Mary Wollstonecraft's *A Vindication of the Rights of Woman*. In one sense, this is true, in that she wrote what is now commonly regarded as the original 'manifesto' of feminism.[3] It is also true that her manifesto anticipated most of the issues that later feminists and their opponents debated, including the fundamental one about women's essential character *vis-à-vis* men, arguing that the weaknesses and lack of rights of women in her own society were the result of poor education and prejudicial attitudes. If you think you have found mention of a new angle in later writers, you go back to Wollstonecraft and find that, to some extent at least, she has probably dealt with it: the importance of a healthy life and physical education for women ('. . . should it be proved that woman is naturally weaker than man, whence does it follow that it is natural for her to labour to become still weaker than nature intended her to be'); whether that physical education should be for beauty or strength; whether supposed feminine characteristics had been correctly identified; whether women should fear to be dubbed 'masculine' and which of the supposed masculine traits they should aspire to (nobility of purpose, not 'coarseness'); the relationship between the role of women and their rank or class;[4] and so on; the list is long. Yet in another sense, Wollstonecraft is not our natural starting point. It is generally accepted that she had no immediate intellectual heirs of stature and influence, that because of her life-style, her associations, and the changing political and intellectual climate after her early death in 1797, her message was largely ignored. Not till the 1850s, the decade in which our own topics begin, did the 'Woman Question' become widely discussed and then generally lead to a wider consideration of gender roles in general.[5] Despite a few precursors, most books on Victorian feminists start their studies around 1850.[6] By then the political climate in which Wollstonecraft located her arguments (the French Revolution and the Radical response in Britain) had long gone and was wisely not referred to a great deal. And the intellectual context, which had had her engaging with Rousseau, had changed, as had the very language itself. So, in one sense, most of her intellectual heirs belong to the great rediscovery of her in and after the 1960s.

It is also often said that the new breed of campaigners for women's rights in that mid-Victorian period concentrated their fire on specific practical issues such as education, the legal status of women with particular reference to married women's property rights and divorce, and eventually the delicate matter of the vote, rather than broader, philosophical issues and the nature of gender. There is some truth in this but inevitably wider issues were addressed, particularly when the topic of women's education was discussed, because this raised the question of just what were women capable of, if properly educated. Particularly important in this respect were Barbara Leigh Smith Bodichon and the Langham Place Group (especially through *The English Woman's Journal*) and those who pioneered higher education for women. This gave the debate a middle-class focus but it raised the vital issue of innate abilities versus socialization. For our present purposes we can briefly illustrate the debate from the perspective of Bodichon and Emily Davies, one of the founders of Girton College.

Bodichon, in her 1857 tract, 'Women and Work', arguing that women were God's children equally with men, found that what should have been lives dedicated to serving God's purpose ('the progress of the world') were, in fact, made redundant to this purpose by social convention and control, which assumed that they were fit to serve only men. Women were unable to stand 'face to face with God'. They languished in purposeless idleness, succumbing to 'hysteria', early ageing, and pettiness. She argued that marriage need not be the ultimate purpose of a woman's life, and might not always be possible – which was certainly true at the time. She cited Dr Elizabeth Blackwell, and even Queen Victoria, as women with other purposes in life. If only women could be educated and put to fulfilling work ('not drudgery'), they would be healthier and happier -- not 'listless, idle, empty-brained, empty-hearted' and even 'ugly' as they too often were. She covered a wide agenda, including even things like the constraining effects of women's long clothes which limited their roles as they limited their movements.[7] That this was a middle-class agenda is not the issue for our purpose, which is to note that she believed that women's characters and current disabilities were the products of what Mill was to call the 'subjugation' of women, not of inherent weaknesses.

Six years later Emily Davies, writing in support of the campaign to allow women to have a university education, reckoned that the arguments of her opponents 'resolve themselves, for the most part, into an "instinct", a prejudice, or an unproved assertion that women ought not to pursue the same studies as men; and that they would become exceedingly unwomanly if they did', losing their 'gentleness', 'grace', 'sweet vivacity' and indeed their minds, and becoming 'cold, calculating, masculine, fast, strongminded, and in a word, generally unpleasing'. She identified the central issue – that 'the differences between a man and a woman are either essential or conventional or both'. She thought that, in most observable respects, they were likely to be conventional, and that in other respects it was simply impossible to comprehend differences if they were truly of the essence of only one gender, in that nobody could claim to have experienced both male and female personalities. If, as was generally believed, women had certain talents and men had their virtues – if indeed

> the strength of the woman . . . is in the heart; the strength of the man, in the head. The woman can suffer patiently; the man can act bravely. The woman has a loving care for the individual; the man an impassioned reverence for the general and the universal

if this really was the case, then these undeniably desirable qualities should still be striven for by all, men and women. Davies was quite prepared to argue that, if men and women did naturally incline to certain behaviours, they should still try to become rounded individuals even if that meant learning from each other's characteristics. However, she distanced herself from 'Amazons', 'Bloomerism and other ugly eccentricities', 'the fast women and the masculine women'. Neither would educated women be 'the hard and cold women', for such were more likely to be created by the current upbringing, in an atmosphere of frivolity and pettiness, of most middle-class women.[8] Davies's attitudes are a good illustration of the complexity of some of the positions adopted on the gender issue.

Women like Bodichon and Davies, like Frances Power Cobbe, Elizabeth Garrett, Elizabeth Blackwell, and Harriet Taylor, although they all knew each other and worked together, represented a variety of views, not all of them as liberal as might be expected. But they set the agenda in the 1850s and 1860s; they asked the questions, and forced others, supporters and opponents, men and other women, to answer them. Harriet Taylor is of special interest because of her link with John Stuart Mill, whom she eventually married. Those women who wanted the vote had to use Mill as their spokesman in the Commons; and, several years after Harriet's death, he finally published what was to become one of the best-known attacks upon the subjection of women.

In 1869, coincidentally at the exact mid-point of Queen Victoria's reign, and after two decades of growing controversy about the 'Woman Question', John Stuart Mill at last published *The Subjection of Women* (it had been written in 1861), and in the same year W.E.H. Lecky published his two volumes on the *History of European Morals from Augustus to Charlemagne*, which contained a substantial last chapter on 'The Position of Women'. Despite his supposed historical purpose, Lecky looked to the future and discussed contemporary issues as much as did Mill, and it was a future that was to see an intensification of the debate particularly in the matter of sexuality, which to some extent Lecky anticipated with a dread of 'wild' theories. Despite this dread, both pieces have in common a typically mid-Victorian Liberal progressivism (both men were Liberal MPs), both claim to be defending women's rights – and both are written by men; though with *The Subjection of Women* there is considerable debate about the input of Harriet Taylor before her death in 1858. Here the similarities end. Mill's is regarded as the classic liberal statement of not only the equality of the sexes but their essential similarity, apparent inequalities and differences being explained as social, not biological in origin:

> I deny that any one knows, or can know the nature of the two sexes, as long as they have only been seen in their present relation to one another . . . What is now called the nature of women is an eminently artificial thing – the result of forced repression in some directions, unnatural stimulation in others.[9]

In contrast, Lecky, proclaiming that 'It is the part of a woman to lean, it is the part of a man to stand', represents the classic view that men and women are inherently different and that in the most important respects, whatever women's merits in some specifics, men are superior. Nature or nurture, society or biology: here we have a fundamental dichotomy. Though it is not, of course, true to say that all those who supported the emancipation of women believed in Mill's ungendered egalitarianism; nor is it true that all those who adopted Lecky's approach, Lecky included, can be regarded as wholly conservative on the matter.

'It is one of the characteristic prejudices of the reaction of the nineteenth century against the eighteenth, to accord to the unreasoning elements in human nature the infallibility which the eighteenth century is supposed to have ascribed to the reasoning elements,' wrote Mill. 'For the apotheosis of Reason we have substituted that of Instinct; and we call everything instinct which we find in ourselves and for which we cannot trace any rational foundation.'[10] For Mill, the subordination of women and the assumption of natural mental differences between the sexes were irrational, unnecessary, indefensible on grounds of instinct or nature, and in need of new attitudes. Men denied women equality of opportunity in order to retain 'their subordination in domestic life', and there was no evidence that, freed from domestic slavery (and Mill drew parallels with slavery), women were unsuited to public life and responsibility.[11] He would have no truck with physiological evidence about brain size or shape.[12] With a typically Utilitarian individualism, he concluded that to disadvantage half the species was to diminish the total of human happiness on a grand scale and leave 'the species less rich, to an appreciable degree, in all that makes life valuable to the individual human being'.[13]

But Mill's approach was not typical of social attitudes as a whole. As Davidoff and Hall have indicated, 'By the 1830s and 1840s . . . the belief in the natural differences and complementary roles of men and women which had originally been linked to Evangelicalism, had become the common sense of the middle class'.[14] And this certainly remained true for the rest of the century. Lecky, who had recently been lionized in London literary society and was at the height of his influence, was much more representative of his attitude, yet in one way he started from the same historical assumption as Mill; both men assumed that the subjection of women began in the barbarian world because of man's physical strength, and the 'value' he attached to women as Mill put it, or because she was 'the minister to his passions' as Lecky, rather more boldly, put it. Both men used a terminology of 'slavery'. Lecky was the most graphic:

> Woman is looked upon merely as the slave of man, and as the minister of his passions. In the first capacity, her life is one of continual, abject, and unrequited toil. In the second capacity, she is exposed to all the violent revulsions of feeling that follow, among rude men, the gratification of the animal passions.

But the essential difference between the two was that Mill regarded this historical explanation of women's subjection as the start of an argument to demonstrate that the existing laws, institutions and attitudes that related to the subjection of women were derived from predecessors that had merely recognized the original brute facts of life, and in no way constituted an argument for maintaining the *status quo*. Lecky, by contrast, saw even the crude early family, which he thought of as originally enslaving women, as the vehicle for reform and transformation: the very fact of a marriage ceremony regularized, according to laws and precedents, the relationships of the sexes, and with the abandonment of wife purchase (which he thought occurred very early on) and the adoption of monogamy, the family was set fair to become, not the vehicle for women's subjugation, but progressively her liberation and her defence, provided that the 'many wild theories' that were probably due to be propounded did not push things too far.[15] In general, to see the family as a vehicle for reform was about as far as most contemporary opinion would go; more frequently, the presumption that it was the earliest form of social relationship, before civil society or the state, and indeed the basis for both, gave it the status of being 'natural' and, therefore, not to be challenged, perhaps even being beyond reproach.[16] And Lecky's partially conservative intents are clear; if the 'wild theories' can be avoided, then perfection is close to hand.

One of the most striking features of Lecky's chapter is that, though entitled 'The Position of Women', it is almost entirely about carnal relationships between men and women. The rest of the book was about other aspects of morals and, thus, by implication, about men not women; nothing could be a better unwitting illustration of the subjection of women. For this reason he approached the subject with, as he put it, 'hesitation' and 'extreme delicacy', aware of the risk of causing 'scandal or offence'.[17] As The Times's reviewer of Elizabeth Braddon's Lady Audley's Secret put it in 1862, with reference to its scandalous heroine, and with remarkable candour, 'Now, the most interesting side of a woman's character is her relation to the other sex, and the errors of women that are most interesting spring out of this relation.'[18] We should remember that women were, quite simply, 'the sex', a terminology which stressed the gendered and, by implication, exceptional character of women,[19] as if they alone were dominated by gender, by their natural biological functions, and as if they were a departure from the norm. For Lecky, carnal lust was truly the original sin because 'the natural force of this appetite' was, in a Malthusian sense, 'far greater than the well-being of man requires'. The family was both the way of controlling and civilizing this natural force, and as such 'the centre and the archetype of the State' upon which the health of society depended, and also at odds with this force, which would break out – by going to a prostitute, for example – 'that unhappy being whose very name is a shame to speak'.[20] Prostitution was currently the subject of great debate and concern, which is very revealing about mid-Victorian attitudes to sexuality and gender roles in general.

At the heart of Lecky's argument was the assumption that, though the trend of modern history was to improve the lot of women, men and women remained essentially different and unequal. Physically, men were stronger, though women had more beauty. 'Intellectually, a certain inferiority of the female sex can hardly be denied', the highest forms of genius being confined to men – an argument refuted, in detail, by Mill.

Specifically, women were 'intellectually more desultory and volatile' – a characteristic Mill had explained in terms of their subjection, if indeed it existed at all. Lecky also believed that women were intuitive rather than reasoning, 'usually superior to men in nimbleness and rapidity of thought, and in the gift of tact' – and so on; probably we could all complete his list of women's supposed intellectual strengths and weaknesses. They were also morally superior, more inclined to self-sacrifice, but they could also fall victim to the petty vices of vanity, jealousy, spitefulness and ambition. They had less 'active courage' than men, but more 'passive' courage – not fortitude exactly, that was stronger and more masculine, but a 'resignation which bears and bends'. 'In the ethics of intellect' they were inferior to men, feeling rather than thinking, inclining to mercy where men inclined to justice. The poor things even aged less well than men: men acquired wisdom, dignity and even greater physical beauty; women just grew eccentric.[21]

Lecky adopted an essentially protective attitude towards women. He regarded himself as a progressive, but feared an anarchy of ideas in a godless age of rapid social change which threatened the family, took the women out of the home, gave rise to prostitution, and left a surplus of women without a male protector in a world that had not been built for them; the family was the essential unit for the protection of women, for population control, for the prevention of prostitution and venereal disease, and to make sexual relations respectable. For Lecky, who expressed all the classic concerns of men confronted with the 'Woman Question', that question was clearly a problem not an opportunity. In all of this he was more typical of his age and of male middle-class attitudes than Mill's philosophical liberalism.

Mill and Lecky wrote explicitly, and they represent a clear-cut division between rationalism and intuitionism, between egalitarianism and separate spheres; Lecky was an ardent critic of the utilitarian tradition from which Mill came. Yet both were reckoned to be Liberals in political terms – and in this respect they were typical of the 1860s. But the age saw much literature that was less explicit in its pronouncements about gender roles, yet just as ideologically committed; the dividing line between philosophical and ethical tracts and creative literature is unclear. In one respect didactic fiction has particular advantages for the historian of ideas; as Dyhouse has said, 'a novel can arguably encompass more complexity, nuance, and ambiguity in stance' than personal testimony or polemic.[22] Yet much fiction that appears non-didactic is also very revealing of attitudes to gender. Thus there is a continuum from works of philosophy and ethics, like Mill's, through histories that make comments on ethical issues of contemporary concern, like Lecky's, novels with a clear didactic purpose, like Mona Caird's, which nonetheless have the quality of 'aesthetic artefacts' (Lyn Pykett), to apparently non-didactic novels, like R.D. Blackmore's, but whose constructions of gender were by no means as naive as might at first sight appear.

This volume involves the interaction of literature and cultural history, and contributors come from both disciplines in roughly equal proportions. They see that literature can be studied as an historical phenomenon. This is not to deny that literature may be other things – even to the same people. But a work of literature constitutes an historical event inasmuch as does an Act of Parliament, a stock market crash or a diplomatic crisis, even though it may need to be treated differently. All but the most dyed-in-the-wool philosophical idealists or the most intransigent materialists would now accept that literature is not simply a vehicle for the ideas that make society, nor solely a product of economic and social conditions. A work of literature is, itself, a social fact; literature is an aspect of society's many activities.

Specifically, literature is an aspect of society's culture; and culture, in general, is now regarded as a legitimate subject for historical inquiry. It can be seen as both a response to and an expression of popular attitudes, and as an influence. We turn to it, no doubt, because we live in an age dominated by the images of popular culture and acutely self-conscious about the nature of its own cultural identity; we experience and observe our own cultural influences. Reasoning by analogy, we can gain insight into recent cultural history, particularly in the last century and a half, as our modern means of communication developed. It was during the Victorian era that widespread literacy and the development of large-scale publishing began a series of radical changes in the way that culture was expressed and disseminated; and it was during that era that first the 'Woman Question' and then wider issues of gender roles and sexuality became topics of discourse.

Some of the best-sellers of this era have remained in the popular consciousness for several generations, acquiring the status of classic texts, though often because they are reproduced in other media; as classic texts they lose their historical specificity; but most works of even best-selling authors sink into obscurity. These 'other' works form an essential context for the better-known texts, and were often popular enough in their own day. Thus Bram Stoker has to be understood by more than *Dracula*; and Blackmore by more than *Lorna Doone*. Neither were campaigning writers, but their books are full of the social prejudices and attitudes of their authors.

Other so-called 'minor' writers such as Olive Schreiner, Mona Caird, and Edward Carpenter addressed social and political issues, including those of gender and sexuality, directly, didactically and radically. Campaigning writers, like these, often fulfilled other roles. Mona Caird was a campaigner and pamphleteer for women's rights; Edward Carpenter was active in the labour and socialist movements. Few writers lived solely by creative writing; Blackmore was a market gardener, as was Carpenter, though even if both used a modest inheritance to purchase their market gardens, they did have radically different ideas about what they wanted to get out of them; Stoker was Henry Irving's business manager. In all cases, it is impossible to separate the author from his or her other activities.

Additionally writers respond to historical events as traditionally defined (political, military, legislative, social, etc.), and there is interaction between their responses and those of the genre they employ. Some of our chapters, therefore, are thematic rather than relating to an individual author. Thus, there is a gender-conscious literature of the Crimean War. Individually, Edward Carpenter had already reacted against the anti-homosexual legislation of the late-Victorian period, just as women writers were responding to a new consciousness of women's rights in marriage, in politics and in society generally, and men sympathetic to women's rights dared to legislate for their education in the correct mores, for their changing role.

One need make no apology for having begun this introduction to gender roles and sexuality in Victorian literature with a consideration of the role of women, for both in the Victorian period itself with the 'Woman Question', and in the modern historiography on gender roles, women have come first, partly because women themselves have raised the issue but partly because – and this is true particularly in the mid-Victorian period – men have become concerned about women's roles as if women were a special or minority problem as far as gender is concerned. Only later does attention turn to the gender roles and sexuality of men. And now it is generally accepted that one can no more study a sex in isolation than one can study a class without looking at class relations. As Sally Alexander has put it: 'Feminism . . . has been . . . the principal contender in the struggles for the reorganization of sexual difference and division.'[23] And Brittan has noted that 'masculinity' did not exist as a topic 'until feminists began to attack the presuppositions of traditional political and social theory', suggesting that studies of masculinity were 'parasitic' on the insights of feminist theory and practice.[24] Once the genie was out of the bottle, masculinity and femininity could both be seen as possibly social constructions which did not conform precisely or unchangingly to biologically determined functions; once women were seen to be capable of challenging the limitations placed upon them in their separate sphere, then the whole question of cross-gender characteristics could come to the fore. Eventually Edward Carpenter was to talk of homosexuals as a third, intermediate sex.

However, the first task in this ultimately mould-breaking trend was to define, in effect, ideal types of gendered behaviour and character; the very fact that this needed to be done was proof of uncertainty, but initially the ideal types conformed to conventional stereotypes. The man exercised will and reason; his was the public sphere of business, or the professions, or the management of inherited property, or political life (from voting to government), or that ultimate test of physical prowess and active courage, of will and command – war. As Brittan has said: 'The way in which masculinism enters into nationalism is nowhere better exemplified than in the conduct of and aftermath of war.'[25] This more aggressive aspect of masculinity was controversial, however. Davidoff and Hall, amongst others, have seen a clash between two ideals:

> Masculine nature, in gentry terms, was based on sport and codes of honour derived from military prowess . . . Since many of the early Evangelicals came from gentry backgrounds they had to consciously establish novel patterns of manhood

which tied in with more middle-class attitudes. There was a new emphasis on sensitivity, steadfastness, conscience, and doing good – a less hearty, less boisterous ideal. These were to be the qualities of a true Christian gentleman – 'dangerously close to embracing "feminine" qualities'. But as the century wore on a less emotional, more stolid, perhaps severe, ideal of masculinity, 'doing God's duty in the world', 'dignified, serious and . . . properly masculine', won favour.[26] In this process it was also useful to present the Regency buck as an effeminate dandy, as well as a womanizer, aristocratic and decadent (to set against the hard-drinking, hunting image of the squirearchy), as a contrast to the soberly dressed, down-to-earth, mid-Victorian paterfamilias.[27]

Thomas Hughes provided one of the classic Victorian statements of 'manliness' in his sermon on *The Manliness of Christ*, in 1879. This was an attempt to reassure pubic-school boys that manliness should also be Christian; and it is even more revealing of his attitudes than Hughes intended: 'The conscience of every man recognises courage as the foundation of manliness, and manliness as the perfection of human character', said Hughes, moving effortlessly from manliness to the full 'human' character, thus elevating manly ideals to human ideals, and denying women the chance of perfection. This was said in the context of the wishes of our 'Father in heaven' and his son, 'our Master', who had set the agenda 'before individual men' and asked them to choose, to struggle for virtue, for 'courage or manfulness, gained through conflict with evil – for without such conflict there can be no perfection of character, the end for which Christ says we were sent into this world.'[28] Even allowing for his audience of Rugby schoolboys and, in a sense, Hughes's innocence of the wider gender issue, never can a gendered language have been more ideologically loaded, for only 'manfulness' allowed Christ's work to be done, only men could struggle and choose – and, in a sense, therefore, only men could be truly Christian and fully human.

The other interesting aspect of Hughes's definition of manliness is the distinction he drew between mere 'brutal', barbarian courage, 'brutal' being a term he used about the lower social orders as well as the lower animals, and a determination to do what was right – moral courage and steadfastness. Despite the rhetoric of war ('For we are born into a state of war, with falsehood, and disease, and wrong, and misery in a thousand forms, lying all around us, and the voice within calling on us to take our stand as men in the eternal battle against these'), and the references to Nelson as the ultimate hero, the true contemporary hero would have to win his wars in the peaceful spheres of everyday life: 'even in our peaceful and prosperous England, absolute truth of speech and rectitude of behaviour will not fail to bring their fiery trials.'[29] Here we have the classic example of the translation of an early warlike image of manliness into a peaceful, earnest one.

The ideal type of womanhood was suited to the private sphere, the home and the family, possessing gentleness, kindness, active sympathy – characteristics directly related to the role of daughter, wife, and mother. But what if men were seduced into adopting this softer role? There is no doubt that Victorians had a clear idea of what constituted appropriate qualities of femininity and masculinity, but they were quite willing to ascribe 'feminine' characteristics to men and 'masculine' characteristics to women, suggesting a fair amount of unease about gender roles once the issue had been opened. 'Unease' is probably the correct word, because, although there are examples of cross-gender characteristics being praised (a man might have his character softened by feminine sensibility, for example), in general femininity and masculinity in the wrong sex were regarded as a misfortune, undermining the integrity of the character. Manliness and femininity 'were constantly being tested, challenged, and reworked both in imagination and in the encounters of daily life'[30] in this period; but this meant that even for those who, like Lecky, argued that defined gender roles were natural and immutable, the paradox was that, once the need to define and redefine had been accepted, then there had been an acceptance that gender characteristics and roles were neither fixed, natural nor obvious. As it happens, one of the most famous attacks upon men supposedly displaying womanly characteristics dates from 1869, the year of Mills's and Lecky's interventions in the gender debate. This was Alfred Austin's attack upon Tennyson, Swinburne and Trollope, an attack of double interest to us for it is an attack on the feminization of literature and it was explicitly written in the context of Mill's protest against the Subjection of Women.

> If we were to sum up the characteristics of Mr Tennyson's composi-
> tions in a single word, the word we should employ would be 'femi-
> nine' . . . We have just had, from a much revered source an essay on
> the Subjection of Women; but we think it would not be difficult to
> show that men, and especially in the domain of Art, are, and have for
> some time been, quite as subject to women, to say the least of it, as is
> desirable.[31]

Swinburne, despite his protestations, was even less 'masculine' than
Tennyson; and Trollope, who was contrasted with the masculinity of
Scott, was 'a feminine novelist, writing for women in a womanly spirit
and', in case we have missed the point, 'from a woman's point of view'.
They all had 'womanly vices' and were 'steeped in the feminine temper of
the times'. Austin was careful to stress that he meant no disrespect to 'the
sex' itself, which was 'fair, devout, dear, and indispensable'. In other
words, feminine qualities were all right in their place, indeed indispensable – their place being women and women's place being in the home,
and certainly not in literature where they had been making quite a splash
in the 1860s through the sensation novels, some of which were written by
women and all of which displayed supposedly feminine qualities.
Tennyson's verses were 'all about women. What is "Maud" about?
Woman. What is "The Princess" about? Woman, woman. What are the
four "Idylls of the King" about? Woman, woman, woman, woman.'
Thus Austin avoided any femininity in his own style, by employing a
bludgeon which he wielded with, no doubt, masculine aggression. And
what was this fatal effeminacy? It was writing of love and emotion and,
intriguingly enough, romance between the sexes, rather than of grander
public themes. The sensational women novelists were even worse, for
they wrote of love and 'lust' – 'which begins with seduction and ends in
desertion', or those variations on the theme, 'bigamy, adultery, and, in
fact, illicit passion of every conceivable sort under every conceivable set
of circumstances'. Worse, the temptress heroines

> are more animal and impassioned than the heroes . . . It is the
> feminine element at work when it has ceased to be domestic; when it
> has quitted the modest precincts of home, and courted the garish
> light of an intense and warm publicity. It is the feminine element no
> longer in the nursery, the drawing-room, or the conjugal chamber,
> but unrestrainedly rioting in any and every arena of life.

This was the result of the fatal step of 'making women too conspicuous in
life and literature'.[32] It has been said that Austin was expressing 'in
extreme form the uneasy suspicions to which thirty years of public
debate had roused even the most scornful conservative on the Woman
Question'.[33]

Women had been breaking out from the domestic sphere, to which they had painstakingly been allotted, both 'in life and literature'. Few men, at least, agreed with Mill when he wrote: 'There remain no legal slaves, except the mistress of every house.'[34] Whatever the law might say about a wife's lack of rights, in particular her lack of a separate legal personality or identity, most would have agreed with Ruskin's comment in a passage from 'Of Queens' Gardens', published in *Sesame and Lilies* (1865), which has become one of the most quoted passages on gender roles in Victorian Britain:

> He is eminently the doer, the creator, the discoverer, the defender. His intellect is for speculation and invention; his energy for adventure, for war, and for conquest whenever war is just, wherever conquest necessary. But the woman's power is for rule, not for battle, – and her intellect is not for invention or creation, but for sweet ordering, arrangement, and decision. She sees the qualities of things, their claims, and their places. Her great function is Praise . . . The man, in his rough work in open world must encounter all peril and trial: – to him, therefore, the failure, the offence, the inevitable error: often he must be wounded, or subdued; often misled; and *always* hardened. But he guards the women from all this; within his house, as ruled by her, unless she herself has sought it, need enter no danger, no temptation, no cause of error or offence.[35]

Though by no stretch of the imagination can Ruskin be called a conventional figure, this passage is in some ways also representative of mid-Victorian middle-class attitudes to the active, public role of men, in the world of work and of national life, and the passive, supportive role of women in the home – attitudes expressed, however, in full consciousness of the stresses that such gender roles imposed, and with awareness that there were alternative views. For as Brian Maidment points out, Ruskin himself demonstrates anxiety as well as a conservative approach. Davidoff and Hall have suggested that, for some time before this, 'the masculine persona' of the middle classes 'was organized around a man's determination and skill in manipulating the economic environment' while recognizing that market forces were actually difficult to manipulate and could bite back.[36] In any case, patriarchal concepts and patrilineal families cut across the notion of the nuclear family home as woman's realm. And, as Lecky realized, industrialization and urbanization changed working roles and, hence, roles within the family.

Lecky, however, would have endorsed this view of separate roles, and believed that the family was of supreme importance to the health of society. In his history of morals he was a stern critic of the ascetic movement in early Christianity, not just because it smacked of fanaticism, but because it involved renunciation of family, and the duties, emotional ties and the ethical sexual intercourse which went with family life, and

because of its misogynist tendency to regard women as agents of the devil sent to tempt men into the sins of the flesh.[37] He may have got this hostility to early asceticism from Kingsley's *Hypatia*, though it was the stuff of his own Broad Church hostility to extremism. Improvement in the status and treatment of women *within* the family was at the very heart of social progress; it was the perfecting of an initially flawed institution, in his view. Coming from an Anglo-Irish Ascendancy background, he was particularly keen to portray the Anglican clerical household as the ideal to which others might aspire; even the best type of hard-working Catholic priest could not match this, he said, because of its exemplary role; and the unwed priest was always at moral risk because of the unnatural asceticism of his calling. He praised the 'gentle clerical households which stud our land . . . the most perfect type of domestic peace, the centre of civilisation in the remotest village'; whereas asceticism had made 'war upon human nature' and introduced 'the notion of sin . . . into the dearest of relationships . . . It is one of the great benefits of Protestantism that it did much . . . to restore marriage to its simplicity and dignity.'[38] The family, then, controlled the natural force of sexual appetite and became the very basis of civil society.

Women too, even feminist women, often thought that they had to choose between the family and a more public role. Emily Shirreff, the first Mistress of Girton College, went further, despite her pioneering role in higher education for women, writing in *The Contemporary Review* in August 1870 that, whereas men could have 'professions *and* marriage', women had to accept that these were alternatives, and that the choice was seldom theirs alone. She also felt that any rivalry with men would be unwise because they had natural advantages, not least greater physical strength. To challenge conventional roles would, therefore, risk everything:

> It might cost too much if it should turn many women who can afford the quiet dignity of home-life to seek the public highways of the world, instead of those secluded paths where their footsteps have been blessed heretofore. Especially may it cost too much if women, in the eagerness of competition, in the visions of ambition, forget that the noblest of human trusts is theirs already, – theirs by right divine. For wide and honourable as we justly consider the field of social exertion, of profitable industry, of scientific research, greater – aye, and nationally more important – than all these is that responsibility for the welfare of each new generation that God has placed in the hands and bound upon the hearts of women.[39]

Thus women's roles as wives and mothers were deemed to be quite literally sacred, more important than any other possible role and, crucially, incompatible with other roles. The unease about competitive, independent-minded women remained, however. As Beatrice Webb recorded in her diary after a lunch-time discussion with Marshall, the economist: '"If you compete with us we shan't marry you," he summed up with a laugh.'[40]

But was the woman supposed to rule her separate domestic sphere? 'We assert the unalienable right of woman to preside over her own home, and to promote the welfare of her own family', wrote Charlotte Tonna in 1844; but she was arguing against working-class women being forced into industrial work and being turned into 'an army of ferocious, fearless women, inured to hardship, exercised in masculine labours' – drinking, swearing, smoking Amazons.[41] Interestingly, however, she did assume that a woman, back in the home, would 'preside'. Accounts and opinions vary, even within the ideal of the middle-class family which increasingly set the tone for what was regarded as right and proper. For some, the woman ran the domestic economy and raised the children, with young boys tied to their mothers' apron strings until forced to become men and face the harsh vicissitudes of the wider world with a hitherto absent father or as an apprentice or at boarding school. In Ruskin's ideal the woman does 'rule' in the home, but only in the sense of 'sweet ordering' and 'arrangement', not in a creative or (to use a military metaphor) strategic sense; in fact, her 'great function is Praise' – of the man, who returned to be soothed and looked after. Norma Clarke has drawn our attention to a case where a middle-class man who actually played a major role in rearing his young children was regarded with utter disgust by his friend; the doting father was Edward Irving and the friend who was shocked to see him play with his babies, praise them and concern himself with them in front of others, was Thomas Carlyle.[42] Davidoff and Hall regard men as the 'absent presence, there to direct and command but physically occupied elsewhere for most of their time'.[43] For some middle-class women the home must have seemed more like a prison than a kingdom, so few were the opportunities for a respectable public presence; one of the early appeals of organized religion, be it church or chapel, was that it was the 'one public arena' from which women were not excluded. And the essence of femininity was dependence, with an idealized fictional wife often portrayed as 'young, dependent, almost childlike'.[44] Nor was the fictional child-bride so removed from reality in many cases.[45]

Also, let us not forget the daughters. Who controlled them as they grew to womanhood? F.M.L. Thompson suggests a real division of labour and responsibility: fathers were formally asked for their daughters' hands in marriage, enshrining 'male authority over the family as well as relocating aristocratic practice'. But women determined 'marrying standards, and their enforcement'. Fathers concerned themselves with the material prospects of their prospective sons-in-law, but mothers (and grandmothers) devised chaperoning techniques to control their daughters' behaviour and contacts, and, therefore, their marriage prospects.[46] There may have been a division of labour, with women able to control younger women, but the daughters' lives were clearly very circumscribed.

Also, for the upper and middle classes there was the patrilineal concept of the 'family' as a dynasty that survived down through the generations, inheriting land and property, relationships and characteristics; inheritance laws, titles, and simple patronymics ensured that this concept of the family was a patriarchal one. The house-bound nuclear family may have been a cosy concept, but the dynasty gave the individual a place in the world, an identity and, frequently, a livelihood. Moreover, for the aristocracy and gentry, and for many members of the middle class, there would still have been no rigid distinction between the affairs of the estate (or business) and domestic affairs; the men expected to preside over both even if they delegated to their wives what they did not delegate to their stewards.

This brings us to the vexed question of 'patriarchy', a concept much debated, refined and developed, often in a highly theoretical way. At its simplest, the modern use of the term is intended to mean the domination of women by men. But, unfortunately, things are not that simple. For some radical feminists it has been so important a concept as to supersede all other concepts of social relationships or structures, notably class, and has been seen as a permanent feature of human society to date. For its critics, its very permanence makes it ahistorical and, therefore, suspect – though why it should be seen in such absolute terms is not always clear. Then there have been arguments about whether it is equally applicable to the public and the private spheres, and whether or not it is essentially the same thing when exercised in both spheres. Its sternest critics see it as something of any empty box; and for many feminists it remains a feature of capitalism and is not always evident in other societies. There has even been debate as to whether or not its fundamentally male character is solely about the domination of females, as opposed to younger males and other dependants.

This last argument has a special interest for us because it goes right back to the original usage of the term as a tool of social analysis in Victorian times by Maine. He conceived of patriarchy as an early form of social organization, as the means of ruling a family-based society before the invention of the state and of statute law, and as a form of power in which the eldest male, 'the eldest ascendant' was the supreme authority in the household. This ascendancy was exercised over slaves, servants, wives, sons and daughters alike.[47] Maine's *Ancient Law* appeared in 1861 and was, in many respects, an interesting cultural product of the 1860s, not least because this version of patriarchy would deny truly masculine status (power, strength, authority) to younger males and lower order males as well as to females; within a kinship only one man was actually able to exercise the potential power of the male. Maine's anthropology may now be deeply suspect, but his assumptions about the primeval family were, as we have seen, typical of his age and will have contributed to the presumptions of others. As a contributor to a recent exhaustive centennial compilation on Maine has put it,

> One of Maine's most potent themes was that the family was the basic social institution, providing the model for other associations including, even, the early state. Similar ideas were taken up and developed, in very different ways, by Engels and Freud, and they have been revived by some modern feminist writers.[48]

These issues have surfaced again fairly recently, when a number of historians and sociologists have set out from a feminist position to try to refine the concept of patriarchy. One has concentrated on the distinction between true patriarchy, meaning rule by one adult male, and 'viriarchy' meaning rule by all adult males; but was also exercised by the distinction between the family sector and a more 'extended' role for male domination; the outcome amounted to a full-blown philosophy of history, ending with the observation that there was a gulf between today's egalitarian and democratic ideologies and the practice of sexism, offering more than a hint of millenarianism.[49]

Another has more simply made an attempt to break the concept down into component parts, defining six different patriarchal structures: 'a patriarchal mode of production in which women's labour is expropriated by their husbands; patriarchal relations within waged labour; the patriarchal state; male violence; patriarchal relations in sexuality; and patriarchal culture.'[50]

It would be inappropriate here, having dwelt only briefly on a very limited selection of the considerable literature on the subject of patriarchy, to do more than pick out a few points of interest to our particular concerns. The patriarchy–'viriarchy' dichotomy is of interest not only in defining the nature of women's subjection but also in defining forms of masculinity and relationships between fathers and sons in particular. The distinction between the private and the public spheres, and the distinction between modes of production, political forms, sexuality and patriarchal culture is also helpful. To conclude, we need to say a little more about the effect of the notion of separate spheres, the implications this had for definitions of femininity and masculinity, and the increasing attention paid, ever more explicitly, to the related question of sexuality, which must have confirmed Lecky's worst fears about 'wild' theories.

We have seen that there was unease about the concept of femininity as a result of the 'Woman Question'. The domestic ideal, so painfully established in the period between 1780 and 1850, as Davidoff and Hall have shown, was under threat at one level from industrialism, as our study of *The Family Economist* shows. It was also challenged by that Victorian icon of womanhood, Florence Nightingale, and by the whole experience of the Crimean War, which tested both gendered ideals, the male as well as the female. It can be argued that, as an ideal, as 'the Angel out of the House', a woman like Florence Nightingale did not challenge men's roles, because she was extending her role as ministering angel from the domestic sphere to a carefully defined woman's role in the wider world.[51] Cynthia Dereli explores the paradox between Nightingale's iconic status and her failure to set a precedent. Yet the careful delimitation of such a role must have raised consciousness of the gender issue. A number of Florence Nightingales would have marked the arrival of women as fully-fledged adults in a Christian community. Unmarried working-class women may have found plenty of employment out of the home despite Mines Acts and Factory Acts, and this had little or nothing to do with improving their status. For middle-class women it was altogether different. If they could find the sort of work to which they could dedicate their lives, emulating men, and Christ, after the manner of Hughes's recommendation, that would be a major change in their status. Like many propertied men, they did not need to work (in a sense, that was the mark of a gentleman and a lady), but they could dedicate their lives to good works. J.R. Green recounted to A.P. Stanley how in 1863, as a young, sceptical Oxford undergraduate, he had been given a sense of purpose and a faith by Stanley's lectures:

> I had withdrawn myself from Oxford work, and I found no help in Oxford theology. I was utterly miserable when I wandered into your lecture room . . . Then and after I heard you speak of work, not as a thing of classes and fellowships, but something worthy for its own sake, worthy because it made us like the great worker.

As both clergyman and historian, this was to be the basis for his own work.[52] Most women had never been able to find solace in 'work' of this kind, to model themselves on 'the great worker', but though many avenues remained closed, like the Church itself, eventually some did find a role as angels abroad as Poor Law Guardians or in the COS (Charity Organization Society), for example. Many writers have spoken of the home as a refuge from the harsh world of work; and Trudgill has talked of this in the particular context of the social upheavals of the mid-Victorian period;[53] but such upheavals could also provide a context for dedicating lives to the sort of public duty that gave a sense of purpose; for women they could provide both a context and an opportunity.

That women should even get involved in that ultimate example of the dangerous, testing public sphere, namely actual war, in however carefully defined a caring role, was shocking to many. In the 1860s the rise of the sensation novel, which had distressed Alfred Austin, particularly when it was written by a woman, with an active heroine going out to right wrongs and challenging traditional roles, or even an anti-heroine, acting in a socially unacceptable, even scandalous, way, suggested that the 'Woman Question' was being posed with new force. Victorians must have asked themselves, in the words of some modern commentators, 'How satisfactory can traditional roles be if adultery, bigamy, and spouse-killing captivate millions of readers?'[54] And even if the heroine was rather more on the side of the angels, she could not be an angel in the house, for as The Times's reviewer of Lady Audley's Secret put it, 'This is the age of lady novelists, and lady novelists naturally give first place to the heroine. But, if the heroines have first place, it will scarcely do to represent them as passive and quite angelic, or insipid – which heroines usually are. They have to be pictured as high-strung women, full of passion, purpose, and movement – very liable to error.'[55] In short, they were out in Ruskin's man's world, and had to live up to it and take its risks. One of the risks was being unsexed: as the Saturday Review put it, two years later (1864), 'A strong-minded woman is like a pretty man; the merit is unnatural to both, and both are certain to be ridiculously vain of it.'[56] More than that, though, the sensation novels were also, as Lyn Pykett has pointed out, a response to the reported sensationalism of the time; if they dealt with 'crime, bigamy, adultery, arson and arsenic' that was in tune with sensationalist reporting of actual crime, which the reading public found equally fascinating. In reaction to this in Eliza Lynn Linton's 'The Girl of the Period', in the Saturday Review (14 March 1868), which Pykett suspects of mounting an organized campaign to reconstruct the image of the properly feminine woman, the strong-minded woman became stereotyped as a danger to society.[57]

One interesting development that has not perhaps received as much attention as it might, despite Wollstonecraft and other early feminists, was not so much the development of strong-minded women as strong-bodied ones. It was assumed, even by the friends of women's rights that the origins of the subjugation of women lay in their relative lack of bodily strength. Working-class women in the home, as well as outside, had always undertaken physically demanding tasks, but middle-class women had to a considerable extent been denied healthy exercise. Quite a lot has been written about the development of sport and physical activity for boys and young men, but the cult of the healthy body did, in the end, affect the education of middle-class girls also. Ruskin, no less, despite his advocacy of separate spheres, was an early advocate of girls' physical education. And, later, Gordon Stables of *Boy's Own Paper* (and *Girl's Own Paper*) fame, was also an enthusiast for the healthy body and healthy mind argument, having no truck with fainting or the faint-hearted; though there was tension in his writings between his advocacy of healthy exercise and his anti-emancipation attitudes; for him womanly exercise was in pursuit of beauty rather than bodily strength.[58]

Colonial experience also provided women with opportunities to escape from the claustrophobic 'domestic' scenes in both senses of the term – the home and the nation. Murray Steele, in his essay on Olive Schreiner, notes the influence of her African experiences and how this fed into an established tradition of portraying the 'Old Country' as 'stuffy'.

Most writers assume that tensions about gender roles had come to a head by the early 1870s, creating a new era of more explicitly sexual controversy, when things were debated that had been little talked of before, at least publicly, or talked of with difficulty in the context of the 'Woman Question'. Witness Lecky approaching the subject of women's sexuality with 'hesitation' and 'extreme delicacy', and being unable even to mention the terms 'prostitute' or homosexual', despite a strangely ambiguous attitude (which provides an interesting gloss on the 'double standard') to the former, who was both the 'supreme type of vice' but also 'the most efficient guardian of virtue' and even 'the eternal priestess of humanity, blasted for the sins of the people' on account of her role as safety valve and, hence, paradoxically a necessary adjunct to the family system.[59] And he claimed that homosexuality, while a regrettable vice of the ancient world, was both 'unnatural' and 'totally remote from all modern feelings'.[60] Once discussion of gender roles gave way to discussions of sexuality itself, of prostitution and contagious diseases, and of homosexuality, all of which were the subject of both public debate and legislation in the last decades of the nineteenth century, this was found to be matched by a new freedom in literature. Trudgill has talked of a generation of younger writers rebelling against 'the constraints their elders had found congenial', about 'the struggle for new freedoms', noting that, 'Increasingly in the seventies, and more especially in the eighties, the press, pulpit and general society were prepared to discuss the Social Evil question with a hitherto unknown frankness', and crediting the writers of the 1870s, like Wilkie Collins, with having 'inched their way to greater freedom'.[61] And in Weeks's view, 'The last decades of the nineteenth century saw the coming together of all the major themes of its sexual discourses: class pride and evangelism, moral certainty and social anxiety, the double standard and "respectability", prurience and moral purity. Moral reforms, from the 1870s, came close to the centre of political debate.' Weeks also regards 1885 as 'an *annus mirabilis* of sexual politics', but this was as much to do with the 'social purity' movement striking back as with sexual revolution.[62] In short, the debate hotted up, and affected practical politics and thereby, through legislation, social behaviour which in turn reaffected social attitudes. Demands for greater sexual freedom went hand-in-hand with moral panics and demands for greater control. The 1890s saw novels about the 'new woman' which dealt with sex in a much more explicit way than had been possible in the sensation novels of the 1860s. Lyn Pykett has noted that

> the New Woman represented a threat not only to the social order, but also, to the natural order. Many doctors believed that the development of a woman's brain induced infertility by causing the womb to atrophy, and hence jeopardised the survival of the race. In addition, the spectre of the 'mannish' New Woman who refused her biological destiny of mother-hood threatened to dissolve existing gender boundaries.[63]

As this coincided with Havelock Ellis's *The Psychology of Sex* (1897) and Edward Carpenter postulating ideas about the mutability of sex and of feminine characteristics in men, it is no wonder that the moral panic of the 1890s appears to outdo that of the 1860s. When linked to socialist ideas this challenge to contemporary mores was intensified. When linked to issues of supposed racial degeneration the reaction could be almost hysterical. In such a heightened atmosphere we need not be surprised to find a great deal of repressed (but very revealing) sexuality in works by authors who purported to be offended by many of these developments. Thus, as Jeffrey Richards shows, the novels of Bram Stoker, an advocate of strict censorship, are as revealing as the writings of Mona Caird or Edward Carpenter. Some historians of these trends have tried to be over-schematic and have got into some confusion by trying to demonstrate clear trends in particular periods, or to simplify 'Victorian' attitudes. But the crucial point is that the period was typified by debate, initially guarded, but increasingly frank. There were a few easily identifiable moments when public attitudes seemed suddenly to change, it is true, most noticeably in 1895 with the trial of Oscar Wilde; but even here the mood had been becoming increasingly fraught in the late 1880s and early 1890s with a number of trials and scandals threatening the openness of debate about sexuality; and the debate continued into the Edwardian era.

Like so many other issues, the debates about sexuality between the 1850s and the end of the Victorian era demonstrate the facile nature of generalizations about 'Victorian values', and in some ways also illustrate the point that many so-called 'Victorian' attitudes actually derive from Evangelical attitudes in an earlier period; and as much effort, in the mid and late Victorian era, was put into debating and challenging those ideals as into maintaining them. It may be that, in the history of ideas and popular culture, an age is more easily identified by the issues that were deemed important and contentious enough to argue about than by the things it agreed upon. On the other hand, 'the refusal to talk about it' can also put something 'at the heart of discourse',[64] and to some extent the absence of explicitness on sexuality in the 1850s and 1860s, while gender roles were already under discussion is, in itself, of importance. A refusal to talk is rarely a matter merely of silence; it is also about allusion and obfuscation, and the study of literature can be particularly revealing in these respects. Yet these mid-century years did see the beginning of a debate that has continued for well over a hundred years, despite periods when attempts have been made to repress it; by looking at aspects of the Victorian debate it is hoped that we too can make a small contribution to the continuing efforts to understand the way gender roles and sexualities are constructed.

Notes

1. E.K. Helsinger, R.L. Sheets, W. Veeder, *The Woman Question: Society and Literature in Britain and America, 1837–1883, i Defining Voices* (Chicago and London: Univ. of Chicago Press, 1983), pp. xii, xiv.
2. D. Daiches, 'General Editor's Introduction', in J. Calder, *Women and Marriage in Victorian Fiction* (London: Thames and Hudson, 1976), p. 9.
3. M. Brody, 'Introduction', in M. Wollstonecraft, *A Vindication of the Rights of Woman* (London: Penguin, 1992), p. 25.
4. Wollstonecraft, op. cit., pp. 79–83, 113, 118–19, 126–7.
5. M. Brody, 'Introduction', ibid., pp. 58–9; P. Hollis, *Women in Public: The Women's Movement 1850–1900* (London: Allen and Unwin, 1979), p. vii.
6. See e.g. Hollis, op. cit.; P. Levine, *Victorian Feminism 1850–1900* (London: Hutchinson, 1987); M.L. Shanley, *Feminism, Marriage, and the Law in Victorian England, 1850–1895* (London: I.B. Tauris, 1989).
7. B. Leigh Smith Bodichon, 'Women and Work', reprinted in C.A. Lacey (ed.), *Barbara Leigh Smith Bodichon and the Langham Place Group* (London: Routledge, 1987), pp. 36–44, 63.
8. E. Davies, 'The Influence of University Degrees on the Education of Women', [first printed in *The Victoria Magazine*, June 1863], reprinted in ibid., pp. 419–22, 425.
9. J.S. Mill, 'On the Subjection of Women' [1869], *On Liberty and other essays* (Oxford: OUP, 1991), p. 493.
10. Ibid., pp. 473–4.
11. Ibid., pp. 524, 536–8. For marriage as slavery see pp. 507, 588. For more on the impact of domestic tasks see pp. 551–3.
12. Ibid., pp. 540–4.
13. Ibid., p. 582.
14. L. Davidoff, C. Hall, *Family Fortunes: Men and Women of the English Middle Class 1780–1850* (London: Hutchinson, 1987), p. 149.
15. Mill, op. cit., p. 475; W.E.H. Lecky, *History of European Morals from Augustus to Charlemagne* [1869] (London: Longmans, 1877), ii, pp. 276, 372.

16. M.L. Shanley, *Feminism, Marriage, and the Law in Victorian England, 1850–1895* (London: I.B. Tauris, 1989), pp. 11–12.
17. Lecky, op. cit., ii, p. 275.
18. Helsinger *et al.*, op. cit., iii, p. 131.
19. S.O. Rose, *Limited Livelihoods: Gender and Class in Nineteenth Century England* (London: Routledge, 1992), p. 14.
20. Lecky, op. cit., ii, pp. 281–3. In general, for prostitution see pp. 282–96.
21. Ibid., ii, pp. 358–60, 366.
22. C. Dyhouse, *Feminism and the Family in England 1880–1939* (Oxford: Blackwell, 1989), p. 185.
23. S. Alexander, 'Women, Class and Sexual Differences in the 1830s and 1840s: Some Reflections on the Writing of a Feminist History', *Hist. Workshop Journal*, 17 (1984), p. 126.
24. A. Brittan, *Masculinity and Power* (Oxford: Blackwell, 1989), p. 178. A similar point is made by E.A. Rotundo, 'Learning about manhood: gender ideals and the middle-class family in nineteenth-century America', in J.A. Mangan, J. Walvin (eds), *Manliness and Morality: Middle-Class Masculinity in Britain and America, 1800–1940* (Manchester: MUP, 1987), p. 35.
25. Brittan, op. cit., p. 196. See also N. Vance, *The Sinews of the Spirit: The ideal of Christian manliness in Victorian Literature and Thought* (Cambridge: CUP, 1985).
26. Davidoff, Hall, op. cit., pp. 110–12.
27. R. Gilmour, *The Idea of the Gentleman in the Victorian Novel* (London: Allen and Unwin, 1981), pp. 85–6.
28. T. Hughes, *The Manliness of Christ* [1879] (London: Macmillan, 1907), pp. 3–4.
29. Ibid., pp. 10–12, 16, 18.
30. Davidoff, Hall, op. cit., p. 450. For 'womanly tenderness' being acceptable in a man, see N. Vance, op. cit., p. 146.
31. Helsinger *et al.*, op. cit., p. 156.
32. Ibid., pp. 157–60.
33. Ibid., p. 160.
34. Mill, op. cit., p. 558.
35. J. Ruskin, 'Of Queens' Gardens', *Sesame and Lilies, Unto the Last and the Political Economy of Art* (London: Cassell, 1907), p. 73.
36. Davidoff, Hall, op. cit., p. 229.
37. Lecky, op. cit., ii, pp. 107–39.
38. Ibid., pp. 334–6. Kingsley had led the way in attacking asceticism, see N. Vance, op. cit., pp. 30–9.
39. E. Shirreff, 'College Education for Women', reprinted in B. Dennis, D. Skilton (eds), *Reform and Intellectual Debate in Victorian England* (Beckenham: Croom Helm, 1987), p. 158.
40. Hollis, op. cit., p. 21.
41. Ibid., p. 289.
42. N. Clarke, 'Strenuous Idleness: Thomas Carlyle and the man of letters as hero', in M. Roper, J. Tosh (eds), *Manful Assertions* (London: Routledge, 1991), pp. 31–4.
43. Davidoff, Hall, op. cit., p. 181.
44. Ibid., pp. 108, 114, 323.
45. See, for example, J. Tosh, 'Domesticity and Manliness in the Victorian

Middle Class: the family of Edward White Denson', in M. Roper, J. Tosh (eds), op. cit., pp. 51–9.

46. F.M.L. Thompson, *The Rise of Respectable Society* (London: Fontana, 1988) p. 103.

47. A modern theorist of patriarchy has drawn attention to Maine's role: M. Waters, 'Patriarchy and Viriarchy: An Exploration and Reconstruction of Concepts of Masculine Domination', *Sociology*, 23, 2 (1989), pp. 193–211.

48. A. Kuper, 'The rise and fall of Maine's patriarchal society' in A. Diamond (ed.), *The Victorian Achievement of Sir Henry Maine* (Cambridge: CUP, 1991), p. 109.

49. Waters, op. cit., pp. 193–211

50. S. Walby, 'Theorising Patriarchy', *Sociology*, 23, 2 (1989), p. 220 and in general pp. 213–34. See also J. Acker, 'The Problem with Patriarchy', *Sociology*, 23, 2 (1989), pp. 235–40.

51. For the concept of 'the angel out of the house' see Helsinger *et al.*, op. cit., i, p. xv.

52. Green to Stanley, Dec. 1863, in L. Stephen (ed.), *Letters of John Richard Green* (London: Macmillan, 1901), pp. 16–19. (In fact, Green was soon wrestling with theological and, consequently, vocational doubts again.) For a similar point with reference to Thomas Hughes, see N. Vance, op. cit., p. 149.

53. E. Trudgill, *Madonnas and Magdalens: The Origins and Development of Victorian Sexual Attitudes* (London: Heinemann, 1976), pp. 40–5.

54. Helsinger *et al.*, op. cit., iii, p. 112.

55. Ibid., iii, p. 131.

56. Ibid., iii, p. 89.

57. L. Pykett, *The 'Improper' Feminine: The Woman's Sensation Novel and the New Woman Writing* (London: Routledge, 1992), pp. 20, 47, 69–70.

58. V. Jones, 'Victorian Child and Youth, as reflected in the works of Dr. William Gordon Stables, M.D., C.M., R.N', unpublished dissertation submitted as part-requirement for MA History (Lancaster University), at Edge Hill College of Higher Education, 1992, pp. 67–84.

59. Lecky, op. cit., ii, pp. 282–3.

60. Ibid., p. 294.

61. Trudgill, op. cit., pp. 229–30, 233–6.

62. J. Weeks, *Sex Politics and Society* (London: Longmans, 2nd edn, 1992), pp. 81, 87.

63. Pykett, op. cit., p. 140.

64. Weeks, op. cit., p. 19. Weeks is referring to Foucault.

CHAPTER TWO

Domestic Ideology and its Industrial Enemies: The Title Page of *The Family Economist* 1848–1850

Brian Maidment

The title page of *The Family Economist* (Plate 1) has been widely used for illustrative purposes by recent scholars and picture editors, to the point where it has almost reached iconic status. It is used, for example, to illustrate the improving 'mission to the home' of the Victorian middle classes in Irene Dancyger's *A World of Women*, where *The Family Economist* is identified, wrongly to my mind, as a women's magazine.[1] It is used for similar purposes in Jenni Calder's *The Victorian Home*.[2] J.F.C. Harrison has pointed out the ways in which mottoes were used as part of the title page design in this study of adult literacy and education.[3] In all three commentaries, the title page is read as being ideologically transparent, as directly transmitting conservative values of domesticity, of gender roles, and of respectability from an entrepreneurial middle class to an artisan readership through the medium of a cheap (1d. a month), mass circulation magazine.[4] Additionally, the three discussions all centre on the original 1848 title page, with its vignette of a male working in the fields seen through a rustic cottage window while his family work and play together round the cottage hearth. Yet, in the 1850 volume of *The Family Economist* (Plate 2), this apparently settled image is replaced by a much more ambiguous one in which the window on to the scene of steadfast rural labour has been blocked off, and the tidy cottage dresser replaced by a half-open door which frames a standing male figure.

Such a radical change to the original image throws in doubt the ideological consistency and certainty which Calder, Dancyger, and Harrison identify in *The Family Economist*, especially as there seems no obvious good reason to redraw the 1848 vignette given that magazines tend to depend on a familiar, easily recognized title page configuration. Accordingly, it may be necessary to acknowledge that the title pages to *The Family Economist* comprise a more complex verbal and visual formulation than immediately apparent, especially when taken together. An interpretation of these title pages requires acknowledgement of a range of component structures – visual, verbal, narrative, and graphic – which together constructs its ideological statement. In trying to give proper

THE

FAMILY ECONOMIST;

A Penny Monthly Magazine,

DEVOTED TO THE MORAL, PHYSICAL, AND DOMESTIC IMPROVEMENT
OF THE INDUSTRIOUS CLASSES.

VOLUME FIRST.

The Cottage Homes of England
  By thousands on her plains,
They are smiling o'er the silvery brook,
  And round the hamlet fanes :
Through glowing orchards forth they peep,
  Each from its nook of leaves :
And fearless there the lowly sleep,
  As the bird beneath their eaves.

The free fair homes of England !
  Long, long in hut and hall
May hearts of native proof be reared
  To guard each hallowed wall,
And green for ever be the groves,
  And bright the flowery sod,
Where first the child's glad spirit loves
  Its country and its God.

LONDON:

GROOMBRIDGE & SONS, PATERNOSTER ROW.

AND SOLD BY ALL BOOKSELLERS.

1848.

EDUCATION IS A SECOND NATURE.

(left margin) LABOUR RIDS US OF THREE GREAT EVILS, IRKSOMENESS, VICE, AND POVERTY.

(right margin) A GOOD TEMPER IS ONE OF THE PRINCIPAL INGREDIENTS OF HAPPINESS.

1   Anonymous wood engraved vignette

weight to this range of possibilities, I should like first to discuss the idea of the 'cottage' artisan magazine as a literary genre; second, the motto and saying as a typographical and cultural event in the Victorian period; third, the traditional narrative of the returning artisan arriving home at eventide from the ardours of the day's labour; and, finally, the ideological vision which sustained this narrative of cottage contentment despite obvious empirical evidence to the contrary.

The discourses of the 'cottage' magazine

The values which *The Family Economist* sought to represent might to some extent be read off from its title, which brings together notions of domesticity and thrift into a single phrase. The implied or intended readership is also made clear through the magazine's title page – the low price of the magazine, the unequivocal address to 'the industrious classes', the vignette of the tidy cottage interior, the improving mottoes which form the typographical border, and the Christianized, patriotic invocation of the verses all suggest a periodical explicitly directed to a respectable, ambitious, but socially deferential artisan readership. *The Family Economist* belongs to the second generation of magazines of popular progress which flourished after the collapse of Chartism in 1848. The first generation of magazines aimed specially at artisans dated from the early 1840s and included *Howitt's Journal, The People's Journal, Douglas Jerrold's Shilling Magazine, Eliza Cook's Journal* and *The Illuminated Magazine*, all of which had grown out of, and modified, *Chambers's Edinburgh Journal* which had been launched in 1832. These magazines sought to offer a cultural, philosophical, literary, and possibly even a political and ideological alliance between progressive elements within bourgeois culture and intellectually ambitious sections of the artisan class.[5] Projected by liberal entrepreneurs and 'friends of the people', these magazines gave artisan readers access to ideas (*Howitt's Journal*, for example, offered the best and most thoroughgoing account of French socialist thought available in Britain in the 1840s) and even, on a limited basis, to print. An underlying ideological purpose – that of constructing an alliance which would merge evident economic and class interests into shared cultural and intellectual values – differentiates these periodicals from political or specifically Chartist journals, which worked through the rhetoric of difference and opposition. Yet there are many similarities of interest, tone and, indeed, format between the artisan and the radical Chartist journals in the 1840s.

Easy as it is now to turn this ambitious cultural project into another manifestation of subtle bourgeois hegemonic impulses, it is nonetheless important to acknowledge that the magazines of popular progress dating from the 1840s did publicize with startling honesty the fractures and contradictions within middle-class ideology. Especially conspicuous now are the tensions expressed within the writings of liberal intellectuals between the wish to encourage and support the development of artisan cultural ambitions while at the same time disassociating them from the political arena. To cite out of context one of George Gilfillan's more memorable remarks about Ebenezer Elliott, the 'Corn Law Rhymer', 'when he writes about corn-fields' rather than 'Corn Laws', 'what a ·pleasant companion does he then become'.

After 1848, the need for a specifically cultural alliance between liberal intellectuals and ambitious artisans was less pressing, and *The Family Economist* makes it clear even on its title page that this is a magazine directed at artisans from above, perhaps largely as a commercial or entre-preneurial undertaking. The contents were largely aimed at reflecting the assumed interests of the readers rather than at ostentatiously shaping or constructing artisan self-images. Yet this distinction may prove to be a false one, as the notion that commercialism disproves or denies ideological purposes can scarcely be seriously maintained.

The Family Economist was published by Groombridge and Sons, one of the new publishing houses of the 1840s which specialized in develop-ing the mass literate or just literate readership. The educational, cultural and economic progress of the artisan classes had, by the 1830s, been suf-ficient to define artisans as a potential mass market for literature, espe-cially periodicals. Other firms which exploited similar readership in comparable genres during the 1840s and 1850s were William Tweedie, Partridge and Oakey, and Cassell, whose post-Chartist *Working Man's Friend* offers a direct comparison with *The Family Economist*.[6] Underpinning these rapid developments lay the outstanding success of huge projects undertaken by the Chambers brothers in Edinburgh – not just the rather earnest and formidable unillustrated *Chambers's Edinburgh Journal*, but also the cheap series of *Popular Information* and *Papers for the People*. Although essentially entrepreneurs, the Chambers Brothers were themselves from an artisan background, and were gen-uinely committed to a vision of a calm cultural progress within the work-ing classes. A generation later than *The Family Economist*, firms like Nelson and Warne, which specialized in chromolithography, moved the mass popular market on to another stage, this time away from self-improvement towards a more diversionary and entertaining kind of liter-ature. All these firms understood the crucial role of illustration, especially the use of the vernacular wood-engraved tradition adapted for the mass market, in selling their books and satisfying the needs of their artisan readers. In this respect *Chambers's Journal*, which was unillustrated, was an isolated phenomenon. The publications of a firm like Groombridge, while ostensibly directed at an artisan readership, nonetheless located their books a notch higher in the cultural scale than another group of mass literature entrepreneurs, the provincial firms of Milner and Sowerby from Halifax, Nicholson of Wakefield, and J.S. Pratt of Stokesley who produced cheap 'cottage library' literature sold in the streets like broadsides and catering for a variety of tastes in a glittering but shoddy format.[7] By making these fine distinctions it is possible as a first step to locate *The Family Economist* in a wave of entrepreneurial publishing ventures of the late 1840s and 1850s which sought to exploit an artisan readership in commercial terms while offering simultaneous encouragement to its cultural aspirations.

Central to this endeavour was the translation of separate popular and vernacular literary and graphic genres into a collective serialized form. The contents of *The Family Economist* suggest exactly such a drawing together of established popular modes. The magazine comprises short improving narratives (derived from tract literature), recipes and advice on thrifty housekeeping (drawn, interestingly enough, from precedents in Chartist periodicals like *The Reformer's Almanac* as much as from Mrs Trimmer and eighteenth-century improving periodicals), calenders of gardening tasks or events of popular interest (invoking the almanac and calender vernacular tradition so brilliantly exploited in the 1820s by William Hone's *Table Book* and *Everyday Book* and in the 1860s by Chambers' *Books of Days*)[8], factual information of the kind popularized in the 1830s by *The Penny Magazine* and *The Saturday Magazine*, direct moral homily (again derived from the tracts), and poetry by the likes of Thomas Hood and Eliza Cook of an exhortatory and elevating kind commonplace in the magazines of popular progress. The textual illustrations in *The Family Economist* are essentially explicatory and demonstrative wood engravings in the *Penny* and *Saturday* tradition. It is important to suggest precedents for all these elements, as the eclectic gathering of popular genres here shows how determinedly *The Family Economist* draws on established forms in order to press its claim on artisan attention. An assessment of the extent to which these sources are reformulated both generically and ideologically in their transition to the commercial artisan literary discourses of the 1850s is one reason for attempting a close reading of this text.

Eclecticism, then, is a keynote of this particular title page. The immediate impression is of a crowded, complex design which seeks, with some success, to integrate a wide variety of elements – a long, explanatory title; a woodcut vignette; exhortatory verses; four mottoes; and the publishing details. The clever use of rules makes the page possible, dividing up the various components with delicate lines, while, through the use of the

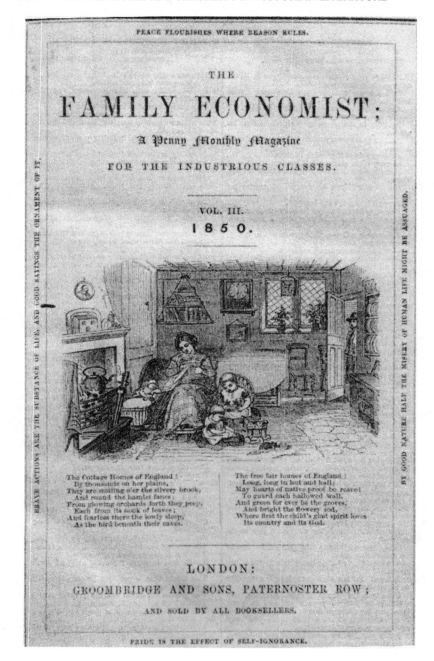

2   Anonymous wood engraved vignette

motto-lined border, providing an overall unity of effect. A similar dialogue between the component elements and the whole page is provided by the typography. A wide variety of sizes is used, but the same type face is maintained apart from the Gothic sub-title, a consistency which again provides unity. Overall, despite a secular insistence on the practical, thrifty, respectable discourses of artisan self-help, the most direct visual analogy for this title page is to be found in tract literature. This analogy is an interesting one given that *The Family Economist* foregrounds secular usefulness against the Christianized knowledge so central to, for example, *The Penny* or *The Saturday*. Of the complex range of popular genres brought together and unified in this title page, the most startling is, however, the visually arresting use of the motto. It is worth saying a little more about the motto as it constituted an important discourse in Victorian Britain.

The motto

In his discussion of 'the literature of success' in *Learning and Living*, J.F.C. Harrison draws attention to the saying within this literary mode: 'the social devices and conveniences of the age acquired the compulsion of moral, even religious, virtues. They were popularized in many forms, but particularly as proverbs and aphorisms.'[9] Harrison cites *The Family Economist* as part of his evidence, and goes on to suggest the reliance of two of the most widely read Victorian conduct manuals, Smiles's *Self Help* and Tupper's *Proverbial Philosophy*, on the epigrammatic method. He might have mentioned Ruskin as a further example, notably in later editions of his works where he differentiated his more memorable statements as aphorisms by printing them in different type faces, or even colours. Certainly Harrison's contention that the widespread popularity of the aphorism was caused by its ability to reduce complex moral choices to simple memorable rules of conduct seems fully borne out by the practice of another widely read popular biographer and ideologue of popular progress, Edwin Paxton Hood.[10] In one of his most interesting books, *The Uses of Biography*, Hood's usual accumulative mode of exposition is continually cut across by typographically distinct comments which attempted to summarize the arguments in simple proverbial formulations such as 'Biography Forms the Museum of Life'.[11] Another book of the same period, *The Mental and Moral Philosophy of Laughter* (1852), italicizes a similar sequence of proverbial wisdom – 'The sources of laughter then lie in incongruity'; 'Wonderful is the detective power of ridicule and mirth'; 'Humour the Teacher, but Wit the Scourge'.[12] This apophthegmatic mode was a deliberate attempt to retain an important element of orality in Hood's work. Through this means, a vast reservoir of effortless cliché wisdom and proverbial anodyne was available as a shared mode to both artisan and middle-class reader. Other sources for the motto as a mode of discourse include the embroidered sampler, a tremendously widely used ornamental form in artisan and middle-class homes,[13] the widespread use of sayings as chapter headings in novels (drawn from many sources or even made up if an appropriate motto did not come to mind), and above all, tract and devotional literature. So once again this *Family Economist* title page depends on the exploitation of widely used and diverse traditions of discourse, all of which sought to translate popular forms into an expression of middle-class values. The annexing of vernacular traditions for ideological purposes is one of the crucial symptoms of the purposefulness and unity of middle-class ideology in the mid-Victorian period.

The visual integration of mottoes into complex or eclectic texts, so obviously a feature of *The Family Economist* title page, and pioneered by samplers, is well illustrated in the pages of another artisan periodical, *The British Workman*, which was published in the mid 1850s.[14] The aim of *The British Workman* was to retain the visual impact and appeal of the handbill and sampler into a type-set page. *The Family Economist* follows *The British Workman* in once again drawing a variety of popular modes, secular and devotional, visual and typographical, vernacular and relatively polite, into a single integrated image. The mottoes in *The Family Economist* are interestingly secular – while there is nothing in them which would contradict conventional Christianity, the stress is on social conduct rather than on individual spiritual self-examination. One, indeed, offers the motto genre itself a moment of self-congratulation – *Brave actions are the substance of life and good sayings are the ornament of it*. The mottoes here are 'ornamental' in two ways, both as a feature of a pleasing typographical lay-out, and as a gloss on, or an epigrammatic summary of, a well-lived life.

At the centre of this title page, however, is the dominating wood-engraved image of a cottage interior. It is to this vignette that I now wish to turn.

The artisan's homecoming

The pastoral trope of the evening return of the agricultural labourer to his family can be traced back to the harmonized Georgic pastoral mode of Theocritus or Virgil.[15] However, a more selective account of this tradition should provide an adequate context here, and the obvious place to start is the evening vision of Gray's 'Elegy', with its famous opening invocation of the 'homeward way' of the 'weary ploughman' whose arrival home occupies a later elegiac stanza:

> For them no more the blazing hearth shall burn,
> Or busy housewife ply her evening care:
> No children run to lisp their sire's return
> Or climb his knee the envied kiss to share.[16]

Gray's poem is, of course, a self-proclaimed elegy, a recognition of the difficulty of sustaining the Georgic vision of nature improved and rendered full of economic and moral meaning through human and social presence, into an era of rapid rural and agricultural change. In this stanza, Gray laments one specific instance of the failure of the heroicizing eighteenth-century pastoral vision: the loss of the interpenetration of work and home in a dialectic of rural contentment. What Gray sees as a necessary and 'natural' interconnection between labour and domesticity is here celebrated just at the moment when the separation of leisure from toil began to become an increasingly powerful economic and social reality.

Gray's works, and especially 'The Elegy', became standard texts for illustrated editions, especially in the latter half of the nineteenth century. Most of these editions were in an untroubled, celebratory pastoral mode, many with engravings by, or in the manner of, Birket Foster's fussily idyllic country scenes.[17] Few of these editions use the domestic or figurative themes in 'The Elegy' as a source of subjects for engraving, but it is nonetheless possible to find popular engravings of the scene of the artisan's evening return described in the quoted stanza. One such vignette from an edition exactly contemporary with *The Family Economist* title page (although the original drawing was made fifteen years previously)[18] locates the scene of the return outside the cottage door, but uses its circular form to emphasize the unity, fecundity, and vigour of the family group, which spirals round the central male figure, relegating the becowled wife to the periphery. The image is sculptural and heroicizing, despite the gaping, apparently doorless, cottage doorway which tells of poverty and cold. My point here is not entirely to do with the specific formulation of this image but rather with a recognition that Gray's work must have been widely known to a relatively large readership in the mid-nineteenth century through a succession of illustrated editions. In some cases, as in this one, there were representations of the scene of the artisan's return which reaffirmed Gray's attempts to formulate a heroic pastoral vision in which, work, family, and leisure were elided into a single ideological statement.

Gray's poem was also important because it served as the source for another powerful formulation of the same narrative, Robert Burns's 'The

3 Wood engraved illustration to 'The Cotter's Saturday Night'

Cotter's Saturday Night', first published in 1784–5. Burns's poem, despite its vernacular subject and diction, alluded to the sophisticated or learned pastoral tradition in a number of ways, notably through the use of an epigraph from Gray's poem and by using a quotation from Pope's 'Windsor Forest'. Burns translated Gray's artisan homecoming into more homely terms, and furnished it with elements crucial to Victorian versions of the theme – the cottage, the hearth, the wife, cleanliness, thrift, order:

> The toil-worn COTTER frae his labour goes,
> This night his weekly moil is at an end,
> Collects his spades, his mattocks and his hoes,
> Hoping the morn in ease and rest to spend,
> And weary, o'er the muir, his course does hameward bend.
>
> At length his Lonely Cot appears in view,
> Beneath the shelter of an aged tree;
> Th' expectant wee-things, toddlan', stacher thro'
> To meet their Dad, wi' flicterin noise and glee.
> His wee-bit ingle, blinkin bonilie,
> His clean hearth-stane, his thriftie Wifie's smile.
> The lisping infant, prattling on his knee,
> Does a' his weary kiaugh and care beguile,
> And makes him quite forget his labour and his toil.[19]

Subversively, this description resolves into a distinction, perhaps even an opposition between 'cares', labour, and 'toil' on the one hand, and the virtues of a domestic family Saturday night, gathered round the hearth, on the other. Burns is claiming the narrative of the returning artisan for a version of respectability, piety, humility and family loyalty. Like Gray's 'Elegy', 'The Cotter's Saturday Night' was a famous poem, widely known at all levels of society, and rendered even more famous by Burns's early Victorian status as a biographical model for artisan or self-taught writers. His writing career, if not his private life, offered an early and obvious example of the 'pursuit of knowledge under difficulties' and had been widely used in middle-class propagandist accounts of artisan cultural development.

Burns's poem, like Gray's, appeared in many illustrated editions, often published by provincial publishers catering for a local, but not entirely unsophisticated, readership.[20] The most famous and enduring of these provincial editions was the Catnach and Davidson edition published in Alnwick in 1808 with numerous wood engravings drawn by Thurston and engraved by Thomas Bewick (or at least by members of his workshop). Volume 1 of this edition contains a superb vignette of the artisan's homecoming (Plate 3), in which a single sturdy toddler greets her returning father, watched by her mother from a distant cottage doorway.[21]

This particular image mediates a quite sophisticated rural narrative back into vernacular terms, but avoids the crudities usually associated with a vernacular visual code. The lack of the heroic here is striking – the artisan's spade and sack, balanced on a thick stave, are given a weight acknowledged, but not celebrated, in the bent form and painful gait of the cotter. The child's pose is sturdy and natural but again without idealization. By all these means the image is stripped of its moralizing and heroicizing codes and becomes a 'simple' naturalistic narrative of family affection. Thurston's drawing also denies the central presence of the domestic in this version of the narrative – the outside/inside divide is represented through a chain of receding figures which smoothes the transition from work to the domestic hearth.

The extent to which Bewick and Thurston deny the heroicizing impulse in their subject can be gauged through a comparison with a very similar, if cruder wood engraving published in the 2d. weekly periodical *Saturday Night* in 1824 along with Burns's poem.[22] The placing of many of the visual elements in this print is directly comparable to that in Bewick's print – the male figure, sack over shoulder and spade in hand, surveys a distant cottage overhung with trees, with wife and child emerging to greet the returning labourer. But here the male figure dominates the scene, towering over and diminishing the cottage. The distance between home and figure has grown enormously, again asserting the centrality of the labourer, who is sturdier and less obviously burdened than Bewick's workman despite the complexity of his tackle. Set against a marine landscape, and with the pilaster effect of the cottage window mullions, this scene seems closer to Arcadia than Arbroath. Even the floppy brimmed hat in the anonymous print lacks the solidity of the discharged soldier's bonnet in Bewick and Thurston's image. The celebratory impulse of the *Saturday Night* print checks the naturalism in the detail of the main figure, so that Bewick's clarity, as well as his focus on the family, are lost. How important or well known these images may have been by 1850 is hard to evaluate, but they certainly serve as another useful reference point in trying to decode the title page of the 1850 *Family Economist*.

Beginning this discussion of the returning artisan motif with Gray and Burns in this context is not solely a matter of iconographic significance. Gray's poem was extremely influential on the artisan and self-taught poets who were beginning to find their way into print in the 1830s and 1840s.[23] That these writers should turn to the neo-classical couplet of Pope or the academic and self-conscious lyric forms of Gray for poetic models is not surprising given their cultural insecurity and their need to prove their intellectual power and formal skill, even if these models ultimately inhibited the potential range of their work. Burns's simple lyrics were also frequently put forward as models for working-men writers by sophisticated and powerful critics like Kingsley and Carlyle, with Kingsley's essay 'Burns and his School' providing a central definition of the arguments.[24]

However, as already suggested, it was Burns's life rather than his work which was most influential, despite middle-class anxiety about his morals. Burns appeared to self-taught writers as an example of the way in which cultural achievement might be linked to social and economic success. The combination of sophisticated literary knowledge and vernacular lyric skill shown in his work also vindicated the ambiguous cultural aspirations found in much poetry by working-men authors.

However, it is clear that in imitating models like Burns, Gray, and Pope, self-taught authors often borrowed not just their language and forms but also whole ideological structures as well. Accordingly, it is not unexpected to find a Manchester self-taught artisan poet, the reed-maker John Critchley Prince, concluding an ostensibly celebratory poem (unlike the elegiac 'Elegy') called 'The Poet's Sabbath' with precisely Gray and Burns's trope of the artisan's homecoming. The poem was first published in volume form in 1843:

> Shadows are round me as I tread the floor
> Of balmy breathing fields; my weary feet
> Bear me right onward to my cottage door; –
> I cross the threshold – take my accustomed seat.
> And feel, as I have always felt, that home is sweet!
>
> My wife receives me with a quiet smile,
> Gentle and kind as wife should ever be;
> My joyous little ones press round the while,
> And take their wonted places on my knee:
> Now with my chosen friends, sincere and free,
> I pass the remnant of the night away . . .[25]

It is noticeable that the fluency of Gray and Burns's lyric forms has here given way to a more anxious and fractured verse form. Prince's resolution of the narrative, as one might expect from an urban artisan whose trade had been destroyed by the technological developments of the industrial revolution, modified the pastoral harmonies of Gray's elegiac vision by calling into the poem the oppositional elements from Burns's poem:

> And wish that human life were one long Sabbath-day.

At this moment the previously absent fact of week-day labour is brought back disruptively into the poem's argument. Prince's cottage vision, unlike Gray's, is built out of a tacit antithesis between home and labour, and even between the reconciling necessity of repose and work. Gray's consoling elision between agricultural labour and domestic repose cannot survive without challenging the obvious divisions between work and home predicated by the new kinds of industrial culture established in the 1830s and 1840s.

Another poem by an artisan writer, despite being published ten years after *The Family Economist* title page, exploits exactly the same narrative trope, and reveals even more clearly than Prince both the persistence of Gray's influence and the consequent shift in meanings brought about by major social change. Philip Connell's 'A Winter Night in Manchester' opens with a direct imitation of Gray and Goldsmith but modulates through a stanza describing street activities into the now familiar trope of the cottage hearth:

> Far other scenes now bless the workman's night,
> In slippers easy, chair, and shirt sleeves white,
> With hair to one side comb'd and well-wash'd face
> Radiant with happiness – while in her place
> The very cat enjoys her evening nap.
> Purring her grateful anthems in his lap.
> And ever as he casts around his eyes
> A look meets his, beaming with hopes and joys,
> And quiet happiness – his own dear Bess
> Nursing their baby boy in fond caress,
> His vermil' lips around the nipple press'd
> And half his cheek hid in her milkwhite breast:
> There sits the workman in his happy home,
> The fire fair blazing round the cheerful room,
> The carpet brush'd, the grate and fender bright,
> The polish'd table glancing to the light,
> The hearth pure white, the chimneypiece array'd
> With dogs and shepherds nestling in the shade;
> The simple shelves with glass and china bright,
> The busy bare-faced clock not always right;
> The baywood bookcase, full, select, but small,
> Curtain'd with crimson, pendant on the wall,
> And hung around – the lovely, good, and wise
> Look from their maple frames, with living eyes.[26]

Connell's entire poem is a prolonged meditation on the question of what constitutes suitable leisure activity for a sensitive and cultured urban artisan. The poet rehearses a series of possibilities – loitering on Victoria Bridge to consider the aesthetic potential of a November night in Manchester; the urban and gregarious pursuits of pub, prostitutes, and the theatre (all rejected as vulgar and demeaning); domestic pleasure; reading; introspection. Thus the poem describes, in neo-classic couplets, a phrased retreat from contemplation of industrial reality via urban alienation and family life into terminal introversion. Such a retreat is not just a personal failure but also represents a defeat for those poetic strategies which might have controlled or structured a resistance to urban anxiety. The poem forms an interesting gloss on one of its obvious poetic sources, Gray's 'Elegy'. In Gray's poem the poetic fluency remains uninterrupted despite growing intellectual tensions within the speaker's perception of the countryside. In Connell's version of the 'returning artisan' (or here the 'just returned artisan') narrative, which occupies the central section of the poem, the verse enacts, probably unconsciously, the failure of poetry as a means of confronting the distresses caused by urban industrial life. The section of the poem quoted above is an almost obsessional attempt to use the ordering precision of the couplet to construct a vision of domestic order by means of locating even the 'very cat' in an exact place in the scene. The result is overstated, but moving in its compulsion to seek order, domestic repose and emblematic tidiness as a means of coping with factory life.

The correlations between Connell's poetic description of a cottage interior in 'A Winter Night in Manchester' and the graphic representation of the same scene in the 1848 and 1850 *Family Economist* title pages are striking, even allowing for the probability that the two vignettes depict rural rather than urban dwellings. The blazing fire, the gleaming table top, the ornamental chimneypiece, the simple shelves, the hanging bookcase, the ostentatious clock are all prominent components of both scenes. These similarities of representation might be further extended through comparisons with other versions of artisan interiors in contemporary fiction. *Mary Barton* and *North and South*, both novels which assert documentary realism as part of their fictional strategies, offer obvious examples of comparably emblematic and ideological coded accounts of artisan domestic scenes. One obvious explanation for these marked similarities might be that all these descriptions were an accurate version of empirical reality. But more persuasive still are the arguments which suggest that these detailed descriptions are structured more by shared ideological expectations than by any coherent factual basis. These cottage interiors seem to me emblematic and value laden rather than intentionally naturalistic.

A further useful contrast with *The Family Economist*, and indeed with Connell's poem, can be found in John Gilbert's engraving for a poem about work by Gerald Massey. Here one can see a confident middle-class annexation of the 'returning artisan' trope for a coherent mid-Victorian celebration of the united stoical working-class family. This engraving was published in a showy illustrated gift book published by Routledge in 1858 made up of a poetic anthology organized around the theme of *The Home Affections*, edited by Charles Mackay and with illustrations by 'eminent artists' under the direction of the Dalziel brothers.[27] Massey, himself from artisan origins, offers in the poem both a bleak and a heroicized version of the work/home antithesis, balancing two stanzas of

4   Wood engraved illustration to *The Poetical Works of Gerald Massey*

denunciation of the struggle of urban labour ('I have fought, I have van-quisht, the dragon of Toil') against two which celebrate home and fam-ily. Yet even in the attack on toil, Massey defends the self-reliance, energy and manliness of labour. Gilbert's engraving thus follows the poem by acknowledging the realities of urban poverty, positioning a single candle against the gloomy shadows which form a backdrop to the scene. But Gilbert centres his image on precisely the same sculptural family shape both monument and dynamic spiral, as in the vignette discussed above, if in reverse, with the women occupying the periphery of the scene. The heroic endurance of the workman is emphasized by the strong vertical of the stand chair in the right foreground, itself a monumental piece of fur-niture. The artist here shows every confidence that a combination of cele-bration and pathos can hold the image together as a sympathetic representation of industrial family life which would gratify both the social concern and the family vision of a middle-class readership.

An additional detail offers an interesting gloss on Gilbert's illustration. In 1861 Routledge published a cheap, single-volume *Poetical Works* of Gerald Massey, something of an achievement for a writer from an artisan background and with professed radical views.[28] Aimed at a slightly dif-ferent, culturally more ambitious, but financially less competent reader-ship than *The Home Affections*, and certainly more meanly produced, Massey's *Work* included a cut-down version of Gilbert's plate (Plate 4). In cramming this quite large and impressively scaled illustration into a small octavo page, the candle and the chair on the right-hand side have been cut away, which brings the focus exclusively on to the family group. By these means this powerfully heroicizing image was given renewed or expanded currency with a potentially wider readership. As a clear exam-ple of how plates were reused as established visual tropes even at quite sophisticated levels of the literary market (and not just in provincial broadsides), this illustration could not be bettered. Having once formu-lated an image into a block, the widest possible use of that block becomes an economic necessity. The function of such re-use in disseminating and extending the currency of particular images should not be underesti-mated.[29]

The issues raised by these uses of the 'returning artisan' motif are com-plex. This narrative trope exercised a powerful and persistent hold on both artisan and middle-class perceptions. It would be easy to cite many late Victorian versions of the same theme, the most interesting of which seems to me Arthur Hughes's late painting 'Home From Work', now in the Russell-Cotes Museum in Bournemouth. It is, however, a trope which originates in a Georgic vision of pastoral harmony between work and home, between Labour and Nature, but which shifts by successive transformations in both literary and graphic formulations into a mode of reconciling an implicit conflict between labour and leisure. The use of this new version of the narrative, in which the house becomes an antithetical element of the factory, is a necessary context for reading the 1850 *Family Economist* title page.

Ideology and *The Family Economist*

In trying to read off the ideological formulation constructed by this vignette wood engraving, it may be best to begin with what is *not* being said, those meanings which are by implication being excluded from this particular representation. In Plate 1, the 1848 version, the setting is uninterruptedly rural, with a country scene continuing the fertile, plant-lined theme of the window sill. A male worker, possibly the householder, is framed by the open window, watering plants in his smallholding. Behind his active figure rises a church spire set alongside a row of tall trees. Along the right-hand wall of the cottage is a large dresser displaying rows of plates in an orderly metonym for domestic organization. Even the bare boards of the cottage floor cannot disrupt this organically composed scene of the interdependence of work, leisure, and family contentment. This formulation of the scene is in direct contrast with the 1850 title page (Plate 2), where the window blots out the world of work rather than celebrating it, and where the emblematic dresser is replaced by a half-open door and a male figure.

But more powerful comparisons still in revealing the potential disquiet which underlies an apparently celebratory image are with two illustrations to tract narratives of almost the same date, the first one of the Chambers' Brothers secular tracts of 1847 (Plate 5) and the second a slightly later S.P.C.K. narrative of 1853 (Plate 6).[30] Both these tracts illustrate narratives which act as direct and unequivocal refutations of the narrative trope of the happy returning artisan learnt from Gray and his successors. Both are from kinds of literature directed specifically at artisan readers with reformist intentions and both interestingly construct the returning artisan in an unheroic and disruptive way in which conventional representation of drunkenness through clothes, posture, and expression is put to use to offer a naturalistic rather than an ideological image. Here the returning artisan is a threatening drunk who creates a stagey but carefully realized panic in the wife and children placed, as usual, in the orderly cottage interior. The two vignettes accompany a similarly direct rewriting of the narrative. In the Chambers' Brothers tract, a rather restless but fundamentally hard-working and conformist servant marries a local workman without finding out his true character. He takes her small savings and launches into dissipation, returning home only to replenish his funds. He beats his wife, who contracts breast cancer as a result, and undergoes radical surgery. Her husband falls into petty crime, and then more serious trouble. He is apprehended and sent to Botany Bay. He eventually dies in Australia. Meanwhile his wife struggles to maintain herself and her child. After many tribulations she is rescued through a chance meeting with a prosperous relative, but, interestingly, the narrative acknowledges its own fictive closure by pointing out that few readers will have rich uncles to rescue them from hastily made marriages. Narrative and woodcut alike insist on both the fictive structures of tract literature and on the fundamental naturalism of representation of the brutalized husband.

The S.P.C.K. tract offers a similar narrative. An inexperienced and stubborn young woman insists on marrying a known drinker who degenerates into brutality and, consequently, poverty. Her children die, she is finally driven into madness by the coincidental death of the last child and the arrival of the bailiffs. She is taken away, but in her absence her husband finds God and is reformed. Trusted by forgiving neighbours, the husband finds work, his wife recovers, and comes home to replace her lost children with new babies. The structure here of a God who manifests himself by clear social vengeance and reward may be a convenient theological simplification, but the ease with which the 'returning artisan' trope can be appropriated to such an alien purpose suggests the difficulty of continuing to use Gray's narrative for ideological purposes in the mid-Victorian period. In order to succeed in its celebration of artisan domestic contentment, *The Family Economist* engraving has to repress a range of interpretative possibilities which enter the narrative through the social changes consequent upon urbanization and industrialization – the returning labourer may be vicious, drunk, out of work, alienated. As the Chambers Brothers and Home Tales tracts suggest, family housing conditions or illness may deprive the narrative of its central action, as the artisan may well choose to seek the pub or some other diversion of the kinds rehearsed by Philip Connell rather than the consolations of family and hearth. The social realities of a harsh industrialized culture threaten the celebratory narrative of the artisan's homecoming with all the possibilities of alienated labour.

Bearing these issues in mind, an interpretation of *The Family Economist* 1850 title page thus depends on the significance of the male figure, who is half hidden in the doorway. His pose is the reverse of heroic, indeed is almost slouching, as he gazes at the orderly domestic interior with both mother and the two eldest children absorbed in their separate activities. The unified grouping of the intent mother and children extends the strong triangular shape of the hanging bookshelves, and emphasizes the separateness of the domestic group from the world

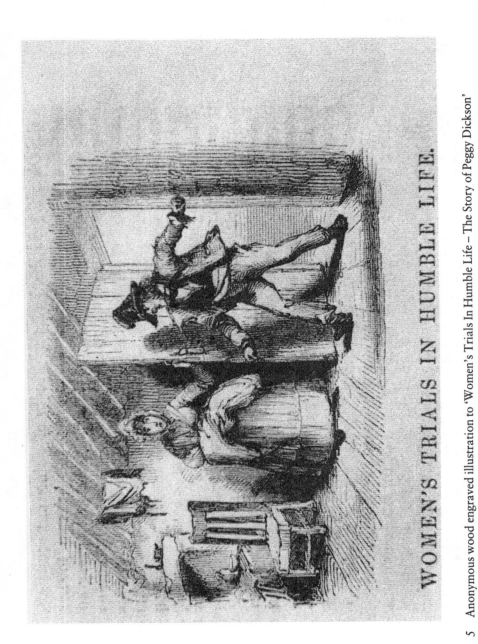

WOMEN'S TRIALS IN HUMBLE LIFE.

5 Anonymous wood engraved illustration to 'Women's Trials In Humble Life – The Story of Peggy Dickson'

outside the cottage.[31] The figures turn away from the outside world glimpsed through the window, focusing on the hearth rather than the doorway. I think it is hard for contemporary viewers to regard the male figure as anything other than a disruptive intrusion into this scene, as he seems to lurk voyeuristically on what is presumably his own doorstep. Is he pausing to contemplate his own domestic happiness, to savour the quiet, respectable activity round his own fireplace? Or does he pause in full consciousness that his male presence will bring the world of work intrusively into the domestic sphere? The threat the male figure offers to the scene is a powerful combination of his gender and his industrial role. Indeed this vignette might stand as a classic exposition of Ruskin's notorious association of gender with work in a famous passage of *Sesame and Lilies*, first published in 1865:

> We are foolish, and without excuse foolish, in speaking of the 'superiority' of one sex to the other, as if they could be compared in similar things. Each has what the other has not: each completes the other, and is completed by the other: they are in nothing alike, and the happiness and perfection of both depends on each asking and receiving from the other what the other only can give.
>
> Now their separate characters are briefly these. The man's power is active, progressive, defensive. He is eminently the doer, the creator, the discoverer, the defender. His intellect is for speculation and invention; his energy for adventure, for war, and for conquest, wherever war is just, wherever conquest necessary. But the woman's power is for rule, not for battle, – and her intellect is not for invention or creation, but for sweet ordering, arrangement, and decision. She sees the qualities of things, their claims, and their places. Her great function is Praise . . . . The man, in his rough work in open world, must encounter all peril and trial; – to him, therefore, must be the failure, the offence, the inevitable error: often he must be wounded, or subdued; often misled; and *always* hardened. But he guards the women from all this; within his house, as ruled by her, unless she herself has sought it, need enter no danger, no temptation, no cause of error or offence. This is the true nature of home – it is the place of Peace; the shelter not only from all injury, but from all terror, doubt, and division. In so far as it is not this, it is not home; so far as the anxieties of the outer world are allowed by either husband or wife to cross the threshold, it ceases to be home; it is then only part of that outer world which you have roofed over, and lighted fire in.[32]

This passage has, not surprisingly, been identified by feminists as a crucially conservative but compelling male definition of gender which expressed a dominant Victorian ideology.[33] But it seems to me that even here the superb rhetoric fails to resolve all the contradictions of Ruskin's position in order to present a unified ideology. More powerful even than this argument about home seems to be Ruskin's tragic definition of the male world of work as inevitably sinful, corrupting, and brutal. As a psychological statement I find Ruskin's fear of his own inadequate masculinity as prominent as his fear of women.

But the crucial issue is Ruskin's association of the male with the heroic if brutalizing world of work and the feminine with the morally sustaining world of home and hearth. In his pursuit of complementary unity, Ruskin works by posing contradictions and differences. *The Family Economist* title page vignette accepts this formulation built on difference and opposition in its simplest possible terms. The aim of the image is to repress difference into a single vision of the domestic, an aim reinforced and confirmed by all the other coded messages of respectability, domesticity, and thrift enacted in this title page. But notwithstanding the unity of purpose expressed here, the vignette is finally at odds with the surrounding ideological formulations. Situated directly under the word 'industrious', directly above verses describing the 'free fair homes' of rural cottage dwellings, and surrounded by mottoes celebrating good sense, rationally, and 'good nature', the engraving seeks to assimilate and extend well-established tropes of domestic harmony, drawn initially from Gray but transmitted, as we have seen, through many popular or even famous subsequent versions. Yet the presence of the male workman here seems to me to disrupt what the image seeks to celebrate. Instead of savouring the cleanliness, respectability, warmth, family affection, and 'economy' of the scene, the male figure at the door seems an essentially anxious even threatening, presence. Despite the conscious use of much of the conventional inconography of cottage contentment, this illustration ends up allowing in all the disruptive possibilities it seeks to conceal. The heroic artisan of Gilbert's image, the sturdy naturalistic labourer of Bewick and Thurston's engraving, the simple swain of Gray's poem, and the pious family man of Burns's, have been allowed to slide into a figure precisely antithetical in nature – the threatening drunk of *Home Tales*. Surprisingly, given the complex of allusions and modes through which it is constructed in the 1850 *Family Economist* title page, the consolatory ideology of respectability is haunted here by fear of its implacable enemies; the alienating effects of hard labour, the violence of the brutalized husband, and the false consolations of drink. If it is possible to regard these illustrations as coded versions of ideological positions, then it is obvious that middle-class ideology is more fractured, more conscious of its own repressions and fantasies than might be expected. In the overtly ideological formulation of the returning artisan motif, aimed at audiences both within and beyond the middle classes, it can be seen that a great deal of idealization occurs. The apparent realism of the wood engraved mode in fact suppresses empirically identifiable reality in pursuit of a literary or mythic construction of an everyday event as it ought

6 Anonymous wood engraved illustration to 'Robert Wilson, or Will He Keep His Promise?'

to be rather than as it was. But in some of the images directed more exclusively at artisan readers, distressing mundane truths insist on being represented so that the heroic artisan seeking the solace of the family hearth becomes the drunken threat embodied in the tract literature. The image then contains, perhaps even expresses, contradictions. While encouraged in the perception that returning workmen offer a vision of domestic contentment, a harmonious alliance between labour and family life, artisan audiences are also reminded that the labourer is potentially brutal and degraded. In looking across this range of images, it is important to recognize the diversity and self-consciousness with which this particular event is constructed in graphic terms. Any notion of the hegemonic power of a unified middle-class version of artisan culture needs to be put alongside the evident variety of interpretation available within these images. The struggle to construct a unified meaning out of social perceptions is precisely that – a continuing struggle between competing possibilities, especially between what ought to be and what was.

One can only hope that the narrative closure of *The Family Economist* vignette is that of Bewick and Thurston and not that envisioned by the illustration of 'Home Tales Founded on Facts'. Indeed, given the confident subsequent use of the same narrative (the family group centred on the mother disturbed by the male presence at the half-open door) in one of the central books of conservative gender definition in the later Victorian period, Mrs Ellis's *The Women of England*, the story ought only to have one happy if non-naturalistic ending.[34] Of such dreams was ideology made, despite the nightmares of observable reality.

Conclusion

In making these links between power, ideology and acts of representation, I have sought to avoid reductiveness. In particular, it is tempting to make an absolute link between social change (here the attack on leisure and on the family caused by new urban industrial modes of production) and its representation in contemporary popular prints (here characterized by a growing pessimism and realism in the depiction of working men returning to their family homes). As Norman Bryson puts it, in a passage which crucially underpins my argument, 'coincidence is not yet determination'.[35] He goes on, more expansively, and using Greuze as his example:

> even if . . . an unprecedented iconography of the family as a unit in separation from society does in fact appear in tandem with the emergence of a new kind of family life and organisation, still it does not follow that related economic and political transformation homoge-

neously *cause* the Greuzian family to appear on the surface of the canvass . . . . Correspondence of an ultimately uni-directional kind (from society to image, and not the reverse) may indeed exist, yet propositions concerning that correspondence remain incoherent until both the specific place of Greuze's mutation of the general iconographic repertoire of familial representation, and the specific role of the image in the social formation as a whole, are clarified, or at least admitted as object of inquiry, say.[36]

Translated into the terms of this chapter, Bryson is warning against reading the changing images of returning artisans as necessary products constructed by new social, economic, or cultural reality. Rather, he argues, we need to read the new images in terms of all those available to the artist as a 'repertoire' of possibilities. This is the reason for my attempt to assemble a range of versions of the same social event from differing levels of social discourse. But Bryson also suggests a further level of necessary awareness – attention to 'the specific role of the image in the social formation as a whole'. In other words, Bryson is stressing the need to acknowledge that images are not merely determined by an economic base, but can themselves be factors in the cultural production of a society, a cultural production which has as its product the construction of social meanings. In this chapter, I have argued that while the images of artisans returning home from labour do have a specific role in social formation, that role is less simply unified than might be expected. Indeed, the images allow themselves to be read (or even demand to be read) ideologically, hence acknowledging their central concern with the construction of specific social meanings. These images are overtly ideological, it seems to me, and do not attempt to conceal their ideological intention under the guise of 'realism' or an unproblematic representation of empirical truths. Their appearance in acknowledged discourses of social instruction, characterized by the generic formulations of cottage magazine, motto, tract and exemplary biography, is itself a recognition of an overriding ideological intention. Yet as Bryson argues, 'correspondence of an ultimately uni-directional kind (from society to image . . .) may indeed exist', and this correspondence is apparent to some extent in the images discussed in this chapter, especially in the apparent linking of realism as a representational code with an increasing pessimism in the social meaning constructed by the image. The happily employed smallholder of the 1848 *Family Economist* gives way to the disruptive lingerer of two years later, the awaited family mainstay of Bewick, Burns and Gray gives way to the threatening drunk of the tract literature. 'Coincidence is not yet determination', but it remains coincidence. While it is dangerous to construct an historical 'truth' from popular prints (yet also to suggest how revealing they can be of ideological structures and

7   Anonymous wood engraved illustration to '*His Hand Upon the Latch* – A Young Wife's Song'

class positions), it is hard to disregard the slide from overtly ideological idealism towards a self-punishing naturalism in the representation of scenes of artisan homecomings between 1750 and 1850. Whether this slide is to be read as a form of progressive, even subversive, increase in social awareness or as merely another manifestation of the power of middle-class ideology to assimilate and accommodate awkward truths, remains a fundamental problem. Certainly the fracture, differences and self-doubts apparent in these images seem to confirm Bryson's denial that images arise directly and necessarily from social and economic realities. Beyond these areas of debate lies the further issue of whether the simple wood engraved vignette is to be read as a realist mode at all. This is an issue which can be fruitfully carried forward into the discussion of a whole range of other Victorian images.

Notes

1. Irene Dancyger, *A World of Women – An Illustrated History of Women's Magazines* (London: Gill & Macmillan, 1978), p. 34.
2. Jennie Calder, *The Victorian Home* (London, 1977), p. 110.
3. J.F.C. Harrison *Learning and Living* (London: Routledge & Kegan Paul, 1961), p. 208.
4. *The Family Economist* ran from 1848 to 1853.
5. See B.E. Maidment, 'Magazines of Popular Progress and the Artisans', *Victorian Periodicals Review*, xvii, 3 (Fall 1984), pp. 82–94.
6. Little has been written specifically on these firms and their role in disseminating literature to a new mass readership, but for the general context see V. Neuburg, *Popular Literature: A History and a Guide* (Harmondsworth: Penguin, 1977) and D. Vincent, *Bread, Knowledge, and Freedom* (London: Europa, 1981). Examples of the development of these kinds of periodicals might be found in *Cassell's Illustrated Family Paper* (1853–1867), *The British Workman* (Tweedie, Bennett, and Partridge, 1855 on), and *The Family Friend* (1848 on – begun as a monthly but weekly after 1852).
7. Some indication of the activities of these firms can be gained from Neuburg, passim.
8. Hone's *Everyday Book* was first published in 1826–7, and *The Table Book* in 1827–28. *The Everyday Book's* sub-title, an 'everlasting calendar of popular amusement', makes clear the popular genres which Hone was reusing. Chambers's *Book of Days* was published in 1862 as a 'Miscellany of popular antiquities', so again the key word 'popular' is given a new currency. William Howitt and Thomas Miller are two other authors who took over and redrew the almanac and day-book tradition for an increasingly literate and serious-minded artisan readership. See Howitt's *Book of the Seasons* (London: Bentley, 1831) and *Year Book of the Country* (London: Colburn, 1850). These books are important not only for the way in which they continue to celebrate a tradition of heroic rural labour into the mid-Victorian period, but also because they suggest in their illustrations a changing representational code for describing the countryside. Howitt's 1831 volume, which was reprinted frequently, has simple vignettes in the

Bewick tradition accompanied by verses. The 1850 volume, however, has pretty and crowded Birket Foster vignettes engraved by Edmund Evans. Miller's *Rural Sketches* (Darton – many undated editions in the 1850s) had comparably pretty illustrations by Branston engraved by Landells and others. Given the wide currency of these kinds of books among artisan readers, it seems possible to infer that these images of the countryside were extremely influential in establishing a representational code for agricultural subjects which mapped a shift from the countryside as a source of aesthetic and moral values perceived by contemplation rather than toil.

9.   Harrison, p. 208.

10. B.E. Maidment, 'Popular Exemplary Biography in the Nineteenth Century – Edwin Paxton Hood and His Books', *Prose Studies* vii, 2 (September 1984), pp. 148–67.

11. E.P. Hood, *The Uses of Biography* (London: Partridge and Oakey, 1852), p. 11.

12. E.P. Hood, *The Mental and Moral Philosophy of Laughter* (London: Partridge and Oakey, 1852), pp. 11, 67, and 73.

13. See R. Parker, *The Subversive Stitch* (London: Virago, 1984). Interesting in the context of this essay is Parker's description of a late eighteenth-century tradition of embroidering samplers with designs taken from landscape paintings.

14. *The British Workman* was published by William Tweedie, Partridge & Co., and A.W. Bennett, a consortium of firms all interested in Christianized popular reading.

The use of mottoes within rules to form a decorative border to the page was used quite widely in exemplary literature. In Godfrey Golding's *How to Get On* (London: Cassell, n.d.) for example, an anthology of 'good devices' and useful exhortatory sayings, the page layout is managed in a manner very similar to that used by *The Family Economist*, with decorative capitals furthering the ecclesiastical resonance of the textual layout. Noticeable in this instance, however, is the difficulty of finding a coherent way of reading a lengthy 'saying' round the page. Where the quotation or epigram runs round two sides of the page, top is paired with bottom margin, left with right. Such fragmentation can be irritating to the reader.

15. Relevant introductions to the conceptual framework of pastoral can be found in P. Marinelli, *Pastoral* (London: Methuen, 1971) and in B. Loughrey (ed.), *The Pastoral Mode* (London: Macmillan, 1984). William Empson's *Some Versions of Pastoral*, first published in 1935, is still central to such debates. For British pastoral painting see J. Barrell, *The Dark Side of the Landscape* (Cambridge: Cambridge University Press, 1980) and A. Bermingham, *Landscape and Ideology* (London: Thames and Hudson, 1987).

I acknowledge, of course, that a full visual history of the 'returning artisan' as a motif in pastoral painting would have to include Gainsborough ('The Woodcutter's Return' [c. 1773] now in Belvoir Castle, offers a good example), Palmer, Morland, Wheatley and many other eighteenth-century landscape painters. Of the many formulations of the image published in print form, William Hamilton's 'The Happy Cottagers' (originally a stipple engraved illustration to Macklin's Poets' Gallery of 1794) and Francis Wheatley's 'The Fisherman's Return' (engraved by Barney from an oil painting of c. 1790) provide powerfully idealized versions. In reducing such a complex representational tradition to a simple ideological formulation, I am seeking a means of entry into mid-Victorian popular versions of the 'cottage' idea rather than attempting any serious exploration of rural themes in British painting.

Feminist historians, in particular, have contributed much to the discussion of the 'returning artisan' motif. The chapter by L. Davidoff, J. L'Esperance and H. Newby in J. Mitchell and A. Oakley (eds), *The Rights and Wrongs of Women* (Harmondsworth: Penguin, 1976), pp. 139–75, called 'Landscape with Figures' is a most important discussion of the themes described here, and it should be read alongside Lynda Nead's excellent study *Myths of Sexuality: Representations of Women in Victorian Britain* (Oxford: Blackwell, 1988). Nead's discussion of Joseph Clark's 'The Labourer's Welcome' in her chapter called 'The Norm: Respectable Femininity' sets the agenda I have followed here, though one of my arguments is that the 'norm' is in fact more troubled and contradictory than Nead suggests. It is, nonetheless, entirely possible to find normative versions of the returning artisan within mid-Victorian popular prints. An anonymous engraving in *Once a Week* for example (8 Dec. 1860, p. 668), which accompanies a poem called '"His Hand upon the Latch" – A Young Wife's Song', implies the kind of rigorously precise female stereotypes described by Nead (Plate 7). In this particular case, the stereotype is all the more powerful because of the absence of the women from the image. The spectator is asked, indeed forced, to construct for him or herself the kind of women actually delineated by Clark.

Other interesting oil paintings on similar themes would include Arthur Hughes's 'Home from Work' (1861) in the Forbes collection – see Susan P. Casteras, *Victorian Children* (New York: Harry N. Abrams, 1986) – and an entirely different reworking of the same theme in the Russell Cotes Gallery in Bournemouth.

16. H.W. Starr and J. Henderickson (eds), *The Complete Poems of Thomas Gray* (Oxford: Oxford University Press, 1966), p. 38.

17. A Birkett Foster edition of 'The Elegy' was published in 1853. He also illustrated Burns (1846), Bloomfield's *The Farmer's Boy* (1857) and contributed to *The Home Affections* (1858, see note 27). Foster's influence on mid and late Victorian wood-engraved versions of pastoral was immensely powerful. Houfe describes his art as 'gentle and subtle', 'much of it in a small scale low key, tiny detailed landscapes with pretty vegetation herds of sheep and cows and cottagers at their doors' (S. Houfe, *The Dictionary of British Book Illustrators and Caricaturists*, Woodbridge: Antique Collectors Club revised edn, 1981, p. 308). As Houfe suggests, Foster is a key figure in sustaining the confident, untroubled pastoral vision of the eighteenth-century landscapists into the mass-produced era of popular wood engraving.

An extremely conservative formulation of the opening scenes of 'The Elegy' can be found in the Westall/Finden steel engraved vignette in the 'gift book' edition of Gray, printed by Whittingham and published by J. Sharpe in 1826. The cottage is excluded in this image, in which the setting sun irradiates the face and smock of the returning swain, merging his figure into the shadowy dusk. The tonal effects possible in steel engraving allow Westall and Finden to create a unified, if sombre, mood of rural harmony, in which the workman 'naturally' fits. The coherent harmonizing tonality of this engraving is not something that can be easily reproduced in wood, however skilfully engraved.

Both Bewick and Constable illustrated 'The Elegy' but neither drew this particular scene.

18. *Gray's Elegy* (Philadelphia: G.S. Appleton, 1850) with illustrations by K.S. Gilbert. Unnumbered pages, but this illustration accompanies stanza VI.

19. J. Kinsley (ed.), *Burns – Poems and Songs* (Oxford: Standard Authors, 1969), p. 117.

20. See, for example, Mackenzie and Dent's Newcastle edition of 1802 with engraved illustration by W. Davidson. This edition does not have an illustration to 'The Cotter's Saturday Night'. The four-volume edition illustrated with Stothard's steel engravings and edited by Currie furthers the metal engraved tradition discussed in note 17. Such engravings are in a quite different graphic mode to the wood-engraved illustrations discussed in this essay, and can be situated in a less naturalistic, more placid tradition derived largely from oil painting and mezzotint.

21. *The Poetical Works of Robert Burns with his Life* (Alnwick: Catnach and Davison, 2 vols, 1808), i, p. 223.

22. *Saturday Night*, i, 1 (London: Hodgson, 1842), p. 1. This periodical appears to be directed at an artisan readership, but I have been unable to find out much about it. It seems to belong to a whole group of twopenny illustrated magazines, usually weeklies, which prefigure periodicals like *The Penny Magazine* and *The Saturday Magazine* but which lack the overt didacticism of the new penny journals of the 1830s. Other titles of this kind would include *The Mirror of Literature* and *The Literary World*. This small format twopenny genre seems to have survived on into the post-penny era in periodicals like *The Literary World*, whose editor went on to become one of the key figures in the development of *The Illustrated London News*.

23. See B.E. Maidment, 'Essayists and Artisans – The making of Nineteenth Century Self-Taught Poets', *Literature and History*, ix, 1 (Spring 1983), pp. 74–91. For further discussions of these issues see M. Vicinus, *The Industrial Muse* (London: Croom, Helm, 1974) and B.E. Maidment, *The Poorhouse Fugitives* (Manchester: Carcanet Press, 1987).

24. C. Kingsley, 'Burns and his School' in *The North British Review* (1848) and reprinted in Kingsley's *Miscellanies* on many occasions.

25. J. Prince, 'The Poet's Sabbath' in *Hours With the Muses* (Manchester: Abel Heywood, 6th edn, 1857), pp. 36–8.

26. P. Connell, 'A Winter Night in Manchester' in *Poaching On Parnassus* (Manchester: John Heywood, 1865), pp. 29–32.

27. C. Mackay (ed.), *The Home Affections* (London: Routledge, 1858). Gilbert's illustration is on p. 257. Gilbert's collaboration with Routledge is important in that it drew the Dalziel brothers into the mainstream of illustrated publishing in 1856 when they engraved Gilbert's drawings for selections from Longfellow. See P.H. Muir, *Victorian Illustrated Books* (London: Batsford, revised edn, 1985), p. 134. The Dalziels' work for *The Home Affections* prefigured their work as art editors for important illustrated family periodicals like *Good Works*, which was founded in 1862. Houfe (op. cit., p. 70) has many interesting things to say about Gilbert, arguing that 'his popular appeal cannot be overestimated'. His popularity

was based, according to Houfe, on his 'majesterial' draughtsmanship, and sense of 'majesty and grandeur on the printed page', specializing in 'lofty sentiments'. Douglas Jerrold's notorious remark about Gilbert – 'We don't want Rubens on *Punch*' – takes on an interesting edge when comparing this group from *The Home Affections* with the more modest and naturalistic versions of the scene suggested by the other illustrations in this chapter.

28. *The Poetical Works of Gerald Massey* (London: Routledge, Warne, and Routledge, 1861). Gilbert's illustration is on p. 225. The illustrators are not named or acknowledged in this edition.

29. The best-known example of this process is the cutting down and reusing of Edmund Evans's blocks for some of William Allingham's fairytale volumes.

30. 'Robert Wilson; or, Will He Keep His Promise?', *Home Tales Founded on Facts*, xiv (London: Society for Promoting Christian Knowledge, 1853).

31. This strong triangle, built out of mother and children, is a central feature of a picture by Gainsborough, 'The Cottage Door' (1780), which is persistently relevant to this chapter. In Gainsborough's oil, the elements of tree-cradled cottage, blank open doorway, and family group built into a unifying triangular form are all influential on the 'returning artisan' pictures, especially as, despite the absent father, the painting is usually read as one of Gainsborough's most powerfully harmonious images. E.D.H. Johnson describes it as 'his most satisfactory resolution of the Arcadian vision' in which 'a natural order reigns of which the simple peasant family is just the human manifestation' – E.D.H. Johnson, *Paintings of the English Social Scene* (London: Weidenfeld and Nicolson, 1986), p. 118. Johnson ably defends the 'Rubensesque' power of the interrelated triangles of the compositional elements here, but, after working on this chapter, I still find the absence of the father disturbing. Barrell (*Dark Side of the Landscape*, pp. 65–72) reads Gainsborough's paintings on this topic of the idyllic cottage family group as idylls which are historically challenged by the social realities of rural labour. To me, the discourse of the later Victorian accounts of the same idea centres much more on the family than on labour as the central issue.

While considering the compositional formulation of the returning artisan motif, it is worthwhile mentioning the obvious neo-classical version of the same event. In Greuze's 'Return of the Drunken Father' for instance, the mother and two children are arranged in a supplicatory frieze on the same plane as the returning drunk with their profiles only available to the viewer. The triangular unity of the images discussed in this chapter as a way of emphasizing the protective centrality of the female figure stands in contrast to an Enlightenment equality of supplication, in which the children are as active as the mother. Albert Boime discusses Greuze's picture as a representation of the potentially disastrous misuse of patriarchal authority in *Art in an Age of Revolution 1750–1800* (Chicago: University of Chicago Press, 1987), p. 42. The painting is in The Portland Art Museum, Portland, Oregon.

32. E.T. Cook and A. Wedderburn (eds), *The Works of John Ruskin* (London: George Allen, 39 vols, 1903–1912), xviii, 121–2. *Sesame and Lilies* was published in 1865.

33. See, for the origins of this debate, K. Millett, *Sexual Politics* (London: Hart-Davis, 1970) and some of the essays in M. Vicinus (ed.), *Suffer and Be Still* (London: Indiana University Press, 1972).

34. Mrs S. Ellis, *The Women of England* (London, n.d.), frontispiece.
35. Norman Bryson, *Vision and Painting: The Logic of the Gaze* (London: Macmillan, 1983), p. 133. Bryson's chapter on 'Image, Discourse, Power' (Chapter 6) is a powerful and coherent exploration of many of the theoretical issues which underpin this chapter.
36. Bryson, pp. 133–4.

CHAPTER THREE

Gender Issues and the Crimean War: Creating Roles for Women?

Cynthia Dereli

War has always been a special case, bringing a whole new set of social relationships and institutional controls into operation. The Crimean War was doubly special. It was the first war in which Britain had been engaged since the country espoused a democratic self-image in 1832. It was also the first war in which advances in technology made possible swifter communication between the war front and the public at home, so that W.H. Russell's detailed accounts of the fighting and the condition of the troops before Sebastopol were read by the British public within a few weeks of the events happening. As a result this war provided the rare phenomenon of criticism of the government of the day being voiced during a war. The government of Aberdeen fell and the politicians who took over were forced, even as the war continued in the East, to countenance a public investigation into the running of the war and the allocation of blame for the catastrophic mismanagement.

It is against this backdrop that I want to consider the roles allocated to women during the war period, as they were presented in the newspapers of the time, but particularly in the poetry of the period. In tackling this subject one is not at first sight overwhelmed with evidence. The politicians of the time were exclusively male, as were the soldiers and the personnel of the army and navy; indeed few references to women survive in the accounts of this war. Interestingly, however, for many today the only figure remembered from the Crimean War may well be a woman, Florence Nightingale. A statue of Florence Nightingale was erected in London during the First World War, clearly an instance where an acceptable and well-known image from a previous war was being used as a rallying point in a later one. This does suggest that the image of Florence Nightingale was quite central to the mythology of the Crimean War.[1]

This study will focus primarily on the central period of the Crimean War, from the landing of the allied troops in September 1854 to the fall of Sebastopol a year later. Within that period it will explore the operation of language in the public discourse on the war as it related to the perceptions of the roles assigned to women. It will examine the presentation of Florence Nightingale's role in the newspapers, and in particular through the medium of poetry, and the relationship between these

images and the more general media references to the role of women during the war.[2] Finally the role of women poets will be considered through
an examination of their contribution to the writing of the Crimean War.

While this study does not espouse any specific theoretical approach,
underpinning the choice to consider specific language uses in relation to
their historical context is the vast theoretical debate which has flowed
from Barthes's focus on the ideological content of 'myths', and
Foucault's meticulous teasing out of the operations of power through
institutions and language.

The point of view on the events which I am primarily concerned to
examine is neither that of the objective historian, nor of the participants
in the central action. It is that of the distant observer. Mrs Seacole, a
Creole woman who found a role for herself in the Crimea during the war,
commented astutely that one's view of the battle being fought depended
on where you were standing at the time. The public in Britain, she noted,
'through the valuable aid of the cleverest man in the whole camp
[William Howard Russell], read in *The Times*' columns the details of that
great campaign, while we, the actors in it, had enough to do to discharge
our own duties well, and rarely concerned ourselves in what seemed of
such importance to you'.[3] It is with the public perception of Miss
Nightingale's mission during the period of the war that I will be centrally
concerned.

Before considering the work of Florence Nightingale, it is useful to
note the social role into which she was born simply by virtue of being
female by gender, and upper-middle by class. F.K. Prochaska, in her
introduction to *Women and Philanthropy,* sums up the position of
women in Victorian England with a list of adjectives popularly applied to
them: 'Moral, modest, attentive, intuitive, humble, gentle, patient, sensitive, perceptive, compassionate, self-sacrificing, tactful, deductive, practical, religious, benevolent, instinctive and mild'.[4]

The extent to which individual women at that time were inclined to
question their lot can now only be guessed at. The views of Florence
Nightingale herself did not agree with those of the activist Barbara
Bodichon, for example.[5] Miss Nightingale's own thoughts on the role of
women can be found in her unfinished work *Cassandra,* where she
analysed her own spirit of rebellion against the role socially allocated to
her. The extent to which she succeeded in her rebellion has been considered by many of her biographers.[6] Sir Edward Cook has commented on
the struggle she faced in her early pursuit of knowledge about nursing:

> Now that the fruits of Florence Nightingale's pioneer work have
> been gathered, and that nursing is one of the recognized occupations
> for gentlewomen, it is not altogether easy to realize the difficulties
> which stood in her way. The objections were moral and social,

rooted to large measure in conventional ideas. Gentlewomen, it was felt, would be exposed, if not to danger and temptations, at least to undesirable and unfitting conditions. 'It was as if I had wanted to be a kitchen-maid', she said in later years. Nothing is more tenacious than a social prejudice.[7]

It will be helpful here, therefore, to outline some of the basic facts about this woman who became so involved in the Crimean War. All her biographers consider her family relations to have been problematical. Florence has left clear evidence of the frustration which she felt as a result of the demands made on her by her family, when she saw herself as having a higher purpose to fulfil. Those demands were in part individual and personal, the results of the health or emotional needs of her father, mother and sister and, at times, of her aunts. The restraints were also the product of social pressures, of the family's perceptions of what was acceptable behaviour for an unmarried woman and of the extent to which they considered that her behaviour touched their own reputations. When Florence wanted to spend her time in hospitals in Italy, Germany or England her family were irate. The experience of nursing institutions which she had acquired before the autumn of 1854 had been gained in the teeth of strong family opposition. However, when she insisted on going out to the East and became famous as *the* nurse of the British army, they all revelled in her reputation, especially her sister Parthe.

Reports of the landing in the Crimea, the subsequent battle on the Alma and the shocking conditions endured by the wounded in the hospital at Scutari all appeared in the newspapers during October 1854. Responding to a call published in *The Times* for nurses for the East, Florence sent a letter to her friend Sidney Herbert, then Secretary at War, offering her services. Her letter crossed with Herbert's asking for her help. The moment was significant. Florence certainly felt that this was the task she had been preparing herself for, and equally Herbert seems to have recognized at once that she was indeed the right person for the role he had in mind. Preparations were made with all speed. The reports on the conditions at Scutari appeared in *The Times* on 9, 12, and 13 October. Sidney Herbert's first letter to Florence on the subject was dated 15 October. Miss Nightingale, with her party of 38 nurses, set off on 21 October and arrived in Constantinople on 4 November.[8]

There can be no doubt from her letters that Florence saw the organization of the nurses as a major part of her role. It was one over which she became at times very tense, and there are various opinions as to her success on that count. By January 1855 quite a few of the original nursing team had gone or been sent home.[9] At Scutari there were supporters and opponents of Miss Nightingale's organizational methods. She had to deal with the problems of dirt and lack of sanitation, of obtaining supplies and preparing food, all of which involved her in difficult relations with doctors and army administrators.[10] Religious issues and prejudices also entered into the debate. The British people were still suspicious of the aims of Roman Catholics,[11] and Miss Nightingale had been instructed to guard against proselytizing by the nurses, many of whom were Roman Catholic nuns.[12]

From November 1854 to May 1855 Miss Nightingale worked unremittingly in the Barrack hospital at Scutari. Later in 1855 and in 1856 she visited the hospitals in the Crimea itself.[13] While in the Crimea she was taken ill, but she soon returned to her duties at Constantinople and did not return to England until after the last patient had left Scutari, in July 1856.[14]

At the end of the war she was a heroine. From 1856 for several years a steady flow of memoirs of the Crimea found their way into print, from those who had been there as officers, soldiers, doctors or visitors, even nurses. This literature served to preserve the memory of Miss Nightingale's efforts, and to reinforce perceptions of their importance.[15] While twentieth-century opinions vary as to the exact foundation of the legend that has been built up around her, the existence of the legend cannot be denied.[16]

It is time to turn to consider what the public learned about Florence Nightingale from the press during this year of war. In October 1854, when the first reports of the chaos in the East were published,[17] Florence Nightingale's mission was widely reported, though it was only one of several antidotes to the national pangs of conscience over the conditions for the wounded that were being publicized, others being the establishment of the Patriotic Fund and *The Times*'s Sick and Wounded Fund. *The Times* seems to have been more concerned with its own project, the 'Sick and Wounded Fund', though it did give space to comments on Florence Nightingale's mission in letters to the paper. Here the tone was not always restrained. A letter of 21 October urged the need for nurses for the East, presenting an image of the role of nurse in glowing patriotic colours: 'The women of England must surely yearn to take a part, however small, in the glorious deeds of their countrymen; nor will they allow themselves to be eclipsed in self-sacrifice and devotion by the French Sisters of Charity'.[18]

A letter from 'One who has known Miss Nightingale' was printed on 25 October, which was full of ardent praise for her and even suggested a comparison with Christ:

> When our Saviour did works of charity, the Evangelists tell us he said, 'See that thou tell no man'; but the more he charged them so much the more a great deal they published it abroad; and we, in like manner, are, [I] think, justified in making it known that Miss

Nightingale gave up everything that education, wealth, and connexion could afford to make this life a life of pleasure, when she first devoted herself to the care of the sick.[19]

The language of the local papers was, as always, less restrained. The *War Express and Daily Advertiser,* 1 November 1854, included Miss Nightingale in a list of the benefits of war:

We owe to the war the merciful mission of Miss Nightingale, the beautiful letter of Mr Sidney Herbert, the noble generosity of the British soldier offering water to the dying lips of his wounded Russian foe on the heights of Alma.[20]

The 'beautiful letter' by Mr Herbert had been printed in *The Times* on 24 October. Restraint was the dominant tone of Mr Herbert's pragmatic pronouncement, as he argued against sending out more nurses, especially untrained ones, to the army hospitals where they might cause chaos:

The Government have felt that it would be impossible to throw open a military hospital, or indeed any hospital, to the indiscriminate nursing of any persons whose benevolence or wish for employment might induce them to offer themselves, without evidence of their experience or fitness to perform the arduous duties they undertake.

On the other hand, he spoke in glowing terms of Florence Nightingale's abilities as an organizer, and hence as offering in her person, a solution to the problems of the moment at Scutari.

The Times's rivals were slow to acknowledge the veracity of its accounts of the suffering in the East. *The Times* had set up its fund and printed calls for nurses for the East, before the *Examiner*, beginning to change its position, printed an article, which was then widely reprinted, 'Who is Mrs Nightingale?'. This piece described as thoroughly orthodox Florence Nightingale's education, her accomplishments, and her family background, though the writer also made reference to charitable excursions which had taken her beyond the ordinary limits, but which were explained as arising from the same 'yearning affection for her kind'. While her mission to the East was described as an act of self-sacrifice, the writer always qualified his praise with a touch of scepticism, implying that her mission was a departure from the norm.[21]

A letter to *The Times* on 13 November also generated more comment and highlighted the issues involved. 'Common Sense' offered grudging praise of Florence Nightingale, but expressed reservations about the 'discretion ' of the politicians who had taken up the offer of her services, and suggested the job would be better done by '50 or 60 hospital orderlies'. Problems of accommodation for women, of tasks suited to women, of control and disciplining of women, were all raised with the underlying implication that Scutari was not a place for women. He also queried the particular role of Florence Nightingale as one subordinate to the medical men but in charge of the women. Sisters of Charity, Common Sense argued, were a different matter because of their religious training. He concluded that the 'reckless devotion' of Miss Nightingale and her nurses was likely to prove an embarrassment to the government department that sent them. In the responses to this piece, whether in support of the women or against them, the sensitivity of the issues raised by their action in going out to the East is felt. For example, a letter in *The Times* of 15 November defended them on the grounds that women were better nurses, and their activities were all charitable, and undertaken for love of Christ.

In December, Herbert's speech to parliament in which he made reference to Florence Nightingale gained wide coverage. A writer in *Blackwood's Magazine* in January 1855, attacking the government, referred to Sidney Herbert as sheltering behind Miss Nightingale's skirts.[22] By January 1855 the *Morning Chronicle,* for one, was now firmly on Miss Nightingale's side and attacks on her as an associate of *The Times* and the government were being upstaged by the factual reports of conditions at Scutari.

Many of the conflicts and frictions inherent in the position assigned to Florence Nightingale were almost unconsciously exposed in a report of her arrival at Scutari from *The Times's* correspondent, published on 23 November:

> The employment of female aid in this way was tried once before in our army and failed, and many experienced officers are doubtful as to the success of this renewed attempt, but in the French service it answers admirably, and there seems no sound reason why those who in the popular belief, as in the poets' language, are 'ministering angels', by the bed of sickness and death should, on fair trial, be found wanting now. The public, ever ready to appreciate acts of devotion, will watch with lively interest the progress of such an experiment, and will be reluctant to admit, except upon the clearest evidence, that Protestant England cannot send forth upon a mission of such high benevolence Sisters of Mercy quite as effective as any Roman Catholic country.[23]

There are a number of problems latent in this summary of Florence Nightingale's role. The suggestion, for instance, that the nurses are to be a Protestant equivalent of the French Sisters of Charity is fraught with ambiguities. A large proportion of the soldiers were in fact Roman Catholic, but then, for lack of other suitable candidates, so were a good proportion of the nurses, while prejudice and fear of Roman Catholicism persisted in England in spite of France being our ally.

In the first months of 1855 the reports from the self-appointed supervisor of *The Times*'s fund, the Reverend S.G. Osborne, and from other correspondents in Constantinople continued to bring the issues at Scutari, if not the figure of Miss Nightingale herself, constantly before the public.[24] The reports of the meetings of the Roebuck Committee which was investigating claims of mismanagement in the East, also had the same effect as, one after another, those responsible for the administration at Scutari in late 1854 were called to give evidence. The nurses were mentioned rarely, but their role and especially that of Florence Nightingale must have been called to mind by every reader, when presented with accounts of the muddle that had preceded their arrival. However, the news of Miss Nightingale's illness in the summer of 1855 received only brief coverage in the daily papers, since by that time, after a long period of inactivity, the allies had at last engaged the enemy, and coverage of the military exchanges and then of the death of Lord Raglan were the main news stories.

Finally it should be noted there must have been hundreds of letters arriving in Britain making reference to the nurses at Scutari from soldiers treated there, and some soldiers at least returning home to spread the word.[25] Such letters and verbal accounts must have played no small part in the creation of the reputation of Florence Nightingale during the war.

An important contribution to the creation of the public image of Florence Nightingale was made by poets. From 1854 to 1855 a steady trickle of poetry about Florence Nightingale appeared.[26] Poetry about the war was becoming extremely popular at this point, and Florence Nightingale took her place alongside the battles of 1854 as a popular subject for such works. During the months of war, step by step, the poets constructed an acceptable image of her role, a vocabulary for this purpose being refined from one poem to another. The now famous image of the lady with the lamp appeared only late in 1855 towards the end of this process.

Punch was among the first to speak of Miss Nightingale in verse, with a poem printed on 4 November 1854, 'The Nightingale's Song to the Sick Soldier'.[27] At this date, when only *The Times* seemed entirely convinced of the necessity of Miss Nightingale's mission, the poem retains an impenetrable ambiguity. It would seem to be one of *Punch*'s tongue-in-cheek productions. The title rather disrespectfully labels the lady 'The Nightingale', and this pun on her name becomes the basic image of the poem. The first verse pushes the joke further, punning on the word 'jug': 'Singing medicine for your pain, in sympathising strain, /With a jug, jug, jug of lemonade or gruel'. The poem is addressed to an ordinary soldier, and its message is about the comfort and care which he personally can expect to receive from the Nightingale. This personalizing of the account of her mission threatens to transgress the boundaries of decorum, but the final verse does offer some muted praise:

> Singing succour to the brave, and rescue from the grave,
> Hear the NIGHTINGALE that's come to the Crimea,
> 'Tis a NIGHTINGALE as strong in her heart as in her song,
> To carry out so gallant an idea.

The ambiguity is deepened by comparing this piece with a prose satire which was printed on 11 November 1854, under the heading 'Nurses of Quality for the Crimea'.[28] This purports to be a report of a meeting of women interested in making the journey to the East to help nurse the soldiers there. The views of the women, who are said to be following 'the noble example of Miss Nightingale' but who are all given satiric names, are characterized as frivolous and ignorant, and the fun is heightened with a touch of double-entendre in the reporting of Miss Piscina Copestole's contribution, where the 'corporal' aspects of the tasks to be undertaken are given satiric prominence. The adjective 'noble' applied to Miss Nightingale in the opening sentence must then be seen as ironic. *Punch* seems to be sticking precisely to the accepted role model for middle-class women, and implying that anyone who wishes to cross that boundary is no better than she should be. The voice of stern decorum is introduced to complete the sketch in the character of Dowager Lady Strong'ith'head, who draws attention to the government's role in this affair, and insists, 'It was the business of the Government to provide proper nurses for military hospitals: and not to leave the duties of the soldier's nurse to be undertaken by young ladies of rank and fashion, who knew not even as yet what it was to nurse a baby'. This succinctly reasserts the parameters of the female role, which was first and foremost to be wives and mothers, any nursing activity being an extension of the latter, carried out as an act of charity. Miss Nightingale's actions are referred to by the Dowager as a 'display of enthusiasm'.

The illustration included with the satiric sketch shows a nightingale with a young woman's head, perched on a chair beside the bed of a wounded soldier, while in the background a nurse with angel's wings offers a drink to another soldier. It would seem likely that this illustration would be intended to extend the satiric attack of the prose passage.[29] To what extent *Punch* expected its readers to make connections with the legend of Philomena is not clear.[30] The mere reference to an individual woman in the pages of *Punch* was in itself a novelty. The paper would from time to time offer its comment on female dress or habits in general, but personal invective or criticism was reserved for the public figures, who were, of course, all men. Even putting aside, therefore, the difficulty of assessing the impact of the satire at this distance, the very fact that Miss Nightingale was named in the paper positioned her beyond the pale of acceptable female experience.

However, the poetry about her which appeared in different papers over the next few months offered almost unmitigated and intensifying praise. A four-verse poem in the *Globe* on 2 December, entitled 'Russian and English Women', compared the Russian women enjoying the bloody battlefield spectacle with the positive role envisaged for the English women newly arrived at Scutari, who were praised directly in the last lines of the poem as 'that blest band of mercy, /Beheld by eyes Divine'. The poem thus utilized the already established opposition between the good allies and the evil Russian enemy, and needed to add very little to produce an effective eulogy on the English women.[31]

Westland Marston's poem 'At Scutari', which appeared in the *Athenaeum* on 20 January, was similarly restrained in not naming Miss Nightingale, though it did refer to her individual activities rather than to those of the group as a whole. The diction points the way for other poetic offerings in the coming months, using the biblical connotations of the imagery of 'light', to foreground the religious nature of Miss Nightingale's role.[32]

By 27 January 1855 *Punch* was defending Miss Nightingale in prose,[33] and on 17 February it printed another poem on the subject of 'Scutari',[34] The imagery of light is once again employed, and religious associations suggested: she is 'a bright star', 'blessed', and her work is 'saintly'. The pun on her name now leaves only a residual image of sweetness: 'Lady – thy very name so sweet / Speaks of full songs . . .', and the final verse describes her, this time with deadly seriousness, as 'noble', shedding 'a saint's glory' around her, and as putting into action 'what Christ preached'.

The public image of Florence Nightingale's role continued to gain credibility, a reflection, perhaps, of a need for national unity even while the politicians wrangled. The poets helped to construct an acceptable public image for her, a period-specific female role, forcing into the background any anomalies in her situation as a woman present at the scenes of war.

The acceptability of this new role for a woman, its religious base, and its assimilation into the public image of war traditionally perceived as a male-dominated event, are all subjects which are addressed by Tupper's poem 'To Florence Nightingale'.[35] Essentially Tupper seeks to establish Florence Nightingale as 'the crown of Christian womanhood', and to this end the language of the poem is heavily weighted with religious associations. Tupper is not presenting an argument about whether a woman should or should not go to such scenes in foreign lands, or constructing a new role model for women. Rather, the process which is at work in the poetry is one of attaching labels to actions which do not otherwise fit to prescribed patterns, to make them acceptable within this specific situation of the war.

Tupper establishes Miss Nightingale's Christian credentials with references to her as 'saint', and 'good Samaritan'. The extent of her achievement, implied in the phrase 'the crown of Christian womanhood', is affirmed through a comparison of her work with that of Christ himself:

> With tender eye and ministering hand
> Going about like Jesus doing good
> Among the sick and dying:

An onomatopaeic, alliterative reference to the horrors of war is used by contrast to foreground the calm and peace which is brought by Miss Nightingale: 'Calm dove of peace amid war's vulture woes'.

This simple opposition suggests that Florence Nightingale solves all the problems out in the East by her very presence. Herein lay her usefulness to a beleaguered government, whether the administration of Aberdeen or of Palmerston. It was not what she did that mattered to the politicians so much as what she represented to the public. Politically conservative, Tupper is clearly seeing Florence Nightingale from this point of view, as an image of stability.[36]

The association of Florence Nightingale with images of peace may be seen to have had another public function. For many months considerable publicity had been given to statements from the Peace Party, in particular those of John Bright, setting them up for attack to provide further opportunities for the editors' own patriotic flourishes. By 1855 editors and poets alike were countering any further calls for peace with the line that peace was actually what the allies were fighting for. For Florence Nightingale, as the agent of the government to be bringing 'peace', must have been a most useful support to the latter argument.

The opposition between peace and war, or the idea of peace in war, is central to the sonnet to Miss Nightingale in the collection of war poems by Smith and Dobell. The reviewer in *Blackwood's* in May 1855 commented: 'The sonnet to Miss Nightingale is as the subject requires, altogether graceful and good, and winds up with a beautiful image'.[37] There is, in fact, a great deal about pain and horror in the first half of the sonnet, but this provides a foil to the presence of Miss Nightingale, the impact of which is expressed through an heroic simile with which the sonnet ends. At the heart of the sonnet is the line which gives the most direct reference to Miss Nightingale: 'Thy perfect charity unsoiled shall stand'. The Christ-like 'perfect charity' had become a familiar image. That she is said to be 'unsoiled' is appropriate to her position in these scenes of bloody war, where she is somehow untouched by the horror, and also to the way in which her female reputation remains miraculously unsullied in spite of having transgressed so many social taboos to create an image of perfect peace amid the strife.[38]

These patterns of imagery are to be found repeated in many other poems about Florence Nightingale. The poem 'The Nurses' from Henry Sewell Stokes's 1855 collection, *Echoes of the War and Other Poems*, is essentially a compilation of these much-used images to which he adds a fresh emphasis on the image of the nurse as 'Angel'.[39] Coventry Patmore's recent poem *The Angel in the House* had developed the comparison of the perfect wife/mother as 'angel'.[40] Applied to Florence Nightingale then it effectively endowed her role with all the positive attributes of the carer, even though she was not herself wife and mother. This was a sensitive area, yet the accounts of her work tended to foreground precisely this personal aspect of the nurse's position as an area with the greatest appeal to the public at that time, in their anxiety about the individuals, husbands, sons, brothers, in the East. Miss Nightingale's role as a substitute carer was referred to most explicitly in the street ballad 'The Nightingale in the East', where she appears not only as substitute mother-carer, but even (with apparently no moral difficulties) substitute wife.[41] The doggerel verse intended for an audience of wives and mothers of ordinary soldiers thus bears witness to the extent to which Miss Nightingale had been placed above the common social taboos in the public perception.[42]

This poem also further assimilates her into the heroic story of war, through the reference to her self-sacrifice: 'She'll lay down her life for the poor soldier's sake'.[43] This heroic aspect of her role is given increasing prominence in the poetry of 1855, and in accounts of her work in the period following the fall of Sebastopol.[44] Her status as national heroine provides perhaps the most striking use of language to eliminate uncomfortable debate. Once subsumed into the category of 'hero' she becomes a symbol of national unity, and as such it becomes inconceivable to question the role she has performed.

The poets were essentially retelling a story which had appeared originally in the newspapers, and as new incidents of the Nightingale story were recounted in the press reports they were quickly transposed into poetic images. A poem in *Punch* on 8 December 1855, for example, included information from recent reports about her nocturnal tours of the wards:

> Upon the darkness of the night how often, gliding late and lone,
> Her little lamp, hope's beacon-light, to eyes with no hope else has shone![45]

That this picture of her should be the one to capture the public imagination is not surprising, as it so effectively draws together all the imagery which has been built up over the previous year in the creation of this acceptable new English heroine. Longfellow's poem 'Santa Filomena', published in 1857, can be seen as completing the transformation of the young lady who wished to go as a nurse to the East into the figure of the national heroine, to be preserved for posterity:

> A Lady with a Lamp shall stand
> In the great history of the land,
> A noble type of good,
> Heroic womanhood.

Her presence passing along the wards, and by implication her role in the war, are compared to a light which shone briefly when a door was opened and then closed:

> As if a door in heaven should be
> Opened and then closed suddenly,
> The vision came and went,
> The light shone and was spent.[46]

As was seen above, such 'light' imagery had from the first been used to establish for Florence Nightingale an acceptably religious image. To this was then added a link with universal womanhood through the concept of charity, extended to project her as the epitome of womanhood and at the same time its zenith, through references to saints and even a comparison of her mission with that of Christ. Longfellow's presentation of the lady with the lamp encompasses all these aspects of the constructed image, 'Florence Nightingale', but the appropriateness of the image must have been reinforced in the public mind by parallels with another very popular visual image of the period, that of Holman Hunt's painting, 'The Light of the World'.

The reputation of Hunt's painting from its first exhibition in April 1854, through the travels of the two versions of the painting in the next few years, in Britain, Europe and America, has been documented in Jeremy Maas's *Holman Hunt and The Light of the World*.[47] William Bell Scott commented on the wide interest in the painting: 'For the first time in this country a picture became a subject of conversation and general interest from one end of the island to the other, and indeed continued so for many years'.[48]

The simplicity and accessibility of the symbolism employed by Hunt was examined by Ruskin in a letter to *The Times* in May 1854[49] The source for the image of Christ, light in hand, was traced to the book of Revelations. George Landow notes: 'The important point is that, since the symbolism derives from what he takes to be essential habits of mind, it would be immediately comprehensible to any audience, because such "natural" symbolism does not require any knowledge of iconographic traditions'.[50] It would seem likely that this ready-made visual image of the biblical metaphor of the divine light 'which lighteth every man that cometh into the world' must have influenced the poets, Longfellow in particular, in their choice of imagery and have contributed to the lasting popularity of this final transcendent image of 'the lady with the lamp'. The image served to make Florence Nightingale acceptable as a woman doing what women should not do, to support the establishment, to vouch for its fulfilment of its obligations to the people, and to build a consensus image for this war in which consensus in the public domain was unusually lacking.[51]

However, for the most part, the copious output of poetry of the war which was working to create images of national unity in spite of political crisis and dissension, reinforced a traditional supportive role for women in the war. Many of the poems of Richard Chenevix Trench, addressed to those mourning at home and advocating resignation, implicitly included women in the audience addressed, and some spoke to them particularly. The special grief of a mother is considered in the poem ''H Tan, 'H 'Ehi Tan', ('This, or on this'). Trench offers an image of Spartan motherhood as an ideal of the mother who can send her son to war with the injunction: ' – Bring home with thee this shield, /Or be thou, dead, upon this shield brought home'. The tears of mothers are praised, but, 'The tenderness of trembling womanhood' is described still as regulating her behaviour by 'duty's perfect law'. To the female reader the poem offers praise for conformity. The verses persuade with flattery, and establish a role model for motherhood, strictly in accordance with national needs. The prioritizing of duty to country over personal emotion is the theme of a number of poems which can be read as addressing female readers, and projecting female role models for war-time.[52]

The personification of England as the mother figure, which is developed in many poems of the period, is a two-edged sword. On the one hand it presents the country, which is asking for personal sacrifice, in a personal, caring role. Thus the relationship of soldier to country is presented in terms of a one-to-one personal relationship, a more potent image than the colder 'duty to country'. On the other hand, the concept of motherhood is itself being redefined, its usual implication of caring being balanced by duty to a higher cause, and an imperative to heroism. This has eliminated from the agenda for the mother any questioning of the process which has led to her son's death in battle, or any resentment or anger at that death.

The effectiveness of such imagery is well illustrated in a poem by Sydney Dobell, 'Our Mother', not because it is especially effective poetry, but because in typical Spasmodic style, by concentrating on emotion and eliminating argument, he has reduced the poem to the very basics of a comparison of mother country with mother. The details he gives of a mother's thoughts in grief are also a metaphor for the mother country, so that by the time we read the injunction to the soldier in the last lines of the poem the two images are conflated: 'Whoe'er thou art, / Thank God if thou art called a son of hers'.[53]

To twentieth-century readers there can be nothing new about these images of the woman's role in time of war. Since the Crimean War, they have been invoked along with a vocabulary of national unity whenever war has occurred. Before 1854 the strength of the social hierarchy carried the presumption of unquestioning obedience from all subjects in the cause of national unity when the monarch declared his country to be at war. This basic relationship, for instance, underlies the thinking of Vattel on war.[54] While the image of 'the mother country' may be now a familiar part of the rhetoric of nationalism, in the period of the Crimean War its operation as a coercive image of national unity is exposed in the contrast between such images created in the poetry of the time, and the debates and criticism of the establishment which prevailed in the press, validated by the new self-conscious interrogating voice of democracy.

There are two other areas I would like to investigate briefly to clarify further the roles allocated to women in this war, which will also elucidate further the social function of the role allocated to Florence Nightingale: the evidence of the presence of other women in the Crimea and their apparent 'invisibility' to the British public at the time, and the role of the female poets.

Information can now be gleaned from memoirs and letters about the presence of other women in Turkey and the Crimea, wives of officers and soldiers and other nurses, though these are only passing references and give little detail of the circumstances of their lives.[55] At the time very little was said of these groups, and the wives of the common soldiers in particular remained almost invisible. In October a letter to *The Times* put the case for employing soldiers' wives as nurses. The letter writer described the dreadful conditions in which women were living in the East, whether from first-hand knowledge is not clear, and argued that since there was work to be done, the country should train these women because otherwise their fate was a 'stain upon our character as a Christian and civilised people'.[56] From the uniqueness of this comment, we can deduce that this solution was not generally considered plausible.

Thereafter the subject was more or less closed. A passing reference to the presence of soldiers' wives in the East occurred in an article 'The Story of the Campaign Part IV' which appeared in *Blackwoods' Magazine* in March 1855. E.B. Hamley, describing the wards at Scutari, noted: 'At some beds, a woman, the wife of the patient, sat chatting with him; beside others stood the somewhat ghostly appearance of a Catholic sister of charity, upright, rigid, veiled, and draped in black'.[57] The question of how these wives came to be there was not addressed, either assumed to be understood or unimportant. When their presence was noted at Scutari, they were treated as a problem, and it was the bad element who were described:

> It has been necessary within the last few days to carry out with some decision, after infinite annoyance, the extradition of 20 soldiers' wives out of a total of 120; of those who remain a portion only are willing to be in some degree useful, and do some kind of labour for the hospitals; the rest are simply mischievous and disorderly, and many of them drunken and profligate.[58]

A rare instance of more attention and understanding being directed to the plight of this group was provided by *Household Words*. In an article on 21 April 1855, 'The Soldier's Wife', Henry Morley made the orgnization of the army the main subject of his attack, illustrating this with the case of the wives. First, the army allowed only a few soldiers in each regiment to marry, and then it provided no married accommodation for them. On both of these counts, therefore, the army could be seen to be encouraging the soldiers and their wives to break the rules. In the new circumstances of war, he notes: 'Even the small proportion of wives allowed to each regiment are not only not cared for, but are surrounded by such circumstances as allow them to escape demoralisation only by a miracle'.[59] Though these women were at Scutari and available for work, no useful role, and certainly no visible role, was allocated to them. In spite of Morley's plea for them the soldiers' wives left stranded in the East seem to have remained at the bottom of the social pile, disadvantaged both by sex and class, a sharp contrast to the public role created for Florence Nightingale.

However, at the time, records of the war written by women did appear in print alongside those by men, were reviewed, sometimes praised and presumably widely read. These included the adventures of Mrs Duberly, an officer's wife who went to the Crimea,[60] and Mrs Davies's account of her work as a nurse.[61] A traveller's account by Mrs Young was widely reviewed and praised, in spite of offering a view of events that was more sensitive and other-centred than is usually acceptable in war. In fact many of the travellers who took a trip to the East during the war and published their commentaries were to a greater or lesser degree critical of the establishment and sensitive to the hardships endured by the soldiers. Within the spectrum of such writing Mrs Young's account, for instance, would appear to be positioned towards the critical and sensitive extreme, but by no means beyond the pale of public tolerance.[62]

The memoirs of Mrs Seacole, which were well received at the time, show a refreshing tolerance and human concern.[63] The role which Mrs Seacole made for herself in the Crimea appears to have been unique. A woman of Creole origin, and independent spirit, who recognized the prejudice of the whites against her, she had worked to provide for herself and make herself useful, in spite of that prejudice. She was also tolerant and apparently without prejudice. She describes the arrival of the Sardinian troops, and her bustle of activity to provide for them,[64] and recounts her adventures on the battlefield tending the wounded of many different nations.[65] She sees herself in a motherly role, grieving for the young men who do not return from the fighting. When she leaves the Crimea she is almost sorry that this period of usefulness is ended.[66]

Mrs Seacole's independent spirit led her into a role which fitted with none of the models available to women at the time. The fact that her efforts have been overlooked since, that she is a newly rediscovered heroine of the Crimean campaign, constitutes history's judgement on her role and implicitly a gloss on the position of its chosen heroine, Florence Nightingale. The role of the former, as Creole and woman, though accepted in the crisis and given brief public attention as the war ended, could not be accommodated in the pages of history.

The role of poet was another publicly visible role which women continued to fill during the war. A number of poems by women writers were published in the journals at this time. The very fact that these poems reached the public would suggest that they were not perceived as different, or specially distinguished from the rest of the vast output of war poetry.

There is certainly little to distinguish most of Mrs E.L. Hervey's poems of the period from others endorsing the nationalistic viewpoint on the war. Her poems describing battle scenes, praising victories, lamenting and praising deaths in battle deserve a place among the main body of poetry of the period which was working to build unity where the politicians had failed to produce it.[67]

However, the familiar province of women's poetry in the mid-nineteenth century as moralistic and emotional pieces was also continued. Many poems by women writers do not tackle the subject of war directly, but have a strong emotional or psychological link with the experiences of war-time.[68] For example, the poem 'The Spirit of May' by Mrs Hervey took as its subject 'a beautiful German legend', through which it explored themes of motherhood and grief.[69] The presentation of the grieving mother in the German story was, however, equally applicable to the mothers in England grieving for their children in the Crimea, though the link was not explicitly made. The final mood of the poem was one familiar from other war poetry – that of resignation.

In other poems by Mrs Hervey there are moments when a deviation from the patriotic vocabulary of war is glimpsed in the personal tone achieved. This is true of the poem 'Alma' where an intense identification with the despair of those grieving is woven into the central section of an otherwise predominantly patriotic poem: 'Bring back to us – alas! the word, it knells what we have lost! . . . Bring back the dauntless hearts ye bore – we claim them – they are ours!' The poem does not, therefore, leave the reader with quite the same comfortable viewpoint as was achieved by other poets through the rhetoric of patriotism alone.[70]

Dinah Mulock's poetry takes a more visibly other-centred stance. Her poems on the war add to the facts of the case an intense conception of individual experience, the presentation of which involves her in crossing boundaries set by the consensus agenda for poetry. For instance, her poem on the death of the Czar asserts the levelling quality of death, considering the Czar as just another human being. In doing so it crosses a barrier which the press and other poets had been working to build up, between the 'human' good allies and the simply evil Russian enemy.[71]

Her contribution to the copious poetry on the battle of the Alma, 'By the River Alma', contains a sprinkling of the usual heroic language, and ultimately advocates a position of resignation. However, it also crosses another boundary, that set between the classes, as the mother putting her child to bed notes: 'Poor the bed is, poor and hard'. The poem's structure is that of a dramatic monologue, in which the mother pours out her thoughts to her child, and this is utilized to explore powerful and essentially other-centred emotions. The issues of war are subordinated to the fate of the loved one, the husband and father, and it is the intensity of the poet's identification with the sorrowing woman that gives the poem its power.

A similar distinctive point of view is evident in her poem 'Looking Death in the Face', which gives the thoughts of a soldier on the night before the battle of Inkermann. The speaker passes through many doubts and anxieties about the battle, to a state of acceptance of his duty and possible death in battle, on the basis that God is over all, and war is 'but God's ploughshare'. While the poem again closes on a note of resignation, the honest identification with the emotions of the soldier rather than the construction of images to pacify and control the perceptions of readers is central to the poem.

While we may now identify here in part a different 'female' position, there is no evidence that at the time these poems were perceived as anything other than patriotic productions. Mulock's 'Looking Death in the Face' was printed in *Illustrated London News* (*ILN*) and must be assumed to have been perceived as essentially in line with that newspaper's patriotic stance. Presumably at that time sympathy for the working class could be accommodated within the newly constructed sympathy for the army.[72] All that can be said is that women were allowed a voice as poets in war as they had been in peace. While the more persistently other-centred poems may now appear potentially to subvert a pro-war consensus, within the unusual debate at the time such difference was not perceived.

However, the poems referred to above were published in newspapers which in their editorial commentaries were essentially supportive of the war. The editorial policy of *Household Words,* on the other hand, under Dickens's editorship, was to concentrate on the issues of concern at home, instead of jumping on the war bandwagon. It is not surprising, therefore, to find that the poetry by women contributors, Mary Jane Tomkins and Adelaide Anne Proctor, printed during the war did not consistently follow the themes of national glory and unity.

Proctor's poem 'Waiting', for instance, presents the thoughts of a working-class woman patiently waiting for her husband's return.[73] The poem reaches out to explore an experience that was common in that year of war, on a personal, individual level. Whether this is essentially a woman's point of view is difficult to argue but it is certainly a departure from the norm and characteristic of Anne Proctor's poetry. Whether she is writing about the poor mother's despair,[74] or the grave of an unknown soldier,[75] she is equally striving to understand another life, another point of view.

Two poems by Mary Jane Tomkins which were published during the period 1854–5 offer a perspective on the war which was unusual in poetry or prose of this period, except in *Household Words.* The poem, 'At Thy Peril', begins with the question ' "Am I my brother's keeper?" ', and explores the relationship between different classes at an individual level, reminding readers that diseases such as cholera do not discriminate between the classes in the East or at home. This link between responses to the events in the East and the issues at home was rarely heard, for it contained the seeds of dissent and a criticism of the establishment which was much more far-reaching and fundamental than even the shocking reports from W.H. Russell on the conditions in the East.[76]

In the poem 'Before Sebastopol' the poet again seeks an understanding of an individual's situation, in this case a soldier encamped before Sebastopol, suffering from cold and hunger.[77] There is praise for his courage, but at the centre of the poem lies a criticism of the role of government, whose 'world-old rules and party faction' are seen as responsible for the fate of the poor soldier. Again, the sympathy with the individual is maintained to create a tone which is quite out of line with the patriotic fervour of most of the poetry of the period, though consistent with the tone maintained by *Household Words* throughout the period.

When Charles Dickens included this poetry by women in *Household Words,* poetry which forced a comparison between the rank and file soldiers and the working class at home, he did intend to challenge the images which were being used to maintain national unity and defuse criticism of the establishment. Though he was not against the war, his primary concern, and presumably that of his contributors, remained to achieve reform at home.

On the whole, however, the sympathy for the individual common soldier which appeared in some of the poems by women was not perceived as challenging the patriotic consensus in poetry. The concern with emotional or spiritual well-being was an extension of the familiar ground for women's poetry, and the volatility of the political debate ironically meant that these concerns were assimilable rather than threatening. It would seem, therefore, that the role of the woman poet remained unchanged, though transposed into the fringes of the male realm of politics for the period of the war, where female sympathy and emotion could serve the cause of national unity with effect, though sometimes coming uncomfortably close to the boundaries of what was tolerable, and assimilable.

In the Crimean war there was no overwhelming consensus of public opinion. Rather, public debate divided between the discourse of patriotism, unquestioningly pro-war, and the others, dissident or critical. The images of Miss Nightingale, the accommodation of the role of women as poets and the poetic constructions of traditional domestic roles for women, fall into the former category, functioning to support the notion of national unity and patriotism. In the case of the public image of Florence Nightingale, the language of poetry had been used to isolate simple unambiguous images and to simultaneously make other problematic aspects of her role invisible, as the acceptable role of carer was brought to the foreground and reinforced through religious imagery. The new period-specific role thus created made it possible for one woman to cross the normal boundaries for female activity in the public domain and in the process to rescue the establishment. Florence Nightingale would have been useless to the government as merely an aberrant female. As a contemporary novelist noted: 'Womanhood will teach you that a fearful penalty must be incurred by any straying out of the bounds proscribed for your sex'.[78] But the new myth of one public female role could coexist comfortably with the traditional supportive role for all other women in war-time.

It is the malleability of language which is illustrated here. The semantic changes are not part of the slow linear development studied by the linguist. Rather, language is demonstrated to be a commodity which can be rapidly beaten into a new shape, used, and with equal speed hammered back into its original form and put back to its old use – Barthes's ideological 'myths' reshaped to meet a need. Such speed of change of language usage and development of new myths has been associated in the twentieth century with the efforts of extreme political wills, authoritarian politics of left or right, or latterly with the managerialism of the 1990s. Considering the function of this body of poetic images in relation to the very specific socio-political circumstances of the Crimean War exposes the temporary ideological framework within which these images originally functioned. The myth creation achieved by the poets cannot be seen as ideologically neutral and is essentially an exercise of power.

During the Crimean War the adapted female role for Florence Nightingale, and the other-centred language of the women poets, were alike subsumed into the war ideology. Then as now the control of language which made this possible has to be seen as an exercise of power. Cardinal Wiseman, defending the work of the Sisters of Mercy, acknowledged: 'These ladies are an illustration of power and organisation'.[79] Only when the creation of these public images is acknowledged as an exercise of power, can the significance of the experience of women in the Crimean war, the adjusted images of some, the complete invisibility of others, be fully appreciated.

Notes

1. For an account of the legend of Florence Nightingale, see M. Goldsmith, *Florence Nightingale: The Woman and the Legend* (1937). Over the last 140 years, studies of Florence Nightingale and references to her in works on the Crimean War have provided a constant reassessment of her role. Almost every period since the Crimean War has rewritten the story of Florence Nightingale in its own image. For instance, Arthur Quiller-Couch included a study of Florence Nightingale in his book, *The Roll Call of Honour* (1911). Noting that in November 1907 she had been 'advanced . . . to the Order of Merit, of all rewards to-day the rarest and most highly prized', Quiller-Couch states her achievement in terms of his own age's views on the highest aims of human existence, namely empire:

   Her true reward, however, lay in the abiding gratitude of a nation; in that, and in the fidelity with which Englishmen who followed the path she had found and carried more and more light to the dark places of human misery . . . (p. 238).

   For later generations her activities in the Crimea are easily conflated with the years of illness and writing which followed, and the question of the basis of her reputation is in this way confused. John Shepherd's account of the work of the doctors in the Crimean War provides another context for the evaluation of Florence Nightingale's work. *The Crimean Doctors*, 2 vols (Liverpool, 1991).

2. Mary Poovey's work on women in the nineteenth century, *Uneven Developments: The Ideological Work of Gender in Mid-Victorian England* (1988), has addressed the question of 'The Social Construction of Florence Nightingale'. Poovey's chapter, however, considers this question within the

the context of Nightingale's contribution to the history of nursing. I will be looking at this subject within the narrower confines of a study of the war itself.

3.   Mary Seacole, *The Wonderful Adventures of Mrs Seacole in Many Lands* (1857); reprint (ed.) William L. Andrews (New York and Oxford, 1988), p. 147.

4.   F.K. Prochaska, *Women and Philanthropy in Nineteenth Century England* (Oxford, 1980), p. 3.

5.   For accounts of her work, see H. Burton, *Barbara Bodichon 1827–91* (1949). For excerpts from her writing, see Candida Ann Lacey (ed.), *Barbara Leigh Smith Bodichon and the Langham Place Group* (1986). Florence Nightingale's views on feminism are noted by Ray Strachey, in *'The Cause': A Short History of the Women's Movement in Great Britain* (1928), pp. 24–5:

> ... she shared with Harriet Martineau an active distaste for the feminist writing and propaganda which was multiplying so rapidly during her lifetime. There is indeed a letter of hers to Harriet Martineau in which she says, 'I am brutally indifferent to the rights and wrongs of my sex' (13 December 1861).

For a view on the position of women from the war period, see Eliza Lynn, 'The Rights and Wrongs of Women', *Household Words*, 9 (1 April 1854), pp. 158–61.

6.   See, for example, Sir Edward Cook, *The Life of Florence Nightingale*, 2 vols (1914).

7.   Cook, 1, p. 60.

8.   For a more detailed account see Cecil Woodham-Smith, *Florence Nightingale, 1820–1910* (1950), pp. 130–50.

9.   S.M. Goldie (ed.) *'I have done my duty': Florence Nightingale in the Crimean War 1854–56* (Manchester, 1987), put the number at 19 (p. 80). F.B. Smith in *Florence Nightingale: Reputation and Power* (1982), comments that by Christmas 1854:

> Nightingale had dismissed – on my estimate, because the evidence is ambiguous – 13 of her original contingent, leaving her with 25 nuns and nurses to help about 11,000 men admitted to the hospitals rotten with disease – only about 100 had war wounds. The total was to rise to its peak in January 1855 (p. 40).

10. Some of her biographers have come down heavily on the side of the doctors. See, for instance, Nancy Boyd, *Josephine Butler, Octavia Hill, Florence Nightingale: Three Victorian Women Who Changed Their World* (1982), p. 184.

11. For a view of these prejudices from the Roman Catholic point of view see the review of *Hospitals and Sisterhoods* in *Rambler* 14 (1854), pp. 209–29. On the other side, see, for example, the review of a new novel, *The Sister of Mercy: a Tale for the Times We Live in*, in *Athenaeum*, 28 January 1854, p. 117. The new novel is described as being 'written to prove that the Sisterhood of Mercy is, virtually, a most unmerciful association, devised by unfeeling priestcraft for the subjugation of morbid, feminine, feebleness and vanity'.

12. Miss Nightingale was accused by some of sympathizing with the Catholics, by others of prejudice against them. Compare *Punch*, 28 (1855), p. 37, 'Religious Objections to Miss Nightingale', and Goldie, p. 231.

13. Miss Nightingale was never alone in her position in the East. The role of the Mrs Bracebridge, for instance, is noted, by Rev. S.G. Osborne, *Scutari and Its Hospitals* (1855), p. 29: 'I must not pass over my friends Mr and Mrs Bracebridge; the latter ever watchful over her charge Miss Nightingale'. The French cook, M. Soyer, also accompanied her to the Crimea. See A. Soyer, *Culinary Campaign: Historical Reminiscences of the Late War* (1857), pp. 166–7.

14. Woodham-Smith, pp. 250–5.

15. See for example, a description of a visit to Scutari in R.C. Macormick, *Two Months in and about the Camp before Sebastopol* (1855), ch. 19; thoughts on Florence Nightingale's role from the author of *Inside Sebastopol and Experiences in Camp being the Narrative of a Journey to the Ruins of Sebastopol . . . Accomplished in the Autumn and Winter of 1855* (1856), pp. 248–9; comments on the hospitals in the East and on Florence Nightingale in *Chambers's Pictorial History of the Russian War 1854–56* (1856), pp. 301, 306–10; details of Florence Nightingale's work at Scutari in Harriet Martineau, *England and Her Soldiers* (1859), pp. 190–6, 208, 214, etc.; views of hospitals at Therapia (pp. 73–4), and Balaklava (pp. 306–7) and of 'this celebrated lady', Florence Nightingale in Istanbul (pp. 150–51), in Lady Hornby, *Constantinople During the Crimean War* (1863).

16. Compare Elspeth Huxley, *Florence Nightingale* (1975), p. 146; Woodham-Smith, pp. 220–1; Goldsmith, p. 188.

17. W.H. Russell's report, 'From Our Own Correspondent', in *The Times*, 12 October 1854, p. 7.

18. *The Times*, 21 October 1854, p. 7.

19. *The Times*, 25 October 1854, p. 7.

20. The editorial in *War Express and Daily Advertiser*, 1 November 1854, p. 2.

21. *Examiner*, 28 October 1854, reprinted for example in *Morning Chronicle*, 30 October 1854, p. 8; *Liverpool Chronicle*, 28 October 1854.

22. W.E. Aytoun, 'The Conduct of the War', *Blackwood's Magazine*, 77 (1855), p. 15. The view that the role of Miss Nightingale was essentially useful to the politicians is expressed in *The History of 'The Times'*, 2 vols (1939), pp. 178–9, and in Evelyn Bolster *The Sisters of Mercy in the Crimean War* (Cork, 1964), p. 235.

23. 23 November 1854, p. 7. See also a short story in which the arguments against a woman of good family going to the East are rehearsed: 'The Hospital Nurse: An Episode of the War', *Fraser's Magazine*, 55 (1855), pp. 96–105.

24. Rev. S.G. Osborne's reports served to provide further publicity for Miss Nightingale's mission when they were published in book form in 1855 as *Scutari and Its Hospitals*.

25. Woodham-Smith, p. 234, refers to a legend growing up as a result of the survivors returning home with their stories of the war.

26. The following is a list of poems about Florence Nightingale which were published in local or national press, or in poetry anthologies during the war. It is, of course, only a sampling, particularly of the local press contributions: *Globe*, 21 November 1854, by L.S.C.; *Punch*, 27 (4 November

1854), p. 184, 'The Nightingale's Song to the Sick Soldier' by Percival Leigh; *Morning Chronicle*, 23 November 1854, p. 5, 'A Lady's Reply to Commonsense', defending women's right to go to the east; *Liverpool Chronicle*, 2 December 1854, poem, anon.; *Athenaeum*, 20 January 1855, p. 81, 'At Scutari' by W.M. [Westland Marston]; *Preston Pilot*, 27 January 1855, 'The Sister of Charity' anon., [taken from the new number of the *Family Friend*]; *Punch*, 28 (17 February 1855), p. 61, 'Scutari' by Tom Taylor; *Liverpool Chronicle*, 17 February 1855, poem, anon.; *Punch*, 28 (1855), p. 229, 'A Nightingale in the Camp'; 1855 Broadsheet poems, 'The Nightingale in the East', reprinted in *Curiosities of Street Literature* (1871; repr. 1969); *Echoes of the War and Other Poems* (1855) by H. Sewell Stokes included, 'The Nurses'; *Lyrics* (1855) by Martin F. Tupper included, 'To Florence Nightingale'; *War Sonnets* (1855) by A. Smith and S. Dobell, included 'Florence Nightingale'; *The Times*, 10 September 1855, 'A Monument for Scutari' by R.M.M. [Richard Monckton Milnes]; *Poems by A & L* (1897) by Arabella and Louisa Shore included, 'War Music' and 'Night in the Soldiers' Hospital Scutari', dated 1854 and 1855; *Punch*, 29 (8 December 1855), p. 225, 'Florence Nightingale'.

27. Percival Leigh, *Punch*, 27 (4 November 1854), p. 184.
28. *Punch*, 27 (1854), p. 193
29. A similar transmutation of Florence into a nightingale was used in a comic illustration by Cpt H.R. Howard a few weeks later on 25 November 1854. 'The Jug of the Nightingale' showed a nightingale with a woman's head, carrying a jug with labels 'gruel', 'embrocations', 'fomentations': *Punch*, 27 (1854), p. 215.
30. Philomena was changed by the gods into a nightingale so that she could escape from the wrath of Tereus, having already been raped by the Thracian king.
31. The poem is dated 30 October 1854.
32. *Athenaeum*, 20 January 1855, p. 81.
33. 'Serious Objections to Miss Nightingale' by Percival Leigh, *Punch*, 28 (1855), p. 37.
34. Poem by Tom Taylor, *Punch*, 28 (17 February 1855), p. 61.
35. *Lyrics* (1855), p. 159.
36. Martin Farquhar Tupper's biographer, Ralf Buchmann, in *Martin F. Tupper and the Victorian Middle Class Mind* (Bern, 1941), sees him as essentially typical of the conservative Victorian middle-class outlook.
37. *Blackwood's Edinburgh Magazine*, 77 (1855), pp. 531–35 (p. 533).
38. The degree to which the construction of the image of Miss Nightingale breaks the rules on female behaviour at a personal level is well illustrated by comparing Dobell's poem about her with his personal views on women, as expressed, for instance, in a letter to his sister, where he stated: 'a woman's first "mission" in this world is to be beautiful': *The Life and Letters of Sydney Dobell*, ed. E. Jolly, 2 vols (1878), ii, p. 11.
39. Stokes, pp. 49–52.
40. Reviewed, for instance, in *Examiner*, 25 November 1854, p. 749.
41. Florence Nightingale is referred to in this poem several times as 'a sweet Nightingale' and an 'angel', 'bounteous and good' and bringing 'peace'.
42. For the text see Charles Hindley, *Curiosities of Street Literature* (1871; repr. 1969).
43. The poem is probably incorporating a new issue here, since Richard

Monckton Milnes wrote to *The Times* stressing Miss Nightingale's self-sacrifice. See letter by 'One who has known Miss Nightingale', in *The Times,* 25 October 1854.

44. See, for instance, repeated references to her bravery in the poem, 'A Nightingale in the Camp', *Punch,* 28 (1855), p. 229.

45. *Punch,* 29 (1855), p. 225. The editorial in *The Times,* 23 August 1855, referred to Miss Nightingale's 'nightly wanderings through those long wards'. Woodham-Smith, p. 236, refers to Mr Herbert reading out a letter to a meeting in November 1855, 'in which a soldier described the men kissing Miss Nightingale's shadow as she passed'. *Eastern Hospitals and English Nurses: A Narrative of Twelve Months' Experience in the Hospitals of Koulali and Scutari* by a Lady Volunteer [F.M. Taylor], confirmed this detail of the Nightingale story: 'Miss Nightingale generally visited her special cases at night . . . [she] carried her lantern, which she would set down before she bent over any of the patients' (quoted in a review, *Athenaeum,* 19 April 1856, pp. 484–85).

46. *The Poetical Works of Longfellow* (1904), pp. 312–13. The poem is dated by Sir Edward Cook as having been written in 1857: Cook, i, p. 237.

47. Jeremy Maas, *Holman Hunt and the Light of the World* (Aldershot, 1987). The popular engravings of the painting were not produced until 1860 by Gambart: see Maas, pp. 72–74.

48. William Bell Scott, *Autobiographical Notes,* i, p. 310, quoted Maas, p. 58.

49. Quoted Maas, pp. 61–64.

50. George P. Landow, *William Holman Hunt and Typolo* (1979), p. 34.

51. The perpetuation of this image for posterity has been documented by Woodham-Smith, ch. 11.

52. See, for example, 'Eastward Ho!: Song of the Women to the Soldiers of Great Britain' by Samuel Lover in *Poetical Works* (1868), pp. 308–9; from *The Crimean War Song Book* (1855), 'The Soldier's Wife' by Henry Russell, p. 10, and 'Weep not for the Heroic Dead' by A. Kirkaldy, p. 9. Several poems from Sydney Dobell's *England in Time of War* (1856) adopt a female voice as narrator, and in this way appraise the female role.

53. Alexander Smith and Sydney Dobell, *Sonnets of the War* (1855), p. 43.

54. See Emerich de Vattel, *The Law of Nations or Principles of the Law of Nature Applied to the Conduct and Affairs of Nations and Sovereigns* (1811).

55. Many of the memoirs of the Crimean War, written by men, make passing reference to women on the scene. See, for example, Robert Beaufoy Hawley, *The Hawley Letters,* ed. S.G. P. Ward (1970). Buchanan and Reid both mention seeing Mrs Seacole, an Afro-American woman who was running 'a sort of privatised N.A.A.F.I.': G. Buchanan, *Camp Life as seen by a civilian 1854–56* (Glasgow, 1871), pp. 177, 217; Douglas Arthur Reid, *Memories of the Crimean War, January 1855 to June 1856* (1911), p. 13. Evidence is collected in Piers Compton's book, *Colonel's Lady and Camp Follower: The Story of Women in the Crimean War* (1970).

56. *The Times,* 24 October 1854, p. 9.

57. *Blackwood's Magazine,* 77 (1855), pp. 349–58. A handful of references to women are to be found in W.H. Russell's letters from the East. See, for instance, *The War: From the Landing at Gallipoli to the Death of Lord Raglan* (1855), p. 35.

58. See the report of the correspondent for the 'Sick and Wounded Fund', *The Times,* 19 March 1855, p. 10. See also a reference to the soldiers' wives in

the Parliamentary debate reported in *The Times*, 17 March 1855, p. 5.

59. *Household Words*, 11 (21 April 1855), pp. 278–80.

60. Fanny Duberly was the most prominent of what appears to have been a small number of officers' wives who went with their husbands to the Crimea: *Journal kept during the Russian War: From the Departure of the Army from England in April 1854 to the Fall of Sebastopol* (1855). For a review of the book see *Athenaeum*, 29 December 1855, pp. 1528–29.

61. Mrs Davies was employed chiefly in the kitchens, at Scutari and in the Crimea. Her comments are down to earth, but not detailed. Her remarks on Florence Nightingale are outspoken and critical: *The Autobiography of Elizabeth Davis*, ed. Jane Williams (1857; repr. Cardiff, 1987), p. 183.

62. *Our Camp in Turkey, and the Way to It*, by Mrs Young. For reviews see, for instance, *Athenaeum*, 23 December 1854, pp. 1555–56; *Morning Chronicle*, 18 December 1854, p. 3; *Morning Post*, 23 January 1855, p. 2; a review by J.M. Capes in *Rambler*, 15 (1855), pp. 127–35. Capes noted that Mrs Young's narrative mentioned the soldiers' wives in the East: 'The sex of the writer of *Our Camp in Turkey* leads her to bring prominently forward another point, unhappily too much overlooked by male writers, even the most determined of abuse-hunters; namely, the condition of the women' (p. 132).

63. Sarah Anne Terrot's account of her own day-to-day activities at Scutari also shows a tolerance which is not consistently matched by any of the male writers of memoirs. This is evident in her tolerance of common soldiers, of Roman Catholicism, of the Turks. Her other-centred attitude leads her finally to exclaim:'What lavish waste of life was there! What accumulated wrecks of hopes and joys, all sacrificed, and for what?': *Reminiscences of Scutari Hospitals in the Winter 1854–5* (Edinburgh, 1898), repr. as *Nurse Sarah Anne: With Florence Nightingale at Scutari*, ed. R.G. Richardson (1977), p. 136.

64. Seacole, p. 149.

65. Seacole, p. 166.

66. Mrs Seacole mentioned her friend W.H. Russell, in the preface to her book. He had mentioned her in his reports to *The Times*: *The War: From the Landing at Gallipoli to the Death of Lord Raglan* (1855), p. 360.

67. See, 'Alma', *Illustrated London News*, 21 October 1854, p. 390; 'A Valentine from the Crimea', *ILN*, 17 February 1855, p. 166. See also two poems by Mrs D. Ogilvy which appeared in *Chambers's Journal* in 1855: 'Our Soldier-Brothers' and 'English Worship in Sebastopol', *Chambers's Journal*, n.s.3 (6 January 1855), p. 16, and 4 (22 December 1855), p. 400.

68. See, for example, 'Losses' by Francis Browne in *Athenaeum*, 7 July 1855, p. 790; 'The Wanderer's Return' by Marie J. Ewen, in *Chambers's Journal*, n.s. 3 (23 June 1855), p. 400.

69. *ILN*, 5 May 1855, p. 430. The legend tells of a mothers's vision of her dead child, dragged back from heaven by the weight of her tears in its shroud. The central point of comparison is presented in the third verse as mother earth is called upon to cease her grieving, May being a time when the showers are to end, as the grieving for the dead must also end.

70. *ILN*, 21 October 1854, p. 390. For a similar tone in a war poem by a women see 'The Patriot's Widow' by Sophia Iselin, *Chambers's Journal*, n.s.3 (April 1855), p. 272.

71. *Chambers's Journal*, n.s.3 (21 April 1855), p. 256.
72. Poem had sub-heading 'Before Sebastopol, November 4th', and appeared in *ILN*, 2 December 1854.
73. *Household Words*, 10 (14 October 1854), p. 204.
74. 'The Cradle Song of the Poor', *Household Words*, 10 (27 January 1855), pp. 560–1.
75. 'The Unknown Grave', *Household Words*, 11 (7 April 1855), pp. 226–7.
76. *Household Words*, 9 (29 April 1854), pp. 248–9.
77. *Household Words*, 11 (24 February 1855), p. 85.
78. Review of 'Women As They Are', *Spectator*, 9 December 1854, pp. 1292–3, p. 1292.
79. *The Future Historian's View of the Present War*, a lecture by Cardinal Wiseman (1855). S. Jay Kleinberg (ed.), *Retrieving Women's History* (UNESCO, 1988), p. 15, gives a summary of Foucault's view on language and sexuality which seems pertinent here:

> For Foucault relationships of power are constructed through 'discourse', a term that means not only particular discussions, but the entire organisational and ideological technology associated with the implementation of ideas.

CHAPTER FOUR

Gender Roles and Sexuality in R.D. Blackmore's Other Novels

Christopher Parker

All Blackmore's novels, from his first in 1864, to his last in 1897, are about inheritance, family strife and dynastic rivalry, ancient pedigree, and the perils of social mobility, especially across the critical divide between yeoman and gentry; the ownership of land and property is crucial. Inevitably, therefore, given the social setting of his stories, the inheritance laws when they were set, and the social attitudes of the majority in his own time, his worlds are patrilineal ones; heiresses are problems – albeit with romantic solutions. Furthermore, an inherited name, often closely associated with a landed property, together with an inherited personality, appears to legitimize the inheritance of the property from its previous owners or guardians. Consequently, the women who marry into the family, if they have any effect at all, can only introduce bad habits and bad blood, often literally foreign blood, into the family's veins, and cause the decline, through loss of the character and, hence, land and fortune, of the dynasty.

The Carne family, for example, in *Springhaven* (1887), once great landowners, now much reduced in circumstances, and villainous to boot, has been brought low by wedding 'flighty ladies' of slender means and expensive tastes;[1] and this trend has been rounded off by Caryl Carne's mother being a Frenchwoman, which, as the setting is the Napoleonic Wars, explains why his wicked efforts to re-establish the family fortunes involve treachery as well as other crimes. In *Perlycross* (1894), the Tremletts had been ruined when 'there came into the small human sluice a thread of vile weed, that clogged everything up. A vein of bad blood that tainted all, varicose, sluggish, intractable'.[2] In a patrilineal world, women are interlopers, except when, as heiresses of established dynasties, they can bring their inheritance of both property and character into fruitful liaison with another healthy dynasty. They can often be surplus to requirements in the humbler home: thus in *Cripps, the Carrier* (1876), while every son of the eldest brother of the Crippses inherits one of the family businesses or trades, in strict order of birth, the daughters have to be carried around the district on the carrier's cart till somebody takes a fancy to them; like the younger sons' sons, they are surplus. In a realistic way, therefore, Blackmore's books, even when, like *Lorna Doone*

(1869), they have women's names, portray men's worlds.

Furthermore, women and servants, serving women especially, should know their place. In *Lorna Doone*, John Ridd believes that if he does not rule the household of his mother, sisters and women servants, it is 'turned upside down'. Lorna, the great love of his life, has, therefore, to be a 'different being' from other women, 'not woman enough to do anything bad, yet enough of a woman for man to adore'. Paradoxically, as an ideal woman, she is also less than a woman, for women are imperfect. This is entirely within the conventions of Victorian heroines and, indeed, of the Christian tradition in Marian form. When vexed, John feels 'that women are a mistake for ever, and hence are forever mistaken'. He dislikes his younger sister, Lizzie, who unlike his favourite, Annie, is not pretty and is too clever, and, therefore, by no means an ideal woman. Betty Muxworthy, the servant, is a constant irritation as both an uppity servant and an uppity woman. The relationship between gender role and social class is clear when intellectual Lizzie questions the social position of the aristocracy, and John is obliged to both put her in her place and defend the class structure. In brief, John Ridd is conservative and a male chauvinist.[3] However, this masculine world is often under threat: his infatuation with Lorna forces him to examine his attitudes towards women; and his frequent perplexity as to how to deal with them is supposed to be humorous – and as much at his expense as at that of the women. John is portrayed in a quite complex way; he is a romantic hero, a morally and physically strong man, a canny upwardly mobile yeoman farmer, a bit of a prig, and a touch naive in his self-importance. In other words, John Ridd, though at one level he is Blackmore's wish-fulfilment figure (there are several obvious biographical reasons for believing this), is not simply that; in his clumsy, naive sexism he is certainly not Blackmore himself. Reclusive, crusty Tory that he was, Blackmore was nonetheless aware that gender roles were an issue; and the complexity of his treatment of John Ridd's attitudes is a clue to the importance of this issue in his other novels.

However, his women, like Lorna herself, appear to be less complex than John Ridd and fulfil fairly stereotypical roles. There are the romantic heroines, beautiful, passive, Lorna-esque; they usually have to be rescued from evil men and unsuitable suitors. Grace Oglander, missing and presumed dead, has been kidnapped or rather duped into going with her abductors; her gullibility and passivity are unbelievable, but, like Lorna who was captured while still a baby, is unsullied by her experience, despite her abductor wishing to marry her off to his son, just as Lorna was meant for Carver Doone. Her passive role, like that of so many women in Victorian fiction, was that of an heiress – to a fortune to which the villain feels he is entitled.[4] The device of abducting a gullible heroine, heiress to a rival family's fortune, was repeated in *Kit and Kitty* (1889).[5] And the eponymous but passive Alice Lorraine, whose brother is throughout centre-stage, has to choose between saving the family fortune by marrying an odious suitor and saving the family fortune by suicide.[6] In the same novel, the hero's intended nearly pines away when he seems to desert her, thus becoming another classic Victorian stereotype, the anorexic in 'decline'.[7] Another eponymous heroine, Mary Anerley, is equally passive and, like Alice, marginal to much of the story.[8]

Some of the livelier women have to play the nurse, of course, in the wake of Florence Nightingale. Esther Cripps turns up at typhus-ridden Shotover Grange to nurse young Russel Overshute.[9] Ruth Huckaback nurses first Lorna, then John Ridd back to health and strength – and, in both instances, by taking their care out of the hands of doctors.[10] The most active of them, the eponymous heroine, Erema, goes to work in an American Civil War military hospital; who should turn up but her long-time estranged sweetheart, desperately wounded! Through suffering they are reunited, and he is nursed back to health.[11]

Blackmore also has his fair share of wronged women, usually the daughters of farmers or lesser gentry deceived by aristocrats; though, usually, the wrong pre-dates the story as we are told it. This is partly because that provides another type of explanation of a family's misfortunes or for a rift between or within families, which is the stuff of all Blackmore's novels; sometimes it is because this allows him to place the indiscretion in the earlier Regency period when, Victorians believed, aristocratic licence had run riot; and sometimes it is because mid-Victorian propriety preferred not to have seduction in the foreground. Noticeably, when in *Springhaven* the villainous Caryl Carne sets out to seduce the flirtatious but innocent Dolly Darling, though he temporarily subverts her loyalty to her family (which is important to the plot), Blackmore draws back from her seduction, and her place is taken by a woman from a lower social order, whose seduction we do not witness, nor hear about, until the vengeful woman appears complete with baby.[12] More typically, an earlier liaison explains the misfortunes of the Nowells of Nowelhurst and the aristocratic Castlewoods, and the suicide of Frida de Wichehalse.[13]

It is noticeable that several of the retiring maidens provide the titles for their stories – *Lorna Doone, The Maid of Sker* (1872), *Alice Lorraine, Mary Anerley* and the exotic, but equally passive *Dariel* (1897) – or rather for the stories of their suitors, guardians or brothers. Additionally, and with more justice, the eponymous and feisty Clara Vaughan (1864) and Erema tell their own tales and stay centre-stage throughout. Three of the later novels are named after places and this fairly represents a shift of emphasis, but why should women figure so prominently in the titles but obscurely in most of the stories? The explanation is simple: Blackmore started out writing sensation novels (though he seemed ashamed of the genre). The women authors of those novels usually made their central character a woman; Blackmore did, too, in his first novel, *Clara Vaughan*. He never rid himself of the plot-line of the sensation novel even when it had become unfashionable. With the sole exception of the farcical and unsuccessful *Tommy Upmore* (1884), all his novels have a classic sensation plot of a lost or disputed inheritance, a crime (usually a murder) to be investigated and revenged, and a family either divided against itself or threatened by a malevolent rival dynasty. In some respects, he was atypical. For a start, he was a man; and though other men, like Wilkie Collins, were associated with the form, it was regarded as a peculiarly feminine one. Unlike most of the women, he made his heroines more sinned against than sinning, Clara's only real offence being to jump to a too-hasty conclusion as to the true villain's identity; and he did not challenge conventional social mores, except in that he did attack prudery. The importance of the women's sensational novel has been much reassessed, most recently and appositely for our purposes, by Lyn Pykett.[14] But the importance of its lasting impact on Blackmore's work has not yet been examined. In his penultimate novel, *Perlycross*, the genre was so out of fashion and his attachment to it so barren that the crime has become body-snatching, not murder, and the 'body-snatching' turns out to be no crime at all but a case of subsidence in the crypt. It was a very attenuated version of the genre that was on offer by the 1890s, but he could not abandon the plot structures he had first worked with. For our purposes the significance of this is that Blackmore's more active women also originate in a stereotype, but they raised issues of gender in his own mind and, therefore, for his reader; he adopted the form and could not entirely escape its consequences. Though he abandoned active heroines fairly early on, in most of his works, and retained only the convention of using their names as titles, the stories of Clara and Erema are revealing.

Clara, who tells her own story, is fighting to recover her inheritance, unmask a murderer, and restore her family's good name. To do this she has to make her own way in London, indulge in dangerous detective work, get imprisoned in a vivisectionist's gruesome cellar, and lead an assault by loyal servants on her ancestral home – and much more besides. Through haste and over-confidence she does make mistakes, but she is a tough, independent woman. Noticeably, Cradock Nowell, the rare eponymous male hero of the second novel, does much less well, suffering mightily, when forced to stand on his own feet in London exile.

Clara is not an original creation, of course; she can be matched in the literature of the time. But Blackmore's intention is not clear. He published *Clara Vaughan* anonymously at first; this was not so unusual a device for a first novel, at the time, but always adopted for a purpose; and in this case the purpose may have been to do with the controversial genre. When his second novel, *Cradock Nowell*, was dubbed a 'sensational novel' he took grave exception.[15] Yet when he wrote the 'Preface' to his third novel, *Lorna Doone*, he was careful to call it a '"romance"' rather than an historical novel,[16] deliberately identifying it as belonging to the less prestigious genre which, in particular, would have protected it from critics who might have attacked it for historical as well as literary reasons. He was always touchy, and his letters about his first two novels show that he had an inflated idea of his own importance as a writer;[17] so ironically he may have been taking lower ground, as the result of early criticism, for the book that was finally to make his name and fortune. In fact, he did research the historical setting for *Lorna Doone* quite carefully, though it is essentially, as he said, a 'romance', with a lot of 'sensational' ingredients. It is evident, however, that he was genre-conscious. He was also aware that genre and gender were perceived to be related.

Not all 'sensational' authors were women, of course, and not all their stories were given women narrators, but so close was the association of the genre with women's writing that *Clara Vaughan* had at first been attributed to a woman and had, indeed, been criticized for displaying all the supposed faults of women's work. Blackmore had adopted the device of having Clara claim that she would try to narrate her tale as clearly as if it were told by a man,[18] perhaps to throw readers off the scent and probably, given his own attitudes, because he believed that clarity, as opposed to intellectual disorder, was a real masculine quality. When faced with criticism that *Clara Vaughan* was 'headstrong and wilful' he explained this away as a deliberate device as it purported 'to be written by an excitable woman'.[19] Intentional it was not. Part of this supposedly feminine wilfulness was the looseness of the plot structure, a feature of all his novels[20] and, to his chagrin, he was criticized for it throughout his career, perhaps adopting his increasingly bluff insensitivity to, for example, the wounds men suffered in battle, as compensation for this supposedly feminine failing. He hated the confusion of his work with Elizabeth Braddon's and thought this was good reason to readvertise the book under his own name, arguing that acknowledgement of its masculine origins would increase sales because of the prejudice against women writers and because 'it might move some curiosity to see how a man can write in petticoats'.[21] When tempted to reissue *Clara Vaughan* with new publishers, in the aftermath of *Lorna Doone*'s great success, he took grave exception to those reviewers who had said it had been influenced by Braddon's *Eleanor's Victory*, which he claimed not to have read at the time but had subsequently found to be very poor. He also claimed to have actually written *Clara Vaughan* several years before it or *Eleanor's Victory* had been published; and he still had a high opinion of it, reckoning that it had 'more of power and "go"' than *Lorna Doone*, if 'not so much style and finish'.[22] He used the device of a woman narrator only once again, and that in an unsuccessful attempt to resurrect the sensational plot, in *Erema*.

Erema, like Clara, is an heiress out to right a family wrong; she has to discover who so ruined her father's life and reputation that he was driven into the wilderness of the American West, where he perished. Erema is, therefore, exiled in America at the outset, while Clara is exiled to Devon, but both have to go to London for their detective work and their stories are very similar. With its partly American setting, and with his heroine returning to America after her adventures, Blackmore was probably trying to cash in on *Lorna Doone*'s success across the Atlantic. Perhaps for this reason he has Erema question the social mores of her class and her mother country to a greater extent than he usually allows. When Erema is led into positively feminist sentiments, therefore, this does not look out of place.

Birth, status, landed property, together with the roles of men and women all came in for critical comment. Blackmore made no secret of his authorship this time and he had become a very well-known writer, so there is no subterfuge intended; what it does illustrate is that when Blackmore portrayed his paternalist worlds and either patronized his women characters or displayed outright misogyny, he knew what he was doing; he could consciously adopt a different strategy. In pursuit of her investigations into the dark deeds that have beset her family, Erema adopts the village postmistress as her confidante and supporter, and the two women are quite conscious of what they are achieving as women, especially in regard to what policemen might achieve, but also in regard to men in general. Policemen were a natural target for Blackmore, as they were for other sensational writers who incorporated detective work into their stories, but Erema's scorn for them extends to men in general. Her friend will stand her in better stead, particularly in terms of active intelligence.[23] And if Erema wavers ('". . . Oh why was I ever born to do man's work?"'), her friend reassures her:

> 'Because, Miss, a man would not have done it half so well. When you saw that villain digging, a man would have rushed out and spoiled all chance. And now what man could have found this? Would Master Withypool ever have emptied the Moon river for a man, do you think? Or could any man have been down among us, all this time, in this jealous place, without his business being long ago sifted out, and scattered over him? No, no, Miss, you must not talk like that – and with me as well to help you. The rogues will have reason to wish, I do believe, that they had only got a man to deal with.'[24]

Thus the weaknesses of her sex are supposedly turned to investigatory advantage, not always in the most politically correct way perhaps, but astutely nonetheless. *Erema* was not a great success, and Erema has no major successors, certainly not as narrators. Christie Fox, in Blackmore's penultimate novel, *Perlycross*, is a pretty lively character but she is only the sister of the hero of the main plot, and her own romance with a Devonshire yeoman farmer (a sort of peaceful, updated John Ridd) is one of the sub-plots. Also her activity and spirit have limitations, as when her independence in insisting on handling a pony and trap ends in the pony bolting, and when her brave confrontation with her brother's false accuser, reminiscent of several such encounters by Clara and Erema, ends with her bursting into tears with the strain of it all. She does reject an unwanted suitor, although even Blackmore's passive heroines were capable of doing that – though perhaps not with Christie's additional device of deterring him by using the latest racy slang, evidence of a degree of emancipation and perhaps of the ageing Blackmore's preparedness to graft a bit of the New Woman onto his characters.[25] In general, though, the feisty heroine turns out to be another fairly stereotypical female character, introduced during the fashion for sensation novels and active heroines; Lorna is the first truly passive heroine, though in her mythic, almost ethereal perfection, she did not turn out to be typical. Her successors were more earthbound characters and could not always count, in their relationships, on the same degree of loyalty that Lorna could command from John Ridd. Their eponymous role belies their true character and significance. In the person of Erema, however, we do have evidence that Blackmore was keenly aware of the gender issue, even as his characters were expressing conventional attitudes to gender roles.

To explore his own attitudes further we need to look at his male characters and his attitude to masculinity. We can start with an issue which refers back to our opening comments about patrilineal inheritance, primogeniture, and the family name, and also relates to the passivity of the women. As we have seen, a family could be brought low, not only by marriages to unsuitable women, but by indiscretions, sometimes bigamous marriages, with innocent women. The only other thing that can blot a family escutcheon is dishonour in battle, but the two types of dishonour are closely linked, as indeed they are in traditional chivalric attitudes. Thus, Hilary Lorraine has been tempted by a treacherous Spanish beauty while on active service in the Peninsular War, and has deserted his first love, an innocent Kentish maiden who has gone into an anorexic decline as a result. His intentions towards her had always been honourable, but he betrayed her nonetheless. As a result of his folly, he loses 50,000 guineas intended as pay for Wellington's army, is disgraced and has to resign his commission. He can redeem himself only by returning to

Mabel, his first love, and then he can once more show courage on the battlefield, which he does at Waterloo, once again under Wellington's command, though he has to suffer mightily, even unto the loss of an arm, to fully expiate his weakness and regain his manhood, his inheritance and his honour.[26] An even clearer-cut case is when Lewis Arthur appears to act in a cowardly fashion in battle, but it is later discovered that he has taken the blame to protect his elder brother, the heir to an Earldom and land, who had been 'unmanned' because of a guilty conscience arising from having seduced the daughter of one of the chief tenants of the Earl's estate; the poor woman had drowned herself and the guilty fellow had imagined her ghost rising from the Tagus, while he was on a nocturnal sortie, causing his flight. Lewis Arthur had to protect his 'unmanned' brother, who had always been unstable and unreliable, in order to protect the dynasty: ' "We have supposed ourselves to be, of many generations, without taint. Taint of cowardice, or treachery, I mean; for the taint of any other vice seems light" '; so, as the younger brother, he had ' "to save the heir of our race, and our ancient title, from ignominy" '. For this, it was necessary that even his own father did not know the truth – a noble sacrifice, in a patriarchal society.[27]

A guilty act and a guilty conscience unmanned Hilary Lorraine and Philip Arthur when their country needed their manly courage and loyalty. Licentious behaviour was considered weak-willed, or self-willed in the sense of allowing one to be ruled by the passions, which, of course, was also the mark of improper feminine behaviour. The best-known and most clearly heroic, in stature as in everything else, of Blackmore's heroes, John Ridd himself, is tempted to flirt, particularly with his cousin, Ruth Huckaback, even though he is normally presented as the epitome of loyalty to his beloved Lorna. Shuttleworth has concluded that John Ridd 'is in control neither of his sexuality nor his feelings. Far from representing an unproblematic image of a "manly" hero, the narrative of *Lorna Doone* actually explores the social contradictions of the male role, and the inward doubt experienced by a "hero" who needs to prove his own masculinity to himself.'[28] This is true enough, but it has to be recognized that dalliance is a weakness and, therefore, unmanly – which is why John Ridd can be allowed only the smallest of peccadilloes, although Blackmore himself clearly thought these scenes quite erotic. Control of the sexual urges and fidelity were manly virtues.[29]

The strongest association of libido and lack of manliness is evidenced in the creation of Clayton Nowell, the flashy twin brother of Cradock Nowell. Clayton, discovered to be the elder brother and therefore true heir to Nowelhurst after a mix-up in babyhood, is, like Philip Arthur, fatally flawed, which can only lead to his early demise and the more suitable brother inheriting, just as Lewis Arthur was to do. Where Cradock is

solid and dependable, popular, open and honest, and a deep thinker –
solidly masculine qualities – Clayton has 'dash and brilliance' and loves
to be admired; 'Clayton loved the thoughts that strike us, Cradock those
which move us subtly'. Lest we are in any doubt as to the way these qualities supposedly relate to gender, it was spelled out: Clayton is 'more
dashing, yet more effeminate, more pretentious and less persistent'.
When Cradock catches him preening himself in his scholar's gown up at
Oxford, he exclaims, '"You effeminate Viley!"', Viley being Clayton's
nickname on account of having been baptized 'Violet Clayton' by mistake when a deaf old vicar misunderstood the request for him to be
named after his mother, meaning, of course, her surname, Clayton. So
Violet Clayton Nowell he became, the twin brother with the feminine
flaws: poor Violet was accident prone, getting the wrong name, losing his
inheritance, and finally getting shot as soon as he was discovered to be
the true heir. But the mistake over the name, and over the inheritance (a
male right) signifies his femininity. He grows daily more like his mother,
his namesake; he blushes 'fair as a lady'; he develops 'feminine' traits – he
is petulant, 'twitching his plaits up well upon his coat collar'; he is vain;
he is devious. When his learning is compared to Cradock's, even his Latin
is 'coquettish'. When he learns he is the true heir, he throws his arms
round his brother's neck and sobs 'hysterically – for he had always been
woman-hearted'. However, Clayton's effeminacy has only this to do
with sexuality – it is a character fault, for his undoing is his failure to control his philandering, which is seen to be of a piece with his other flaws;
he is shot by the father of the girl whose virtue he is threatening. The
point is further emphasized by the fact that, unbeknown to him, the girl's
father is also his uncle because of just such a piece of philandering, in the
debauched Regency period, by his own grandfather.[30] It is determined
that history shall not repeat itself; and so this weak strain in the Nowells
does not reproduce itself.

The theme of weakness and femininity as synonymous appears also in
Dariel, this time as acquired characteristics rather than inherited ones. A
young man has been deceived as to his true identity, as part of a complicated tale of tribal and family rivalry and treachery in the Caucasus
Mountains; his false mother has done her best to ruin his character and
now plots that he shall be the unwitting agent of his own father's death.
All depends on her unnatural ability to dominate him through his lack of
will, that essential ingredient of a true man: '"Thou hast done thy best
from my birth to make me what thou art not – a woman"' he tells the ter-
magant. Despite a fine physique, when he appears in flowing robes before
his long-lost real father to carry out the deadly deed, he is at first mistaken for his own long-dead mother; he is 'a tall young figure in a long
white robe, timid as a woman, and as graceful; but with supple strength,

quivering for the will to man it'.[31] It would, of course, have been the perfect dynastic revenge to get a young man to kill his father, having first unmanned the son.

The only example of the displacement of supposed gender role in relation to one of Blackmore's major women characters is the far less explicit one of the relationship between Clara Vaughan, the original plucky heroine, and her cousin Isola. Clara weds her cousin, Conrad, thus being able to retain the patrilineal name and reunite the family property, but there is a displaced sensual relationship with Conrad's sister, Isola, before this. Clara has been forcing herself into an independent, masculine role in her pursuit of her family's enemies, and one day she is in 'stormy' and 'bitter' mood when she is comforted by Isola's 'sweetest smiles' and the 'loveliest' of faces, and by her 'soft caresses'. Though they have never met before and do not know of their cousinage, Clara's first contact with Isola is to feel 'an arm steal round my waist'. After this unusually tactile start to the relationship she wakes the following morning having 'dreamed of Isola'. When she meets Conrad, he is basically the male version of Isola: 'How like he is to Isola, and yet how different! So much stronger, and bolder, and more decided, so tall and firm of step' – a perfect matching of his masculine qualities of physique and character.[32] Clara does not, however, desert Isola, indeed at one point their sensual relationship becomes quite ardent when Clara undresses and then dresses Isola:

> 'Isola, off with that nasty dark frock . . . Pull it off, or I'll tear it. Now out with the other arm'. In a moment or two I had all her beauty gleaming in white before me; and carefully taking from the box a frock of pale blue silk, I lifted it over her head, and drew her dimpled arms through the sleeves; then I fixed it in front with the turquoise buttons, and buckled the slender zone.

After rhapsodizing about Isola's beauty, of which both women now have a heightened consciousness, she becomes aware that the dress reveals 'too much of the lifting snow for our then conceptions of maidenhood: so I drew a gauzy scarf . . . over the velvet slopes of the shoulders, and imprisoned it in the valley'. Isola is told 'to love herself in the glass' and Clara kisses her 'darling' on her 'sweet lips'. Isola responds by declaring Clara to have the finer looks, but Clara, though taller and haughtier, knows that Isola is the real feminine beauty – '"Don't talk nonsense, my pretty; if I were a man I should die for you"'.[33]

It is a fairly erotic scene, despite the coyness of the language. What is its significance for our purposes? Clara is obviously playing the man's role just as she had had to do throughout the book. But at this stage of his career Blackmore may have been using Clara to make the scene more, not less, acceptable to his audience. In his second novel, *Cradock Nowell*, he was to get into trouble, at the height of the controversy about fleshly women in the sensation novel, for passages of supposedly bad taste and for sensual descriptions of beautiful women, and he was, understandably, anxious, and typically aggressive, about this. In a letter to his publisher, Macmillan, he railed against the false 'prudery', the 'pretence to refinement', the 'virginity of a prostituted age', the hypocrisy of people who would be as coarse as could be if they thought it fashionable, while fainting 'if my hero blows his nose. How can you fail to see the rottenness of such refinement?'[34] He refused to accept that references to 'a lady's back or bosoms, without even the slightest suggestion of voluptuous ideas' should give offence; surely, he complained, 'you do not suppose that because I object to a sham refinement, a perpetual consciousness of sexuality, that I advocate savage nudity'.[35] Though his letters to Macmillan and others betray an irascible and difficult character, few would today quarrel with his strictures against the sham refinement of the age; and his explanation of this as a perpetual consciousness of sexuality is interesting in the context of the debate about repression in the nineteenth century. He revised *Cradock Nowell* for these and other reasons, though even the revised edition of 1873 retains elements of what had given offence.[36] The truth is that sexuality was a part of Blackmore's consciousness as a writer; it is evident in the controversial passages in *Cradock Nowell*, in John Ridd's flirtations, and in the Clara–Isola relationship. In this last case Clara's role is primarily to camouflage the sexuality of the scene rather than to say anything about gender roles, although without her forceful character, with its masculine quality, the scene would have had to be very different.

Although the erotic passages in Blackmore's first three novels provide an interesting context for Blackmore's authorial insistence that inability to subjugate the passions, the lack of a stern will, makes a man less of a man, it is to his portrayal of men themselves that we must return to complete this study of gender roles, and initially to more of his weak and ineffective men. By seeing what men should not be, we can understand what they ought to be. Apart from the 'unmanned' men and those with overtly 'feminine' qualities of lack of control, next in line come the milksops – like the stereotyped women, fairly conventional characters in Victorian fiction. One such is 'Pet' Yordas Carnaby, presumed the heir, through his mother, to the Yordas estates. The squires of the Yordas family have generally been a rough lot, and 'Pet' has inherited some of their spirit but, lacking their physical strength, he lacks the means of enforcing his will in a tough man's world; thus his spirit comes over as mere petulance, as signified by his name, which also signifies that he has been spoilt by the women who have reared him. His physical weakness is matched by a 'feminine' beauty; but his character is, at first, far from beautiful – he is 'a bully, a coward, a puling milksop' with 'all the viciousness of a Yordas, without the pluck to face it out'. However, he is not without prospect of reform: he falls head-over-heels in love, is man enough to attack a more powerful adversary and, though beaten, wins respect; and in the end he is sent off to 'a marching regiment', under a tough colonel, to be toughened up. As his crusty old grandfather remarks: '"Now betwixt love and war, we shall make a man of "Pet".' Love and war, the twin occupations of the manly, when honourably pursued, ruination when dishonourably practised!

Milksops inhabit several of Blackmore's novels, but even more frequent is the ineffectual brother. We can explain this largely from Blackmore's own experience. His half-brother, Henry John Blackmore, who took the name Turberville when he was disappointed by his share of the family inheritance, was an eccentric drifter, who claimed various intellectual pursuits but achieved nothing; he was estranged from the rest of the family.[37] Weak, ineffective and, therefore, unmanly young men start to appear after the death of Henry in 1875; usually they are elder brothers, unsuited to inherit the family farm or estate. There is Willie Anerley, the eponymous Mary's elder brother: he is spoilt by his mother ('she worshipped her eldest son, perhaps the least worshipful of the family'), is unreliable and 'flighty', lacking patience or persistence. The more deserving younger brother is driven to leave home.[38] There is Frank Darling, elder brother to Dolly, in *Springhaven*, who publishes a slim volume of poetry about 'freedom' and other such fancies, during the Napoleonic Wars; this 'lofty rubbish' and his radical ideas get him into trouble with his patriotic father. Above all, Frank is seduced politically by the half-French villain, Caryl Carne, just as his frivolous sister is nearly seduced in the carnal sense.[39] Harold Cranleigh, in *Dariel*, leaves all the worries of trying to mend the family fortune to his hard-working younger brother, George, the hero of the tale; Harold is referred to ironically as a 'Genius', an 'inventor' (Henry's supposed calling); but he is hopelessly impractical, has a grasshopper mind, and is quite unsuited to act as head of the family.[40] There are several such characters, who cannot measure up to the patriarchal role to which they have been born. Their great failing is lack of will-power and application; they lack these essential qualities of manliness.

When will-power becomes not just the power to subjugate one's own impulses, something that all Blackmore's heroes, like so many Victorian creations, have to learn, but the power to dominate others, then the man becomes truly heroic in the Carlylean sense, an ideal man, a leader of other men, the ultimate manly man – the antithesis of feminine weakness. Such heroes were very important to the Victorians and none of Blackmore's leading men were intended to even approach such superhuman status; but a true hero does appear – none other than that mid-Victorian icon, Nelson. An extraordinary number of Blackmore's men end up fighting directly under Nelson, often on the *Victory* at Trafalgar. In the case of Dan Tugwell of Springhaven he redeems his earlier misdeeds by shooting dead the Frenchman who shot Nelson.[41] Robin Lyth, Mary Anerley's sweetheart and reformed smuggler, is present at Nelson's deathbed, and saves both the *Victory* and, therefore, the dying Nelson from capture by the French; Mary's brother, Jack, is among Robin's followers.[42] If the historic timing is right, those that are not at Trafalgar are at Waterloo ten years later, fighting directly under Wellington's command but, though the Duke is an heroic figure,[43] Nelson is the absolute hero. In *Springhaven*, Blackmore, like other admirers, had to write Nelson's physical weaknesses into his heroic character; they were too well-known to be ignored or denied; so conquering them becomes part of the legend. His small stature and notoriously weak stomach when at sea were handicaps overcome by his ' "wonderful spirit" ', – ' "your nature was to fight, and you fought through, and you always will do" '. Though he was careless of his appearance or of his clothes, he always impressed because of 'the vigour of the man inside them, who seemed to animate the whole with life, even to the right sleeve, doubled up for want of any arm inside it'. Missing an arm was compensated for by sheer hard-working energy. But he did not dominate by bullying or by force; he had an easy command – 'a gaze and a smile which conquered history'. He had an essentially British simple-mindedness and honest patriotism, yet he could see through the tricks of others. 'He was one of the simplest-minded men that ever trod British oak. Whatever he thought he generally said; and whatever he said he meant and did. Yet of tricks and frauds he had quick perception, whenever they were tried against him, as well as a marvellous power of seeing the shortest way to everything.' He has uncontrollable energy and a natural gift of command. Badly treated by his government, his 'sense of duty and love of country' never deserted him. His truthfulness was 'simple and solid as beefsteak is'.[44] The imagery of oak and beefsteak says it all: this is a man in a man's world.

This had been Nelson's second appearance; he had been portrayed before, in *The Maid of Sker*, as 'no common mortal', who could command men by his very nature, by his natural 'genius': 'If this is done by practised subtlety it arouses hatred, and can get no further. But if it be a gift of nature exercised unwittingly, and with kind love of manliness, all who are worth bringing over are brought over by it . . . If it were not hence, I know not whence it was that Nelson had such power over every man of us' proclaims Davy Llewellyn, the cynical old seaman. Others call it witchcraft; so there is the hint of something supernatural about the power to command officers and men alike.[45] Nelson, then, was the ultimate man among men, commanding through love of manliness, almost innocent in his greatness.

One is reminded forcibly of Carlyle's heroes, especially

> The Commander over Men; he to whose will our wills are to be sub-
> ordinated, and loyally surrender themselves, and find their welfare in
> doing so, may be reckoned the most important of Great Men. He is
> practically the summary for us of *all* the various figures of Heroism
> . . . to *command* over us, to furnish us with constant practical teach-
> ing, to tell us for the day and hour what we are to do.

Carlyle's heroes were sent from heaven and great in their sincerity; but
we should also note that, though Carlyle's 'heroes' exercised a divine
authority, if false, they practised a diabolic wrong;[46] for in *The Maid of
Sker* Nelson is explicitly contrasted with the super-villain of the piece,
Parson Chowne. Blackmore specialized in some impressive villains:
Carver Doone is the best known; Caryl Carne matches him for wickedness and exceeds him in ability to manipulate others, though not in bodily strength; and there is a fine array of repellent villains in most of the
other books; but Chowne is evil incarnate, a dramatic contrast to all
Blackmore's other clerics who are either gentle scholars or hunting-and-
fishing parsons, and in both instances good pastors. Chowne is the
antithesis of the good pastor: he terrorizes his neighbours, his parish-
ioners and tenants, his succession of unfortunate wives, and his fellow
churchmen, high and low. He is a murderer, a kidnapper, an arsonist, a
schemer. He is often referred to as the devil, the devil's partner, the
devil's servant, or even the devil's master, and with devilish allusions.[47]
And yet Davy, who is a bit of an old rogue but definitely on the side of the
angels where opposition to Chowne is concerned and whose life has been
sought several times by Chowne, says of 'Satan's own chaplain', in an
astonishing passage:

> . . . to tell the whole truth, upon looking back at the Parson, I
> admired him more than any other man I had seen, except Captain
> Nelson. [This was in the early years of Nelson's career] For it is so
> rare to meet with a man who knows his own mind thoroughly, that
> if you find him add thereto a knowledge of his neighbours' minds,
> certain you may be that here is one entitled to lead the nation. He
> may be almost too great to care about putting his power in exercise,
> unless any grand occasion betides him; just as Parson Chowne
> refused to go into the bishopric, and just as Nelson was vexed at
> being the supervisor of smugglers. Nevertheless these men are ready
> when God sees fit to appoint them.[48]

Chowne is the complete anti-hero, the dark opposite of Nelson, a violent
Satan to Nelson's sacrificial god-hero. Yet he supposedly has elements of
greatness and could have played the hero. He wages his own petty, vin-
dictive, violent wars against his neighbours because nothing big enough
has come his way, while Nelson fights and suffers for king and country.

Everybody he meets fears Chowne; even battle-hardened naval officers fear the very environs of his house. He commands fear where Nelson commands love. Davy has to drop his eyes – 'my spirit owned this man's to be its master'. His face is 'lost to mankindliness, lost to mercy, lost to all memory of God'. He controls men 'of ten times his own fortune' by sheer will power; he binds men 'prisoners of his will'. This and his nocturnal habits (which he shares with *Springhaven's* Caryl Carne), create his reputation for witchcraft; only Davy, common rogue that he is, can see that Chowne's power is natural, not supernatural, and only because he knows this can he resist it.[49] Chowne is an intriguing creation, a violent gothic villain, and a fallen angel; crucially he has a dominant will.

The historical villain with heroic qualities, against whose conquering will Nelson was pitting himself, makes one appearance, in person, in Blackmore's works. Once again it is the clash of wills that is the theme, when Napoleon grants his secret agent, Caryl Carne, an audience. Carne binds men like Dan Tugwell and Frank Darling to his will, and women like Dolly Darling and Polly Cheeseman, but before Napoleon he has, like Davy before Chowne, to acknowledge his master. Napoleon had

> An astonishing face, in its sculptured beauty, set aspect, and stern haughtiness, calm with the power of transcendent mind, and a will that never met its equal. Even Carne, void of much imagination, and contemptuous of all the human character he shared, was the slave of that face when in its presence, and could never meet steadily those piercing eyes. And yet, to the study of a neutral dog, or a man of abstract science, the face was as bad as it was beautiful.

Carne cannot even stand upright in Napoleon's presence, stooping unconsciously before the shorter man, 'to lessen this anomaly of nature'. We are given a sight of the vast army and fleet of transports gathered at Boulogne waiting for just one word of command from Napoleon, the ultimate man of war. Only when his master has departed can Carne's bile and jealousy break out from the superior will: he reckons his own ambition matches that of Napoleon and 'The little gunner has made a great mistake if he thinks that his flat thumb of low breed can press me down shuddering, and starving, and crouching, just until it suits him to hold up a finger for me.'[50] As a villain, Carne is betwixt and between the random wickedness of Chowne and the grand ambition of Napoleon – he has ambition and a revenge motive, and war is his opportunity.

It needs a war to channel this masculine will and fighting spirit into both good, patriotic channels and treacherous, overweening ones. Like most Victorian Englishmen, Blackmore never went to war (nor even abroad) but he was prepared to let his narrators hymn its praises. 'It calls out the strength of a man from his heart, into the swing of his legs and arms, and fills him with his duty to the land that is his mother; and scatters far away small things, and shows beyond dispute God's wisdom, when He made us male and female.' For, after a long peace, women ruled; but in war their role was to have men, real men, die bravely in their arms, 'when the blood flows, and the bones are split into small splinters'. He concludes that 'war is good, no doubt'.[51] It is good because it puts men in control, because big issues are at stake, because patriotism, courage and, above all, a disciplined will are called for.

In comparison, women are trivial and unreliable. Davy in his private war against Chowne is forced, at one point, into 'the almost fatal difficulty of having to trust a woman'.[52] Dan Tugwell, building a fishing boat, and approached by coquettish Dolly Darling, provides the opportunity for the observation that 'Curved and hollow ships are female in almost any language, not only because of their curves and hollows, but also because they are craft – so to speak.'[53] As we have seen, Blackmore's works are filled with misogyny; the world of women is trivial, domestic, and full of small schemings; the world of men is, or should be, on an heroic scale whether for good or evil. When women do exercise a powerful will it spells trouble because it is unnatural, and leads to well-meaning, but weak, men being dominated by wrong-headed, imperious wives, or mothers, or teasing, disarming daughters.[54] Erema and Clara remained the exceptions; and in their own ways both test the rule, in that Erema is allowed to express feminist sentiments, suggesting that Blackmore was fully aware of the issues and not just socially conservative in an inert, unthinking way; and Clara, while providing a useful disguise, at one point, for Blackmore's eroticism, is essentially a product of the fashion for 'sensational' novels which Blackmore, despite his pretensions to higher things, allowed to influence his plot structures throughout his career. Constructing a plot was always one of his problems; and, except in *Lorna Doone*, his loosely structured plots of vendettas and revenge, and coincidences, never really worked. Ironically, he remained rooted in what he seemed to regard as a trivial, female world of sensationalism, while all too often growing ever more jingoistic and callous in his treatment of the supposedly grand masculine theme of war. For ultimately the masculine will, which commands others, is put to the test in war, by the truly heroic Nelson, rising above his physical infirmities, or by the flawed, 'beautiful' but 'bad' Napoleon. This command gives power. Power is what arch-villains, Carver Doone, Chowne and Carne, exercise over others; it is his loss of power in Napoleon's presence that embitters Carne. Blackmore's women, and his weak men with their women's qualities and ineffective lives, do not have this power.

Notes

1. R.D. Blackmore, *Springhaven, a tale of the Great War*, Everyman edn (London: Dent, n.d.), p. 90. Where no author is stated in future references, the author is Blackmore.

2. *Perlycross, a tale of the Western Hills* (Bampton: Three Rivers, 1983), p. 213.

3. *Lorna Doone, a romance of Exmoor*, World's Classics edn (Oxford: OUP, 1989), pp. 248, 330, 392–393, 550; see also the 'Introduction' by S. Shuttleworth, pp. ix–xxvi.

4. *Cripps the Carrier, a woodland tale* (London: Sampson Low, Marston, Searle, Rivington, 1890), pp. 27, 149, 151, 164–172, 277–288, 302–308, 380–385.

5. *Kit and Kitty, a Story of West Middlesex* (London: Sampson Low, Marston, 1894), pp. 408–420.

6. *Alice Lorraine, a tale of the South Downs* [1875] 4th edn (London: Sampson Low, Marston, Low, Searle, 1875), iii, pp. 130–134, 263–266.

7. Ibid., ii, pp. 241, 244.

8. *Mary Anerley* [1880] (repr. edn Bath: Cedric Chivers).

9. *Cripps*, p. 215.

10. *Lorna Doone*, pp. 686–692.

11. *Erema, or my father's sin* [1877] (London: Sampson Low, Marston, Searle, Rivington, 1883), pp. 421–423.

12. *Springhaven*, pp. 406–413.

13. *Cradock Nowell, a tale of the New Forest* [1865–1866] (London: Sampson Low, Marston, 1893). A revised edn was published in 1873, and reissued in 1893, pp. 361–363; *Erema*, pp. 373–385; 'Frida, or the lover's leap: a legend of the West Country', *Slain by the Doones and other stories* [1896], new edn (London: Sampson Low, Marston) pp. 69–134.

14. L. Pykett, *The 'Improper' Feminine: The Women's Sensation Novel and the New Women Writing* (London: Routledge, 1992): see especially pp. 47–54, 73–134.

15. British Library Department of Manuscripts, Macmillan Archive, Add. MS 54965 f. 45: Blackmore to Macmillan, 'Saturday evening', 1864.

16. *Lorna Doone*, 'Author's preface'.

17. See, for example: Macmillan Archive, Add. MS 54965 f. 2: Blackmore to Macmillan, 6 Nov. 1863; ff. 30–31: Blackmore to Macmillan, 28 Mar. 1864; ff. 48–49: Blackmore to Macmillan, 'Tues' 1864, etc. Also: Devon Record Office 329: Blackmore to Sampson Low and Co., 22 Mar. 1873 (marked 'Not sent. Too cocky.').

18. *Clara Vaughan*, 'new and cheaper edn' (London: Sampson Low, Marston, n.d.), p. 54.

19. Macmillan Archive, Add. MS 54965 ff. 48–49: Blackmore to Macmillan, 'Tues' 1864.

20. M.K. Sutton, *R.D. Blackmore* (Boston: Twayne, 1979), p. 41.

21. W.E. Buckler, 'Blackmore's Novels before "Lorna Doone"', *Nineteenth Century Fiction*, 10 (1955), p. 178.

22. Devon Record Office, 237: Blackmore to Low, 7 Jan. 1871.

23. *Erema*, pp. 286, 292, 314.

24. Ibid., pp. 312–313.

25. *Perlycross*, pp. 125–128, 173–176, 236.

26. *Alice Lorraine*, iii, pp. 4–22, 41, 344–346.
27. *Christowell, a Dartmoor Tale* [1881], 'new and cheaper edn' (London: Sampson Low, Marston, n.d.), pp. 315–323, 399–401, 407–408.
28. *Lorna Doone*, 'Introduction', p. xxv.
29. M. Roper, J. Tosh (eds), 'Introduction', *Manful Assertions: Masculinities in Britain since 1800* (London: Routledge, 1991), p. 3: '. . . sexual purity was a major preoccupation for many proponents of manliness'. For the 'improper' feminine, see Pykett, *The 'Improper' Feminine*.
30. *Cradock Nowell*, pp. 5–8, 11, 15, 24, 29, 31, 39–40, 77–78, 126, 361–362.
31. *Dariel, a romance of Surrey*, 'new and cheaper edn' (London: Sampson Low, Marston, 1990), pp. 417–418, 469, 483.
32. *Clara Vaughan*, pp. 103, 133, 147.
33. Ibid., pp. 331–332.
34. Macmillan Archive, Add. MS 54965 f. 69: Blackmore to Macmillan, 27 January 1866.
35. Macmillan Archive, Add. MS 54965 ff. 72–73: Blackmore to Macmillan, 2 March 1866. Actually, though he did no advocate it, he did have naked savages in *The Maid of Sker*, but without any detectable eroticism.
36. *Cradock Nowell*, p. 153.
37. For the original account of his life and strangely controversial death, possibly by his own hand, see: Devon Record Office, 138 M/F 1070–1103: *The Late Inquest at Yeovil: with additional remarks and correspondence by Jonathan Wybrants, Coroner for Somerset* (Shepton Mallet: Albert Byrt, 1875). See also: Sutton, *R.D. Blackmore*, p. 25.
38. *Mary Anerley*, pp. 25–27.
39. *Springhaven*, pp. 207–216, 220–221.
40. *Dariel*, p. 13.
41. *Springhaven*, pp. 427–428.
42. *Mary Anerley*, pp. 431–433.
43. *Alice Lorraine*, pp. 264–266, 342–346.
44. *Springhaven*, pp. 9–11.
45. *The Maid of Sker*, 'new edition' (Edinburgh: Blackwood, 1887), pp. 301–303, 401.
46. T. Carlyle, 'The Hero as King' [1840], *Sartor Resartus, Heroes, Hero-Worship* (London: Chapman, Hall, n.d.), pp. 161, 163, 173–174.
47. *The Maid of Sker*, pp. 167, 168, 172, 183, 227, 249–250, 251–253, 259–262, 461.
48. Ibid., pp. 327–328.
49. Ibid., pp. 462–463, 160–166 passim, 177, 205.
50. *Springhaven*, pp. 227–229, 331–332.
51. *The Maid of Sker*, p. 347.
52. Ibid., pp. 433–434.
53. *Springhaven*, pp. 41–42.
54. See, for example: of the first instance, *Perlycross*, p. 85; of the second, *Alice Lorraine*, ii, pp. 114–128; of the third, *Springhaven*, pp. 25–26. In all three instances, problems or outright disasters result.

CHAPTER FIVE

A Humanist Bible: Gender Roles, Sexuality and Race in Olive Schreiner's *From Man to Man*

Murray Steele

'. . . One day I'm going to write a book something like the Bible . . .'[1]

While *Story of an African Farm* continues to win accolades, Olive Schreiner's other South African novels still languish in relative obscurity. This may be merited in the case of her first novel, *Undine*, written between 1873 and 1876, which attempts to confront the hypocrisy of contemporary Victorian sexual double standards through the doubtful expedient of allowing its eponymous heroine to sell herself into a loveless marriage in exchange for a £50,000 cash settlement.[2] Uys Krige is surely justified in describing it as being 'in the worst traditions of the Victorian novelette'.[3] However, the relative neglect of her favourite work,[4] *From Man to Man*, set in the same period of South African history as *Undine* (1860s–1870s), is more difficult to understand: over half a century intervened between the posthumous edition of 1926 and the Virago edition of 1982.

Schreiner's biographers and critics have meantime registered its faults as a novel. Buchanan-Gould referred to its wide range of subject matter;[5] Meintjes praised the first part ('Prelude: the Child's Day') but condemned the rest as a 'juxtaposition of excellence and mediocrity';[6] while more recently First and Scott have termed it 'melodramatic and derivative'.[7] Even a commentator as sympathetic as Paul Foot thought it necessary, albeit with kindly intent, to plead with readers to be 'patient' with those parts of the novel that interrupt the flow of the plot, such as Rebekah's thoughts.[8]

The problem is, basically, that *From Man to Man* has been judged from the standpoint of the conventional novel. It is more than that. As Rebekah's vow – quoted above – indicates, it is also a worked-out text, a 'Bible',[9] providing moral instruction in the principles of Schreiner's humanism, to govern and direct relationships between people, a relationship that she avers should be based on truth, love, mutual respect and, above all, an empathy for those who are different from ourselves. This is achieved in two different ways: through the interaction, typical of the conventional novel, of Schreiner's fictional characters; and Rebekah's development of these truths by means of 'Biblical' devices such as the illustrative story and the parable. As Patricia Stubbs has pointed out, the cadences of Schreiner's novels resemble those of the King James Bible,[10] although it needs to be emphasized that Rebekah's is a rationalist's 'Bible', elevating the ideal man (and woman). Also, it is perhaps significant that in following her common practice of employing family Christian names[11] to identity her fictional characters, she has Hebraized the spelling of her mother's name Rebecca into the Old Testament form. Rebekah is, however, the prophet of the new, humanist, dispensation.

Schreiner's choice of the Biblical idiom and method was conditioned by her cultural background. As the daughter of a missionary father, she could hardly escape the moral, as opposed to the dogmatic, influence of Christianity, even if her agnosticism had become well-established in childhood. It is more than just a matter of language and style, however; there is a strong ethic in her novels that led early biographers like Hobman to declare – without any supporting evidence – that she cherished 'a secret love of God'.[12]

Another possible influence – direct or indirect – is suggested by references in the novel to Swedenborg, whose works form the staple reading of Rebekah's father.[13] The Swedish scientist and Christian mystic Emanuel Swedenborg (1688–1772) experienced a succession of dreams, some with an explicitly sexual content, from which he elaborated an anthropocentric theological system regarded as heretical at the time.[14] Swedenborg is credited as a major influence on visionary writers and poets like Blake, Emerson and, in particular, Whitman, whose works Schreiner greatly admired.[15] It is just possible that the volume Rebekah's father was reading was his *Journal of Dreams, 1743–44*, which was translated into English only in 1860 – during Olive's childhood. A parallel can in fact be drawn between some of Swedenborg's dreams and Schreiner's own allegorical writings, although she dispenses with his Christian theology: in one dream, he describes how he tried to climb up a mountain floating over a gulf, representing the limitless depths of hell.[16] The climbing image appears especially in Schreiner's more elaborate vision, 'The Sunlight Lay Across My Bed'.[17]

The intention of this chapter is to investigate what Olive Schreiner has to say about human relationships, particularly gender roles, sexuality and race, in *From Man to Man*. The main themes of the ensuing discussion will be her condemnation of women's sexual exploitation by men and Victorian double standards about sexual morality; relationships between women; and the South African dimension to gender relationships typified by the existence of black and coloured men and women in the context of its 'patriarchal racism'.[18] The discussion will embrace both aspects of the novel outlined above – the conventional narrative, and Rebekah's various discourses.

Since so much of Schreiner's fiction is based on her personal experiences, some initial reference should be made to these experiences. Arguably, there is more of Schreiner herself in this work than in her other fiction[19] in that it reflects exactly her own thought and the way it developed from the late 1870s and 1880s, when the bulk of the novel was written, through the various refinements made in the 1890s and the first years of the present century. Schreiner herself gives credence to this in the notes and correspondence published as an appendix to the book by her husband, Samuel Cronwright-Schreiner.[20] She is both Rebekah, the self-taught scientist and self-sufficient woman, and Bertie, the hapless victim of male sexual rapacity and female gossip. The reader senses that emotionally Schreiner identified more closely with Bertie than her sister; Bertie is, after all, named after her. As she protested to Havelock Ellis in 1884: 'I can't have Bertie and Rebekah die'.[21] Almost certainly, it explains why, despite two extensive revisions and many redraftings of individual chapters, she did not complete the novel.

Bertie's degradation and eventual drift into prostitution forms one of the poles of the novel. It is also the least original part: there are parallels with *Undine* and it is a common, almost stereotypical theme in Victorian fiction. The portrayal of her seduction by Percy Lawrie, her tutor, has invited enquiry about Olive Schreiner's own girlhood sexual experiences, much of it speculative.[22] It is largely irrelevant to any assessment of her work, and runs the risk of trivializing it, to wonder whether or not she was seduced by Julius Gau. It is much more significant that she broke off her engagement to him by the end of 1872, having uncovered aspects of his personality that had been hidden to her before. Buchanan-Gould is surely right in describing this experience as the one that 'brought the soul of the artist to creation point'.[23]

There are parallels, however, between Gau and Lawrie. Both are outsiders: Gau was a Swiss, Lawrie 'a delicate young man from England' (p. 81) bringing the superficial glamour of the wider world to the unsophisticated environment of the South African frontier. In addition, Lawrie was Bertie's tutor, a role which he abused to pressurize her into a sexual relationship:

> '. . . I liked him very much. – He was very kind to me. I liked him at first, then afterwards I hated him –' The hands she had now folded together in her lap were covered in the palms with a cold perspiration; ' – I did not know – he said he would be angry with me – I did not want him to be angry with me – I didn't want to – I didn't know, you see! . . .' (p. 135)

The priggish response of John Ferdinand to this incoherent confession, embodying typical Victorian hypocrisy, is predictable: Bertie has sinned (p. 136). Less predictable is the way Schreiner now develops that destruc-

tive instrument, gossip,[24] to bring about Bertie's ostracism. Even her aunt
Mary-Anna is influenced by it:

> '. . . It may be all perfectly untrue, my dear' – there was something
> almost of kindliness in Aunt Mary-Anna's tone – 'but a woman's
> character is like gossamer, when you've once dropped it in the mud
> and pulled it about it can never be put right again. With a man it's
> different; he can live down anything. People say, "Oh, he was young,
> he's changed"; they never say that of a woman; but the soap isn't
> invented that can wash a woman's character clean.' (p. 326)

Bertie's offer to 'talk about it' seems to scandalize her aunt even more
than Bertie's original 'offence', and completes the process of their exclu-
sion from 'decent' society.

Schreiner's decision to use the 'Jew' as the next instrument in Bertie's
degradation has upset some commentators. First and Scott regret her
'disappointingly racist stereotype'.[25] Hobman notes that the 'Jew' is not
even given a name,[26] although in this he is not unique; several other men
in the novel are not named either. While unfortunate, Schreiner's choice
of a marginalized agency like the 'Jew' is the next logical step in Bertie's
downward path, signifying her isolation from 'polite' society: she
becomes a rich man's plaything. However, Schreiner's 'Jew' is not the
coarse stereotype paraded by Hobson in his contemporary writings
about South Africa's Jewish millionaires.[27] She has taken the trouble to
explain his possessive behaviour: we learn that when the Jew was a boy
in Hamburg, his parents had shut him up all day in a garret. He, too, had
had dreams and expectations (p. 331), but has been corrupted by wealth
into believing that everything – including a sexually compliant woman
like Bertie – could be bought. Within the limits of his distorted philosophy, the Jew is kindly, and offers Bertie everything she wants, including surrogate (but not real) infants (p. 386). She is thrown out only when
the Jew believes that his cousin is trying to entice her away.

The English locale of Bertie's incarceration is of importance in the way
Schreiner defines gender and class relationships. In his Marxist analysis
of *From Man to Man* – influenced also by the ideas of Andre Gunder
Frank – Anthony Voss identifies the metropole as the focus of exploita-
tive forces, spreading out in the 1870s and 1880s to pre-capitalist societies like South Africa.[28] Although Schreiner was by no means a socialist
in the modern sense of the word,[29] she had no affection for upper-class
English society. Long before her critique of 'the effete wife, concubine or
prostitute' in *Woman and Labour*,[30] she condemned the 'decadence' of
London's 'idle' classes in the 1890s: 'They are so enervated they have no
will and no ideal but the seeking after pleasant sensations.'[31]

The contrast here with the bracing air of the South African frontier, to
which John-Ferdinand and Veronica Grey had gone – like Cecil Rhodes –

to recover their health (p. 105), certainly owes much to Schreiner's Social Darwinism, but also reflects a far older tradition: the impatience of the colonial visitor with the stuffy ways of the 'Old Country'. Elsewhere in the novel, her portrayal of the grey sea and grey skies of St Leonards on Sea (p. 381), and Bertie's homesickness for South Africa mirrors the experiences of many 'colonials' who longed for open spaces in the crowded vistas of southern Britain.

Bertie's relationships with men are uniformly destructive, and lead – according to both versions of Schreiner's intended ending of the novel[32] – to her death from a 'loathsome and terrible disease' during which she is nursed by her sister. Despite earlier intentions to encompass her death as well, Rebekah is spared: her intellect rescues her from the trough of sexual humiliation. Bertie in contrast is childlike, unsure of herself, dependent on others – especially, and fatefully for her, men. While Rebekah is no blue-stocking – like her sister, she is accomplished in all the domestic arts – she is resourceful and ultimately gains independence: she is not afraid to redefine her sexual relationship with her husband.

The circumstances which enable her to gain that independence need to be examined in detail, as they form the basis for Schreiner's own definition of gender relationships in her 'ideal' society. The environment of the frontier is one contributory factor: white women living there in the early to mid-Victorian period had to be self-reliant, with their menfolk often away from the homestead for days at a time, farming or trading; or for longer periods when war erupted. The frontier produced redoubtable women like Anna Steenkamp,[33] related to the Trek leader Piet Retief. Olive Schreiner herself left home at 17, and over the next few years stayed with relatives, lived in Kimberley (as described in *Undine*) and worked as a governess until she went to Britain in 1881. In contrast, many middle-class girls in Victorian Britain experienced what Walters has described as a 'protracted adolescence', trapped in a cycle of daughterly duties.[34] The frontier thus created a sense of relative freedom, associated with the wide open spaces so admirably depicted in *The Story of an African Farm*, although *From Man to Man* is in no way deficient in conveying the world of the solitary child with a lively imagination, growing up on the frontier and inventing new worlds for herself there.

Roman-Dutch law also helped the position of the white married woman in South Africa. Unlike her English cousin, who was denied by coverture from any independent right over property she brought into the marriage or acquired after it until after the promulgation of the Married Women's Property Act in 1882,[35] women like Rebekah who married by ante-nuptial contract could – albeit with their husband's signature to the legal documents – buy a farm in their own right. Thus Rebekah is able to secure her eventual economic independence from her husband Frank; the proceeds of her fruit farm are sufficient to sustain her, and Frank's daughter Sartje (pp. 156, 444).

Nevertheless, Rebekah pays a high price for this independence. She lives in the more bourgeois world of Cape Town suburbia, with its etiquette and decorum, a world that is distasteful to her and from which she eventually isolates herself. Like her sister, she is wronged by a man, in this case her husband Frank. The marriage vow binds her to him, even though it is strongly implied that sexual relations ceased after her confrontation with him (p. 309).[36] As First and Scott point out, the price Rebekah pays is the denial of her sexuality; she becomes what Walters has described as Mary Wollstonecraft's ideal woman, 'a monster of self-denial'.[37] Even the consolation of finding a soul-mate in Drummond, after years in the intellectual wilderness of middle-class suburban society, is overshadowed by the reality of Rebekah's marriage vow. When he invites her to see his fossils, she refuses despite being tempted to flout social convention: 'She hesitated a moment. "No, thank you", she said' (p. 481).

Her husband Frank's betrayal of their marriage forms the second pole of the narrative. Rebekah's letter (pp. 252–98) may be a clumsy literary device, and as Schreiner admitted, could hardly have been written in four hours,[38] but it is a succinct chronicle of deceit and male sexual arrogance, an arrogance that shrugs off charges of sexual infidelity as mere fancy on Rebekah's part. Frank's conquests reflect the excitement of the chase, and the 'terrible sex-desire of a man' (p. 279), but they also indicate the widening pattern of his sexual exploitation. His affair with Mrs Drummond is one between social equals, unlike his next liaison with the station-master's niece, who is only 14 or 15. The difference in status becomes even more explicit in the case of Sartje's mother, the Coloured girl, who is in his employment and thus an easy target for his lust. However, Rebekah's letter reveals a much deeper cause for the breakdown of their marriage: a lack of understanding between men and women. Men tell each other the truth, why not men and women?

> 'Oh, can't we speak the truth to one another just like two men? Can't we tell each other just what we think and feel? If you can't love me, tell me so; do not be afraid of hurting me. If you feel you cannot love one woman long and that only a succession of women can make you happy, I will try to understand. I will try to be a man with you. Oh, nothing can be so terrible as this awful silence that has been between us through these long years . . .' (pp. 297–8)

Schreiner's frequent references to men treating women as if they were men, or women wishing they were men,[39] has generated much speculation about her sexual orientation. Buchanan-Gould, Hobman and (particularly) Meintjes talk of 'bisexualism' and 'lesbian strains', citing as evidence her fondness for wearing male clothing.[40] This is hardly credible; many other notable Victorian women such as George Sand (an important influence on Olive Schreiner) also wore male costume and were similarly accused of masculinity.[41] The essential femininity of figures like Sand, George Eliot and Schreiner cannot be doubted:[42] even if it were important in any consideration of her work, a comparison between the personalities and behaviour of Olive Schreiner and Havelock Ellis' first wife, the lesbian Edith Lees soon dispels this claim.[43]

Schreiner's 'masculinity' can only be grounded upon her repeated insistence that the strong should help the weak: a great man is he who uses his strength to protect, not dominate (p. 441). But not men alone. Strong women share a responsibility to help their less fortunate sisters. In real life, she felt she lacked the physical strength to accomplish this; as she lamented in a letter to one of her women friends: 'I wish I was large and strong and could put my arms round all the tired lonely women in the world and help them'.[44] Ill-health, the result of asthma and addiction to bromides and other sedatives,[45] prevented her from taking the active role she sought. However, in the world of *From Man to Man*, her other persona Rebekah is able to help and protect wronged women. Significantly, apart from two difficult childbirths, she enjoys excellent physical health.

Several examples of this solidarity between women are developed in the novel. The first is that between the two sisters, Rebekah and Bertie. With great sensitivity and insight, the 'Prelude' shows how a child's instinctive jealousy of a new baby is transformed into a strong sibling bond – a bond so intense that it makes the otherwise very restrained Rebekah exclaim to her sister's suitor John-Ferdinand: 'If I knew . . . that you would ever fail her, I, I, with my own hand would rather take her life . . .' (p. 123). The dedication to her younger sister Ellie, who died when Olive was nine years old, suggests that the novel portrays what 'might have been': her sisters were in fact much older (in the case of Kate) or too different in personality (Ettie had strong religious views). Then there is the woman-to-woman solidarity exemplified by Bertie's gift of a baby's robe to her rival Veronica, who will shortly experience the pain of childbirth (p. 322). But Bertie's generosity of spirit is dwarfed by her sister's decision to accept Sartje, not her child, into her household. Rebekah sees Sartje first and foremost as a woman, like herself a blameless victim. Indeed it could be said that gender is thicker than blood: Sartje is closer to Rebekah than her sons, even though she is not white nor biologically related to her. As she tells her sons:

> 'Sartje is alone in the world. Her mother does not want her; her father does not even know that he has even such a daughter in the world. She has no one but us to take care of her. I shall not even ask one of you to walk with her again. She shall walk with me.' (p. 439)

The relationship in each case is an unequal one, a relationship between 'strong' and 'weak' women. This is explicit in the case of Bertie, described as 'Baby-Bertie' in the early chapters; her face has an 'infant-like expression' (p. 107); she defers to the 'clever' Rebekah; she is one of nature's innocents who needs protecting – in a phrase, 'she needs to be mothered'.

This mothering imperative that runs through Schreiner's life and works has so far been little explored. More often, the adjective 'patronizing' is used to describe her attitude: a more appropriate term might be '(m)atronizing'. The key to her 'matronizing' lies in the dedication of *From Man to Man* to her daughter, who died the day after her birth in 1895. An earlier version of the dedication movingly sums up Schreiner's own feelings: 'She never lived to know she was a woman'.[46] Her husband dismisses this episode in less than a page of his biography,[47] while First and Scott are just as brisk in covering it, and her later miscarriages up to 1899.[48] Of her biographers only Buchanan-Gould[49] really appreciates the impact of this on Schreiner, who had considered the possibility of adopting a child as early as 1879,[50] and later set down the prophetic notion that unmarried women over 30 should be able to have a child without 'social disgrace'.[51] Schreiner's thwarted maternal instincts led her to take the coffin of her child on the various peregrinations around South Africa, and were later sublimated in the menagerie that also travelled with her.[52]

The 'patronization' label has been applied also to her portrayal of non-white peoples, most recently by Margaret Strobel,[53] while other biographers have expressed disappointment with what they conceive to be an irredeemable racism. Hobman doubted whether she had ever moved away from her childish notions of putting black people in the Sahara,[54] while First and Scott conclude somewhat reluctantly that 'her position on race was made ambiguous by her attachment to social Darwinism'.[55] There is of course abundant evidence to sustain the charge that the younger Schreiner had profoundly racist ideas. *Undine* contains several unflattering stereotypes of black people: the migrant workers from the interior with their 'big-jawed foreheadless monkey-faces' and the 'swell nigger', aping the white man.[56] Her *Thoughts of South Africa*, published posthumously, abounds with several often-quoted examples of social Darwinist observation,[57] although she emphatically dissociates herself from the prevailing racist idea that, because of their 'inferiority', black people should not be 'taught'.[58]

However, there is also evidence that her views on race changed substantially onwards from 1891/92, when those particular sections of *Thoughts on South Africa* were drafted. I have suggested elsewhere that

Samuel Cronwright, a leading spokesman for Cape liberalism whom she married in 1894, may have influenced her views on race.[59] Schreiner could write to him in December 1892: 'You are mistaken in thinking I have any affection for the natives of this country',[60] yet only five years later express the following more sympathetic (if rather paternalistic) views in correspondence with the Cape politician J.X. Merriman:

> We shall reach the bottom at last, probably amid the horrors of a war with our native races, then not the poor savage, but generous races whom we might have bound to ourselves by a little generosity and sympathy.[61]

The rest of the transformation is set out in Schreiner's later correspondence, and the pages of *From Man to Man*. A reading of Rebekah's contemplations on the subject of human evolution shows that Schreiner has thought through the principles of conventional social Darwinism and found them wanting:

> You say that keen perceptions and the power of dominating are characteristics of the to-be-preserved races: but what if to me the little Bushman woman, who cannot count up to five, and who, sitting along and hidden on a koppie, sees danger and stands up, raising a wild cry to warn her fellows in the plain below that the enemy are coming, though she knows she will fall dead struck by poisonous arrows, shows a quality higher and of more importance to the race than those of any Bismarck? What if I see in that little untaught savage the root out of which ultimately the noblest blossom of the human tree shall draw its strength? Who shall contend I am not right? (p. 197)

Social Darwinism is thus a false creed, as it was rooted in a crude, physical, determinism. Schreiner erects in its place a diametrically opposed philosophy that elevates the spiritual values of empathy and self-sacrifice as the cardinal virtues; a philosophy that bears some resemblance to the claims that the contemporary black nationalist Edward Blyden was making about African religiosity and communality.[62]

The true gospel, based on these principles and rooted in Schreiner's humanist beliefs, is introduced at a later stage of Rebekah's contemplations:

> Has not the time come when the slow perfecting of humanity can find no aid from the destruction of the weak by the stronger, but by the continual bending down of the stronger to the weaker to share with them their ideals and aid them in the struggle with their qualities? (p. 223)

This gospel is developed further in the closing sections of the novel, employing the Biblical devices of the parable and the story. The purpose of the parable is to draw an extended analogy that will provide moral instruction to the listener/reader. Schreiner's parable of the superior race from the stars who enslaved mankind and called them 'the inferior races' (pp. 418–23) invites immediate comparison with the behaviour of the white race in South Africa, although as Rebekah points out, at least the 'superior race from the stars' had the excuse that, unlike the (human) white race, they were ignorant of the world (p. 424). Rebekah supplements this parable with the stories of the Xhosa women, the first one who sacrifices her life to enable her menfolk to face the white men's canons; and the second, who is driven to kill her children and herself because of a 'trouble' – possibly another errant husband? Rebekah sees these black women as sharing a common humanity with herself, bridging the racial divide; as suffering women, she can empathize with them, visualize herself in the same predicament.[63] In this way, she shows how error based on ignorance can be swept away: the wall erected by the child to confine black people in the Sahara can be lowered –

> 'And so you see,' she said, 'as I grew older and older I got to see that it wasn't the colour or the shape of the jaw or the cleverness that mattered; that if men and women could love very much and feel such great pain that their hearts broke, and if when they thought they were wronged they were glad to die, and that for others they could face death without a fear, as that young Kaffir woman with the assagais did, then they were mine and I was theirs . . .' (pp. 437–8)

It is Hughie – the son most like his mother – who responds most positively to his mother's message, even though he is too young to understand it fully; and it is Frank – the son most like his father – who misses the point, and offers to walk with Sartje, though only in places where he will not be seen by other white boys (p. 440).

Once again, the moral responsibility of the strong to help the weak has been asserted, this time in the context of race relations. We may dismiss this as a m/paternalist doctrine, but in the context of the late nineteenth–early twentieth century, it must be acknowledged as a progressive view.[64] After all, there was much to protect black people against, not least 'speculators' like Cecil Rhodes who, in Schreiner's view, regarded them as a 'commercial asset'[65] to maximize their profits.

Similarly, Schreiner develops the feminist part of her gospel through the medium of Rebekah's thoughts. Her analysis of Greek civilization as the product of a small elite that excluded women, even though they were nominally part of the 'dominant class' (p. 189), points the way to her conclusion that there could be true advancement only when there was 'a perfectly free and even comradeship between men and women at large in human society' (p. 194). In *Women and Labour* (1911), Schreiner was to develop this idea further in her homely analogy of the yoked oxen, who can only make progress if the one moved forward at the same time as the other.[66]

Ultimately though, *From Man to Man* is not just a feminist[67] or anti-racist testament: it is a tract addressed to all humanity, setting forth the basic principles for a transformed society, one based on the willingness of the fortunate to empathize with and help the less fortunate – in short, the exercise of human compassion. Yet this compassion is different from, and should not be confused, with the Christian virtue of 'charity'. That *From Man to Man* is a humanist testament is underlined in Rebekah's (provisionally titled) story 'The Spirit of the Ages', where the chained figure of Humanity is told that only she can release herself:

> 'Despairing one, no deliverer will ever come. You, you, yourself must save yourself. From those weak limbs strike off the fetters; with your strong hands bend down and heal the wounds your hands have made; remove the sand about the heavily sunken feet. When they are healed and free and strong, they, and not another, will bear you to the mountains where you should be.' (pp. 224–5)

Notes

1. O. Schreiner, *From Man to Man* (London: Virago, 1982), p. 53. Page numbers given in the text below refer to this edition.
2. O. Schreiner, *Undine* (New York: Harper and Bros, 1928).
3. U. Krige, 'Introduction' in U. Krige (ed.), *Olive Schreiner: a selection* (Cape Town: Oxford University Press, 1968), p. 2.
4. V. Buchanan-Gould, *Not Without Honour: the life and writings of Olive Schreiner* (London: Hutchinson, 1948), p. 203.
5. Buchanan-Gould, *Not Without Honour*, p. 217.
6. J. Meintjes, *Olive Schreiner: portrait of a South African Woman* (Johannesburg: Hugh Keartland, 1965), p. 160.
7. R. First and A. Scott, *Olive Schreiner* (London: Andre Deutsch, 1980), p. 172.
8. P. Foot, 'New Introduction' in O. Schreiner, *From Man to Man* (Virago edn), p. xiv.
   For a useful survey of Schreiner's biographers, see P. Morris, 'Biographical accounts of Olive Schreiner' in M. van Wyk Smith and D. Maclennan (eds), *Oliver Schreiner and After: essays on Southern African literature in honour of Guy Butler* (Cape Town: David Philip, 1983).
9. Anthony Voss has also picked up this allusion, but develops it in the context of the epic tradition in literature – see A. Voss, '*From Man to Man*: heroic fragment', in I. Vivan (ed.), *The Flawed Diamond: essays on Olive Schreiner* (Sydney: Dangaroo Press, 1991), p. 139.
10. P. Stubbs, *Women and Fiction: feminism and the novel* (Brighton: Harvester Press, 1979), p. 115.
11. Specifically in this case, Bertie (from Schreiner's second name, Albertina) – see D.L. Hobman, *Olive Schreiner: her friends and times* (London: Watts and Co. 1955), p. 55.

12. Hobman, *Olive Schreiner*, p. 15.
13. E.g. Schreiner, *From Man to Man*, pp. 33, 343.
14. The standard biography is G. Trobridge, *Swedenborg, his life, teachings and influence* (London: Frederick Warne, 1907).
15. I. Algulin, *A History of Swedish Literature* (Stockholm: The Swedish Institute, 1989), pp. 47–51; Schreiner to Havelock Ellis, 3 July 1884 in S. Cronwright-Schreiner (ed.), *The Letters of Olive Schreiner* (London: T. Fisher Unwin, 1924), p. 21.
16. G.E. Klemming (ed.), *Swedenborg's Journal of Dreams, 1743–1744*, trans. J. J. G. Wilkinson (London: Swedenborg Society, 1989), p. 7.
17. In O. Schreiner, *Stories, Allegories and Dreams* (London: T. Fisher Unwin, 1923).
18. Ania Loomba uses this phrase to characterize white male attitudes in the British Raj – see M. Sinha, ' "Chathams, Pitts and Gladstones in petticoats": the politics of gender and race in the Ilbert Bill controversy, 1883–1884', in M. Strobel and N. Chaudhuri (eds), *Western Women and Imperialism: complicity and resistance* (Bloomington: Indiana University Press, 1992), p. 105.
19. *Undine* has been regarded as more autobiographical. On the other hand it may be significant that unlike her other female protagonists, Undine is not given a Schreiner family name. Schreiner may have linked Undine Bock with the 'Undine legend' through the images of drowning and water that appear in the novel (pp. 78–80, 279, 282) – cf de la Motte's romance published in 1811, and Lortzing's 1845 opera, both entitled *Undine*.
20. S. Cronwright-Schreiner, 'A note on the genesis of the book', in Schreiner, *From Man to Man*, pp. 483–93.
21. Schreiner to Ellis, 12 July 1884, in Cronwright-Schreiner (ed.), *Letters*, p. 28.
22. Meintjes has been singled out for especial responsibility by First and Scott, although it was A. Calder Marshall's biography *Havelock Ellis* (London: Rupert Hart-Davis, 1959) – not acknowledged by Meintjes – that seems to have been the source of this particular story (p. 91).
23. Buchanan-Gould, *Not Without Honour*, p. 51.
24. This may mirror Schreiner's own flight from the French Riviera in March 1889, when some South Africans who knew of her relationship with Gau are reported to have arrived (Calder-Marshall, *Havelock Ellis*, p. 103).
25. First and Scott, *Olive Schreiner*, p. 174 fn.
26. Hobman, *Oliver Schreiner*, p. 61.
27. J.A. Hobson, *The War in South Africa: its causes and effects* (London: John Nisbet, 1900) – see especially his ironic description of Johannesburg as the 'New Jerusalem' (p. 190).
28. Voss, '*From Man to Man* …', p. 143; First and Scott, *Olive Schreiner*, p. 174.
29. E.g. Schreiner to Ellis, 29 March 1885, in Cronwright-Schreiner (ed.), *Letters*, p. 67.
30. O. Schreiner, *Woman and Labour* (London: T. Fisher Unwin, 1911), p. 81.
31. Schreiner to Cronwright, 4 July 1893, in Cronwright-Schreiner (ed.), *Letters*, p. 237.
32. Voss, '*From Man to Man* …', p. 136.
33. Although unlike her male Voortrekker counterparts, she usually merits only a sentence in the standard general histories – e.g. E.A. Walker, *A*

History of Southern Africa (London: Longmans, 1957, 3rd edn), p. 199.

34. M. Walters, 'The rights and wrongs of women: Mary Wollstonecraft, Harriet Martineau, Simone de Beauvoir' in J. Mitchell and A. Oakley (eds), *The Rights and Wrongs of Women* (Harmondsworth: Penguin, 1976), p. 343.

35. See C. Rover, *Women's Suffrage and Party Politics in Britain, 1866–1914* (London: Routledge and Kegan Paul, 1967), p. 178, and B. Anderson and J.P. Zinsser, *A History of Their Own: Women in Europe from prehistory to the present*, ii (Harmondsworth: Penguin, 1990), pp. 360–1.

36. This in turn suggests that she had decided to abandon the ending as told to Karl Pearson in 1886 (see First and Scott, *Olive Schreiner*, p. 174).

37. First and Scott, *Olive Schreiner*, p. 174; M. Walters, 'The rights and wrongs of women . . .', p. 318.

38. S.C. Cronwright-Schreiner, *The Life of Olive Schreiner* (London: T. Fisher Unwin, 1924), p. 350.

39. Especially the often-quoted passage beginning 'How nice it would be to be a man' (p. 226), introduced somewhat abruptly into Rebekah's thought pattern.

40. Buchanan-Gould, *Not Without Honour*, p. 115; Hobman, *Olive Schreiner*, p. 87; J. Meintjes, *Olive Schreiner*, p. 57.

41. P. Thomson, *George Sand and the Victorians* (London: Macmillan, 1977); see especially p. 20.

42. In addition to P. Thomson (above), see I. Taylor, *George Eliot: woman of contradictions* (London: Weidenfeld and Nicolson, 1989), especially p. xv. Schreiner's sexuality is discussed below, n. 45.

43. P. Grosskurth, *Havelock Ellis: a biography* (London: Allen Lane, 1980), p. 135 *et seq.* Havelock Ellis refers to Lees' 'passionate attractions' for women in his autobiography *My Life* (London: Heinemann, 1940), p. 218.

44. Schreiner to Mrs J.H. Philpot, 17 March 1889, in Cronwright-Schreiner (ed.), *Letters*, p. 156.

45. First and Scott, and Grosskurth link both her asthma and bromide addiction to guilt about her sexuality, the result not so much of her relationship with Gau as that with an unidentified 'sadist'. (This latter story seemed to have originated from Calder-Marshall's interpretation of Ellis' notes (*Havelock Ellis*, pp. 91–2), but was suppressed from Olive Schreiner's published correspondence by Cronwright-Schreiner and Havelock Ellis. In his own autobiography, Ellis merely refers to a great emotional crisis from which she was recovering when he first met her early in 1884 (*My Life*, p. 185)).

Of greater importance in any consideration of her work was the likely effect of this bromide addiction: the high dosage needed to dull the libido (cf First and Scott, *Olive Schreiner*, p. 116n) would have had long-term effects, including a lack of concentration, irritability, mental confusion, and possibly even delirium – see H.M. van Praag, *Psychotropic Drugs: a guide for the practitioner* (London: Macmillan, 1978), pp. 4, 356–7. Her husband's view – which would have been unpopular with her English friends – that her six years in Britain had destroyed her health and permanently affected her powers of concentration (*Life*, p. 175) may not be too wide of the mark.

46. Cronwright-Schreiner, 'Introduction' in Schreiner, *From Man to Man*, p. 497.

47. Cronwright-Schreiner, *Life*, pp. 274–5.
48. First and Scott, *Olive Schreiner*, pp. 229–36 passim.
49. Buchanan-Gould, *Not Without Honour*, pp. 144, 151.
50. Schreiner to Mrs Cawood, 14 May 1879, in Cronwright-Schreiner (ed.), *Letters*, p. 10.
51. Cronwright-Schreiner, *Life*, p. 182.
52. Hobman, *Olive Schreiner*, p. 104; Buchanan-Gould, *Not Without Honour*, pp. 162, 180.
53. M. Strobel, *European Women and the Second British Empire* (Bloomington: Indiana University Press, 1991), p. 66.
54. Hobman, *Olive Schreiner*, p. 146.
55. First and Scott, *Olive Schreiner*, p. 277.
56. Schreiner, *Undine*, pp. 281, 357.
57. O. Schreiner, *Thoughts on South Africa* (London: T. Fisher Unwin, 1923) – e.g. the Bushman as a 'little human in embryo' (p. 152).
58. Schreiner, *Thoughts on South Africa*, pp. 360–1. For contemporary views on the educability of black people, see C.H. Lyons, *To Wash an Aethiop White: British ideas about black African educability, 1530–1960* (New York: Teachers' College Press, 1975).
59. M. Steele, Essay Review: 'Olive Schreiner and the liberal tradition', *Zambezia*, ix, 2 (1981), pp. 179–80.
60. Schreiner to Cronwright, Dec.1892 – quoted in Hobman, *Olive Schreiner*, p. 147.
61. Quoted in Hobman, *Olive Schreiner*, p. 156.
62. On Blyden's racial philosophy see especially R.W. July, 'Nineteenth century Negritude: Edward W. Blyden', *Journal of African History*, v, 1 (1964), pp. 73–86.
63. Kate Flint's recent study *The Woman Reader, 1837–1914* (Oxford: Clarendon Press, 1993) comments that the popularity of *Story of an African Farm* lay in its depiction of suffering of something shared 'implicitly' across races (p. 244). In *From Man to Man*, the sharing quite explicitly transcends the barriers of race.
64. See also R. Davenport, 'Olive Schreiner and South African politics', in van Wyk Smith and Maclennan (eds), *Olive Schreiner and After*, p. 101.
65. Schreiner, *Thoughts on South Africa*, p. 310.
66. Schreiner, *Woman and Labour*, p. 251.
67. Cf her letter to Ellis, 2 May 1884: 'The question of woman's having the vote, and independence, and education, is only part of the question, there lies something deeper' (in Cronwright-Schreiner (ed.), *Letters*, p. 19).

CHAPTER SIX

Edward Carpenter, Whitman and the Radical Aesthetic

John Simons

In 1868 or 1869, Edward Carpenter, Fellow of Trinity Hall, Cambridge (a 'gentlemanly College')[1] was reclining in his room. He was an academic success but increasingly bored and dissatisfied by the ease and facility of the privileged life of University and Church into which a man of his talents and background had so easily and naturally slipped. He was made uneasy by the social injustices he saw around him. He was also unaware that an event was about to take place which would not only lead him to reject his positions in the University and the Church but also inspire him to produce a body of writing in both prose and verse which would shape the thinking of a generation of radicals. This work was enormously influential in his own life but while it is now somewhat less well known it still provides the basis of a critique of the relationship between society, sexuality and gender which speaks to us vibrantly and urgently and still appears radical.

Into Carpenter's room came H.D. Warr, another Fellow of Trinity Hall. In his hand he carried a small, blue-covered book:

> 'Carpenter, what do you think of this?'
> I took it from him and looked at it, was puzzled and asked him what he thought of it.
> 'Well', he said, 'I thought a good deal of it at first, but I don't think I can stand any more of it.'
> With those words he left me, and I remember lying down then and there on the floor and for half an hour poring, pausing, wondering. I could not make the book out, but I knew at the end of that time that I intended to go on reading it.[2]

This first encounter with the poetry of Walt Whitman through the mediation of Rossetti's selected English edition set Edward Carpenter on the road to the near sanctity which he seems to have achieved in the radical mind by the time of his death in 1929. The purpose of this chapter will be to trace some of the major themes in Carpenter's work and to show how his thinking centred on a complex and formal interplay of socialist thought and poetry that serves to articulate a sexual politics which places the homosexual man at the centre of a generally liberational social project, and which seeks to understand the politics of gender in a strikingly modern fashion.

The two salient facts of Carpenter's life are that he was a socialist and that he was a homosexual. These twin themes and their intricate intertwinings form the basis of any consideration of Carpenter's contribution to the analysis of power as this is expressed through the forms of gender asymmetries characteristic of late nineteenth- and early twentieth-century Western society. This concern continues to be at the centre of our analysis of both Victorian society and our own and, given the recent vogue for a revisitation of Victorian values, presses on us as urgently as ever. Carpenter's work precedes and prefigures the major themes of the debate as it is currently understood and for this reason alone would be worth studying, but he offers us more than that. In *Towards Democracy,* he offers us one of the few examples in modern times of the attempt to work out a thoroughgoing philosophical system in verse form. He also offers us some insights into the processes of literary canonization and the ways in which these are related to other kinds of political and social preoccupations.

Edward Carpenter was, without any doubt, one of the best-selling authors of the late Victorian period and its Edwardian-Georgian hinterland. After a slow start his massive poem, *Towards Democracy*, had, by 1916, sold 16,000 copies – not bad for poetry but especially noteworthy for a philosophical epic – and by 1926 it had had 30 reprints. His treatise *Love's Coming of Age* was reprinted 16 times in Britain after 1896 and had an estimated minimum circulation of 100,000 copies internationally – this for a book championing the right of men to be homosexual.[3] Yet for most of his life Carpenter was not acknowledged by the literary public – although his market garden at Millthorpe near Sheffield was a place of resort for literary intellectuals of a liberal or radical cast like Woolf, Forster and Lawrence; he depended instead on a genuine mass readership and today his reputation is only slowly beginning to be reviewed.[4] There can be little doubt that Carpenter's homosexuality is largely the cause of this neglect and it does not take a diligent search to uncover a 'black museum' of homophobic exhibits from the works of the literary critical academy.[5] Carpenter championed free love (both homosexual and heterosexual) and set about the construction of a masculinity which tried to reunite the individual man with a world of feeling and emotion, and to disestablish the power which accrued to him solely by virtue of his gender. This revision of inherited ideas about masculinity is what truly defines Carpenter as a radical, and true radicalism does not easily respond to the politics of apparent consensus which are needed to devise a canon.

This chapter will concentrate on some aspects of Carpenter's redrawing of the map of masculinity. His writing attempted to break down the models available to the late nineteenth century, whether these were drawn from the Arnoldian heritage of muscular Christianity or the Marxist view of the noble worker. Carpenter strove to show how models of maleness carried within themselves the mechanisms by which social injustice operated between classes by enabling the reproduction of these injustices in relationships between the sexes. Indeed, he argues that received models of masculinity are indispensable to the continuation of the social structures which create inequality, an insight that, I believe, one might find confirmed in Victorian writers as diverse in time and outlook as Thomas Hughes and Robert Tressell.

To understand Carpenter the best strategy is to start with a consideration of the place that Walt Whitman had in his thinking. As I have already suggested, Whitman changed Carpenter's life, but this was not solely because he provided a model of literary and aesthetic practice. Rather it was because he provided a role model and a paradigm of homosexual masculinity which escaped the stereotypes that had hitherto been available to a man of Carpenter's class. The early reception of *Leaves of Grass* in the USA had been graced by the approval of no less a figure than Ralph Waldo Emerson, but it had also been marked by a good deal of outrage against the alleged indecent and obscene content of many of the poems.[6] This hostility was much augmented by the addition of the 'Calamus' group of texts to Whitman's third edition of 1860.[7] In this group of poems the homoerotic and homosexual themes that had disturbed earlier readers found a new explicitness and concentration of purpose which set a new pattern for the aesthetic construction of sexuality and sexual relationships.

When Rossetti came to *Leaves of Grass* to make his selections for the first English edition of 1868 he chose to steer a course of discretion, in order to ensure that the reception of the poems would not be overwhelmed by a storm of hostile commentary directing attention to only one section.[8] However, he was immediately plagued by the inquisitions of John Addington Symonds, who included the following query in a letter of 1868:

> I should also have liked to see the poems of Calamus (old edition), 'Long I thought that knowledge alone would suffice me', in your collection – the more so perhaps because it has been omitted in the last edition by Mr Whitman himself. Do you happen to know what induced him to suppress it?[9]

The *faux naïveté* which I catch in Symonds's final inquiry is one that sets off an interesting chain of association leading to the centre of Carpenter's thought. That Symonds was himself a homosexual there can be little doubt but his relationship to his sexuality is difficult and, ultimately, tragic and mean. He wrote a treatise, *A Problem in Greek Ethics,* which Jeffrey Weeks has noted as 'probably . . . the first serious work on homosexuality published in Britain', but had it privately published.[10] Shockingly, as a pupil at Harrow, Symonds (although himself deeply involved in the homosexual ethos that permeated the school) chose furtively to foment a scandal which led to the resignation of the talented headmaster Charles Vaughan and the subsequent ruination of his promising career.[11] This first experience of the dangerous powers of 'outing' seems to have enabled Symonds to engage with the turmoils of his own inner life while, at the same time, distancing him from it. After the failure of his attempt to draw Rossetti into a semi-public dialogue which the latter must have feared could become deeply compromising, Symonds turned his attention to Walt Whitman himself. Between 1871 and 1890 Symonds corresponded with Whitman and endeavoured to draw him out into an explicit statement of the true significance of the 'Calamus' poems. Eventually Whitman seems to have understood the potential dangers of this line of inquiry and responded with a fierce affirmation of himself as a promiscuous heterosexual, letting drop the hitherto unsuspected and unknown (and thus far unconfirmed) fact that he had six illegitimate children by different women.[12]

Given the overwhelming mass of evidence, often from Whitman's own papers, of the wide range of his intimate contacts with other men it is hard to know how to understand his letter to Symonds. Plainly it grows out of a canny recognition of the prurient and possibly treacherous nature of Symonds's letter but, if it is true, it opens up an area of Whitman's life that it is hard to believe could or would have been kept secret for so long only to be disclosed in such an apparently casual and callous manner.

Symonds now had to be satisfied, but for Carpenter, who had been an associate and correspondent of Symonds for some years, the public revelation in the letter appears to have proved problematic in the extreme. Here was the man on whom he had built the edifice of a new masculinity, socio-sexual theory and poetic practice, now revealed as possessing the worst kind of insensitivity and a sexuality that was seemingly irresponsible and rapacious. The project by which *Leaves of Grass* and its author could inspire his dismantling of traditional sexual relationships and analysis of the power of gendering lay, potentially, in ruins.

Carpenter had visited Whitman on two occasions (in 1877 and 1884) and plainly his own impression of the man as recorded in the volume *Days with Walt Whitman* did not square with the disclosure which Symonds now laid before him.[13] In 1902, therefore, some 12 years after Whitman's letter, Carpenter published an essay entitled 'Walt Whitman's

Children' in which he attempted to make some sense of the evidence.[14] In this essay Carpenter first tried to disentangle the facts of the matter as they presented themselves to him, and included a quotation from the problematic letter:

> My life, young manhood, mid-age, times South &c, have been jolly bodily, and doubtless open to criticism. Though unmarried I have six children – two are dead – one living Southern grandchild, fine boy, writes to me occasionally – circumstances (connected with their fortune and benefit) have separated me from intimate relations.[15]

Carpenter admits that very little is known of Whitman's early life and that, until the question of children arose, the evidence all pointed to the fact that 'Whitman never had any intimate relations with women'.[16] This reasonable assumption was further borne out by a letter from Peter Doyle, Whitman's long-term partner:

> I never knew of a case of Walt's being bothered up by a woman. In fact, he never had anything special to do with any woman, except Mrs O'Connor and Mrs Burroughs. His disposition was different. Woman in that sense never came into his head.[17]

As Carpenter commented:

> Though there are points in the interpretation of this passage which are not quite clear, it at any rate conveys the impression of Whitman's reserve towards the other sex; and seems in one part to suggest that his 'disposition' was unfavourable to close relations with women.[18]

This view was confirmed by Whitman's own brother who said that 'he [Walt] did not seem to affect the girls'.[19] Yet Carpenter's view of Whitman is such that he cannot allow himself to assert that the great man was ever less than totally truthful, so he sets out to understand how the mismatch in perceptions might have come into being. Carpenter plainly understands that there is absolutely no reason why a male homosexual should not have children (a fact which ought to be clear to everyone but is, unfortunately, all too often not) and that simple truth enables him to preserve the image of Whitman's complete veracity and, thence, the entire structure of the system which he has built on the bedrock of Whitman's life and work. However, Carpenter also wants to argue – and this is a theme he elaborates later – that sexuality and, from it, sexual preference is not solely a social construct but is, in some way, natural and innate to the individual. This enables him to drive a wedge between the contingent fact of Whitman's apparently extensive heterosexual experience, which had manifested itself in such an unpleasant guise in his early life, and the mature man whose nature and inner life was so frankly and fearlessly revealed in the pages of *Leaves of Grass*:

> Walt's attitude in Leaves of Grass towards men is, as I have already remarked, singularly uniform. Both sexes seem to come equally within the scope of his love . . . Whether this large attitude towards sex, this embrace which seems to reach equally to the male and female, indicates a higher development of humanity than we are accustomed to – a type super-virile, and so far above the ordinary man and woman that it looks upon both with equal eyes; or whether it merely indicates a personal peculiarity; this and many other questions collateral to the subject I have not touched upon.[20]

Carpenter subsequently shows how this inner life expressed itself outwardly, by quoting from Pete Doyle's account of his first meeting with Whitman and Whitman's own records of his relationships with and attractions to other men:

> We were familiar at once – I put my hand on his knee – we understood. He did not get out at the end of the trip – in fact went all the way back with me. I think the year of this was 1866. From that time on we were the biggest sort of friends.[21]

Carpenter is thus able to retrieve the 'super-virile' Whitman who presided over his own sexual theories from the merely macho one that Whitman had presented to Symonds. Far from destroying the picture of Whitman as a homosexual sage offering to the world the new vision of a society in which the inequalities in power produced by the imposition of compulsory heterosexuality are replaced by a coming-together of the sexes in a jubilant physicality, of which 'the love of comrades' is paradigmatic, the letter to Symonds enables Carpenter to strengthen his own theorization of the intermediate sex and of male homosexuality as not only corrective of oppressive masculinity but also socially subversive. It is to this view that we may turn.

In the last quarter of the nineteenth century it would be true to say that there were available four major constructions of male homosexuality: repressed (like J.A. Symonds); homosexually active yet claiming heterosexual identity (like the messenger boys and Guardsmen who provided sexual services to the flâneurs of the Strand and figured heavily in the scandal surrounding the trials of Oscar Wilde – the backwash of which Carpenter caught when his publisher lost his nerve and would not continue to issue his books);[22] Camp (the model which has perhaps done most to produce damaging stereotypes of gay men and which may be associated with the circle of Wilde, with the Beardsley of the *Yellow Book* and *The Savoy*, and which reached its apogee some 30 years later in the work of Ronald Firbank);[23] and Mary Anne (a genuinely homosexual sub-culture building on the eighteenth-century figure of the Molly).[24] For a man of Carpenter's background and position the only viable options were surely repression or the sort of furtive contact with prostitutes recorded, for example, by Sir Roger Casement.[25] Fortunately, the effect on his imagination and intelligence of his reading of *Leaves of Grass* offered him a larger vision of the place of sexuality in his own life and that of his society, and also an example of heroic confession which inspired his own practice. More importantly, Whitman's verse enabled Carpenter's construction of a masculinity which would be viable in a socialist (or, at least, post-capitalist) society where changed relationships of class would demolish both narrowness of moral vision and oppressiveness in the mutual dealings of men and women.

Carpenter's socialism was essentially derived from his reading of H.M. Hyndman's *England for All* and tempered by his experience as a University extension lecturer in the industrial north and midlands.[26] Hyndman was a gentleman Marxist – it has been argued that his fury against his own class was the result of his failure to win his Blue for cricket – whose economics were characterized by an intensely Romantic view, surely comparable to that of William Morris, of life in the Middle Ages.[27] The picture of social relationships under feudalism as portrayed in his writing would have come as news to a thirteenth-century English peasant, but it introduced Carpenter to a harder economic analysis and a more specifically class-based politics than he had previously encountered. Considering the relationship between his reading of Hyndman and his life in industrial towns, his eventual establishment of the market garden at Millthorpe seems an entirely natural and logical progression towards the living-out of a political position and not, as could easily be imagined, a turning away from direct action and involvement in the working-class movement.

While Carpenter saw socialism as the route to a just society, the Marxist analysis that derived from Hyndman did not offer a theoretical or practical space for the full integration of sexual politics into the dialectic. Carpenter's vision of sexuality was an intriguing blend of the essentialist and the constructivist, and, while there can be little doubt that he saw dominant social relations as acting on the individual with almost irresistible force,[28] he also left open the possibility that the strength of natural inclination within the individual could be sufficient to enable him or her to break through into a new social space – a space defined not by externally imposed norms but by the reasoned and passionate application of a politics based on the inner life of the personality. As my analysis of his brief essay on Whitman's children has hinted, Carpenter believed in the innateness of homosexuality and in the potential of an experience so varied that it makes the simple polarity of maleness and femaleness untenable as a social heuristic.

Carpenter was further influenced in his melding together of socialism and sexual politics by his contacts with feminists like Olive Schreiner and radical thinkers like Havelock Ellis, for whose *Sexual Inversion* he provided a self-analysis.[29] He was also much moved by his reading of the Austrian sexologist Karl Ulrichs. From this source Carpenter learned the theory of Uranian sexuality – or rather found an authoritative exposition of ideas that had already formed in his own mind – which formed the basis of his important treatise *The Intermediate Sex*. Here Carpenter followed Ulrichs in arguing that:

> there were people born in such a position – as it were on a dividing line between the sexes – that while belonging distinctly to one sex as far as their bodies are concerned they may be said to belong mentally and emotionally to the other; that there were men, for instance who might be described as of feminine soul enclosed in a male body (*anima muliebris in corpore virili inclusa*), or in other cases, women whose definition would be just the reverse.[30]

For Carpenter this provided the ground on which to build a bridge between the antagonistic sexes, and in *Towards Democracy* his poem 'O Child of Uranus' provided an almost precise translation of Ulrichs' quasi-psychopathological definition:

> Thy Woman-soul within a Man's form dwelling
> [Was Adam perchance like this, ere Eve from his side was drawn?]
> So gentle, gracious, dignified, complete,
> With man's strength to perform, and pride to suffer without sign,
> And feminine sensitiveness to the last fibre of being;
> Strange twice-born, having entrance to both worlds –
> Loved, loved by either sex,
> And freed of all their lore![31]

Thus, the key to the revision and revolutionizing of gender relationships was to be found not so much in a reformation of traditional models of masculinity, whether gay or straight, but in the recognition of the Urning as a member of a natural group which can mediate between men and women.

Following Whitman, Carpenter plainly understood the act of writing itself as capable of articulating a somatic politics in which social change and revolution can, in some way, be inscribed in the physical experience of the writer. This is why Carpenter took so much time and trouble in the description of Whitman's personality and domestic life, why it was so necessary for him to analyse the meaning of the letter to Symonds and why, after his death, the memorial volume edited by Gilbert Beith contained so much in the way of comment on the experience of life at Millthorpe.[32] This tendency to hagiography was a weakness picked up by E.M. Forster, whose own sexual consciousness had so famously been pricked by George Merrill, Carpenter's partner, who 'touched my backside' on his visit to Millthorpe:

He will always be known to students of the late nineteenth and early twentieth centuries for his pioneer work; for his courage and candour about sex, particularly about homosexuality; for his hatred of snobbery while snobbery was still fashionable; for his support for Labour before Labour wore dress clothes; and for his cult of simplicity. But I do not think he will be remembered long either as a man of letters or scientist. He will not figure in history.[33]

Carpenter's work strikingly prefigures the complex of theories which tends to lump together under the grab-bag heading of 'French' or 'poststructuralist' feminism. In particular it would be apposite to see in his practice as writer precisely the revolutionary effect analysed by Julia Kristeva in her early work on poetic language or, in his re-evaluation of the nature of the activities biologically assigned to the different sexes, a shadow of her later work on the Mother. Similarly, the interplay of essentialist and constructivist positions that emerges from his work is forcibly reminiscent of Irigaray's analysis of the shimmering effect by which sex and gender appear in the highly charged intersections of psychoanalytic theory, linguistics and poetic practice. We can also see in Carpenter's view of the intermediate sex, a set of positions that sits well with Kristeva's analysis of the operation of the phallocentric within the very nature of the symbolic order under capitalism, and of the ways in which the prescription of the subject takes place through the agency of gendering. While contemporary feminism is obviously far more than an unconscious homologation of Carpenter's theories it is, without doubt, the case that many of the broad outlines of its own theoretical positions can be found in his writing, which seems to me to meet many of the conditions that would enable it to be identified as an example of gynécriture.

Carpenter plainly would have recognized any analysis of capitalism and its superstructural civilization which exposed the operation of a privileged phallogocentric masculinity as its chief means of ideological reproduction. It is, therefore, not surprising to note that this promotion of the Uranian as cure for the ills of civil life can be discovered in other aspects of the styles of homosexual masculinity in the later nineteenth century.[34] Generally, it would be accurate to claim that homosexuality existed as not only a form of sexual transgression, but also as part of a more extensive pattern of transgressivity which challenged norms of social and class position and aesthetic value. The highly provocative language of Camp fixes one such aspect of this pattern as described in a novel like *Teleny*.[35] The gentlemen who dealt with Guardsmen and messenger boys provide a model for social interaction quite outside traditional class relationships, even if their transactions have a monetary aspect which superficially make them appear to be organized on simple master–servant lines.[36] To understand this we may best look at Carpenter's own self-analysis:

> . . . my ideal of love is a powerful, strongly built man, of my own age
> or rather younger – preferably of the working class . . . Anything
> effeminate in a man, or anything of the cheap intellectual style,
> repels me very decisively.[37]

This would have been well understood by Forster whose novel *Maurice*, posthumously published to avoid a scandal, is genuinely subversive in its intelligent portrayal of the deep connections between sexual transgressivity and social subversiveness through the violation of 'normal' class relationships. In Carpenter's work a non-exploitative masculinity, defined outside of the world of Camp, offers a mediation between men and women. It also offers an analytical tool that prises open the ways in which capitalism operates as oppression, not only by the exploitation of one class by another, but also by the reproduction of that exploitation in the patterns of conventionalized heterosexuality. Ultimately, Carpenter argues, I think, that capitalist civilizations are oppressive because they deny the freedom to love and it is that, above all, that makes his re-evaluation of homosexuality dangerous and subversive.

In this analysis Carpenter – although he would not admit it: to the end of his life remaining in the position of an adoring disciple – goes further than Whitman in his vision of the nature of democracy. For where the American poet imaged democracy through the pluralizing of individual personal encounters, Carpenter grafts into this a social and political element which, while retaining the personal, simultaneously transcends it. This can easily be seen in a representative passage from *Towards Democracy*:

> The young heir goes to inspect the works of one of his tenants;
> (Once more the king's son loves the shepherd lad;)
> In the shed the fireman is shovelling coal into the boiler furnace.
> He is neither specially handsome nor specially intelligent, yet when
> he turns, from under his dark lids rimmed with coal-dust shoots
> something so human, so loving-near, it makes the other tremble.
> They only speak a few words, and lo! underneath all the dif-
> ferences of class and speech, of muscle and manhood, their souls
> are knit together.[38]

Repeatedly, studies of free love and unbound sexuality are used as the vehicle for the penetration of the barriers which class places between individuals. It is instructive here to remember the very different attitudes of Marx and Engels and the latter's dignified response to Marx's callous letter on the death of his working-class partner Mary, whom Marx plainly saw as being sexually exploited in just the way he was apt to use his wife's maids.[39]

Whitman saw *Leaves of Grass* as the aesthetic expression of a social vision and Carpenter followed him by borrowing both his comprehensive gesture and the loose long-line verse form which seemed sufficiently expansive for such great ideas. Indeed, Carpenter saw conventional verse form (again a strikingly modern perception) as being in some way implicated in the oppressions of capitalist morality. He defines Whitman's poetry as male and his own as milder and more feminine, and thus draws on a conventional aesthetic comparison of the sublime and the beautiful.[40] He seeks an expansiveness that is not available in conventional poetics, letting the poem, quite literally, come out and drawing it away from the polite aesthetics which characterize the narrow bourgeois consciousness. In his artistic life Carpenter brought together the themes of his politics and social philosophy in a highly systematic fashion. He understood the deeply subversive power of love and its transformational potential. Carpenter did not invent the slogan 'the personal is political' but, if we wish to find its harbinger in the Victorian world and to discover some Victorian values to which we can happily aspire, we will do well to pay attention to his writing and thought.

Notes

1. Edward Carpenter, *My Days and Dreams* (1916) quoted from Edward Carpenter, *Selected Writings, Volume 1: Sex,* ed. by Noel Greig (London: GMP, 1984), p. 86.
2. Op. cit., p. 88.
3. See K. Nield, 'Edward Carpenter: The Uses of Utopia' in *Edward Carpenter and Late Victorian Radicalism,* ed. by Tony Brown (London: Frank Cass, 1990), pp. 17–32. On early readers of Carpenter see also *Between the Acts,* ed. by K. Porter and J. Weeks (London: Routledge, 1991), pp. 24, 36, 61, 86 and 110.
4. See Brown, op. cit.
5. On this see Mark Lilly, *Gay Men's Literature in the Twentieth Century* (London: Macmillan, 1993), pp. 1–14; *Lesbian and Gay Writing* ed. by Mark Lilly (London: Macmillan, 1990), pp. 1–13; and Eve Kosofsky Sedgwick, *Epistemology of the Closet* (Hemel Hempstead: Harvester, 1991) See also M. Cadden, 'Engendering F.O.M.: the Private Life of *American Renaissance*' in J.A. Boone and M. Caden (eds), *Engendering Men* (London: Routledge, 1990), pp. 26–35, which points out that whereas in *American Renaissance* Matthiessen was very circumspect concerning Whitman's homosexuality, there is no such caution in his private correspondence.
6. *Walt Whitman, The Critical Heritage,* ed. by Milton Hindus (London: Routledge and Kegan Paul, 1971), pp. 21–109.
7. M. Moon, *Disseminating Whitman* (London: Harvard University Press, 1991), pp. 158–70.
8. Hindus, op. cit., pp. 125–30.
9. Hindus, op. cit., p. 129.
10. J. Weeks, *Coming Out* (London: Quartet, 2nd edn, 1990), p. 51.
11. J. Chandos, *Boys Together* (Oxford: OUP, 1984), pp. 307–16.
12. Moon, op. cit., pp. 11–13. See also *A Queer Reader,* edited by Patrick Higgins (London: Fourth Estate, 1993), pp. 102–3.

13. E. Carpenter, *Days with Walt Whitman* (London: George Allen and Unwin, 2nd edn, 1906). Material relating to Whitman's relationships with other men has been collected in C. Shively, *Calamus Lovers: Walt Whitman's Working-Class Camerados* (San Francisco: Gay Sunshine Press, 1987) and C. Shively, *Drum Beats: Walt Whitman's Civil War Boy Lovers* (San Francisco: Gay Sunshine Press, 1989).

14. This was originally published in the *Reformer* in 1902 and was reprinted in *Days with Walt Whitman*, pp. 137–52.

15. 'Walt Whitman's children', pp. 142–3. In 1978 *Gay Sunshine Journal* published an article, 'The Gay Succession', by Gavin Arthur in which he described how, in 1924, he had visited Carpenter and had sex with him. Carpenter described how Whitman was 'ambigenic . . . his contact with women was far less than his contact with men. But he did engender several children and his greatest female contact was that Creole in New Orleans. I don't think he ever loved any of them as much as he loved Peter Doyle.' These and other remarks in the same article hint at a deeper knowledge of the facts on Carpenter's part or suggest that Whitman was prepared to talk about his children more frankly – or more imaginatively – in private to Carpenter than he was in public to Symonds. Note that the woman from New Orleans has, in this account, become a Creole. Carpenter did not, however, use any of this personal material – which included the revelation that wealthy women with sterile husbands had asked Whitman to impregnate them – in his essay. The whole article was reprinted in W. Leyland (ed.), *Gay Roots: Twenty Years of Gay Sunshine* (San Francisco: Gay Sunshine Press, 1991), pp. 323–6.

16. Ibid., p. 144.

17. Ibid., p. 145.

18. Ibid., pp. 145–6.

19. Ibid. p. 146.

20. Ibid., pp. 151–2.

21. Ibid., pp. 148–9.

22. See J. Weeks, 'Inverts, Perverts and Mary-Annes' in *Hidden from History*, ed. by M. Duberman, M. Vicinus and G. Chauncey Jr (London: Penguin, 1991), pp. 195–211; N. Bartlett, *Who Was That Man?* (London: Penguin, 1993); K. Beckson, *London in the 1890s* (New York: Norton, 1992), pp. 186–212.

23. See Bartlett, op. cit.; R. Le Gallienne, *The Romantic Nineties* (London, 1926); *Ronald Firbank, Memoirs and Critiques*, ed. by M. Horder (London: Duckworth, 1977), *The Savoy*, ed. by S. Weintraub (London: Penn. State UP, 1966), L.G. Zatlin, *Aubrey Beardsley and Victorian Sexual Politics* (Oxford: OUP, 1990).

24. See Weeks, 'Inverts' and R. Norton, *Mother Clap's Molly House* (London: GMP, 1992).

25. Weeks, *Coming Out*, pp. 40–1, Higgins, op. cit., p. 92.

26. H.M. Hyndman, *England For All*, ed. by C. Tsuzuki (Brighton: Harvester, 1973).

27. B. Green, *Cricket Addict's Archive* (London: Pavilion, 1985), p. 10.

28. For these terms see R. Padgug, 'Sexual Matters: Rethinking Sexuality in History' in Duberman *et al.*, op. cit., pp. 54–64; see also J. D'Emilio, 'Capitalism and Gay Identity', in *The Lesbian and Gay Studies Reader*, ed. by H. Abelove, M. Barale and D. Halperin (London: Routledge, 1993), pp. 467–76.

29. Reprinted in Greig, op. cit., pp. 289–91.
30. Edward Carpenter, *The Intermediate Sex* (1908) quoted from Greig, op. cit., pp. 190–1.
31. Edward Carpenter, *Towards Democracy* (London: GMP, 1985), p. 331.
32. *Edward Carpenter, In Appreciation,* ed. by G. Beith (London: George Allen and Unwin, 1931).
33. E. M. Forster, 'Some Memories', in Beith, op. cit., pp. 74–81, p. 80.
34. See, for example, his *Civilisation: its Cause and Cure* (1889).
35. Oscar Wilde *et al., Teleny,* ed. by J. McRae (London: GMP, 1986), see also Bartlett, op. cit.
36. For some correspondence on this matter between Carpenter and Symonds see Higgins, op. cit., p. 101. See also the discussion on Marxism and sexuality in J. Weeks, *Sexuality and its Discontents* (London: Routledge & Kegan Paul, 1985), pp. 246–60.
37. Grieg, op. cit., p. 290.
38. *Towards Democracy,* p. 322.
39. Karl Marx and Friedrich Engels, *Selected Letters,* ed. by F. Raddatz (Boston: Little, Brown & Co., 1981), pp. 102–7.
40. *Towards Democracy,* p. 415.

CHAPTER SEVEN

The Cause of Women and the Course of Fiction: The Case of Mona Caird

Lyn Pykett

Recent feminist interrogations of the aesthetic of high modernism have both exposed its masculinist assumptions and facilitated a revision of the traditional history of modernism – a history from which women writers had, for the most part, been erased.[1] This work also provides an important new perspective on turn-of-the-century writing, and, in particular, on what W.T. Stead called the 'Novel of the Modern Woman',[2] that fiction of 'revolt' and protest against 'the fundamental fact that in society as at present constituted woman has the worst of it'.[3] In this chapter I will use the perspectives of the revisionary history of modernism as a means of re-examining the work of Mona Caird, a prominent contributor to both journalistic debates on, and fictional representation of, the New Woman. Caird will be used as a kind of test case of the woman writer who has not only been hidden *from* history, but also hidden *by* history.

Literary history and its conventional valuations, traditionally neglectful of women writers, has been particularly unkind to the women writers of the *fin de siècle*. Anyone who scans the sales figures for fiction in the late 1880s to the mid 1890s, or who examines the pages of the newspaper and periodical press during this period, might conclude that the New Woman writing was perhaps the single most important literary phenomenon of its day. The 'Novel of the Modern Woman . . . written by a woman about women from the standpoint of Woman'[4] commanded a large and eager readership. The New Woman fiction was also debated in heated terms by journalists and literary critics, commentators on the literary scene and on the woman question, and most of all by those who saw the literary scene as being invaded by the woman question and women's questions. 'Things have come to a pretty pass', complained Edmund Gosse in 1895, 'when the combined prestige of the best poets, historians, critics and philosophers of the country does not weigh in the balance against a single novel by the New Woman'.[5]

However, almost from the moment of its production, the New Woman writing was being consigned to the dustbin of history by the hostile judgements of a literary criticism whose canons of value were constructed around a series of gendered concepts in which the feminine invariably represented the negative term.[6] Not least among these canons of value was the notion that great art is 'virile' and austere, that it transcends its moment of production and concerns itself with large and abstract questions rather than local and political issues. The prevailing view was that true art, or truly great art, does not take sides. Thus the very timeliness and topicality of the New Woman fiction, and its engagement with the pressing social, political and ethical issues of its day, ruled out any claim it might make to be taken seriously as art, and diminished it survival power.

The fiction of the New Woman did not fare much better at the hands of those revisionary literary historians who first re-examined the forgotten women writers of the past in the wake of the second-wave feminism of the late 1960s and 1970s. Gail Cunningham and Patricia Stubbs restored the New Woman writers to critical view, but did so largely that they might gain a better perspective on the male writers who, 'for the first time and quite accidentally,' 'dominated' literature.[7] Perhaps the most surprising aspect of the revisionary scrutiny to which the New Woman writing was subjected in the late 1970s was the way in which that revision reproduced the critical valuations of the 1890s. 'The feminist novelists arrived at fiction mainly because their interest in . . . women's emancipation coincided with a need to earn money', Stubbs avers, but they 'were just not good enough *as* writers to turn their material into an important challenge to the literary tradition'.[8] Gail Cunningham also argues that the female New Woman writers were 'minor'; that, although their works sold in 'enormous quantities', they 'produced nothing of lasting value' because they lacked skill and 'were content . . . to parade their arguments unencumbered with the literary trappings of imaginative power or psychological plausibility'.[9] The most influential dismissal of the 'portentous anthems'[10] of the New Woman writers came in Elaine Showalter's landmark book, *A Literature of Their Own*. Like the commentators of the 1890s, Showalter finds the New Women writers to be neurotic and aesthetically deficient. Indeed in a later essay she sees them as aesthetically conservative, in comparison with their male contemporaries.[11] She also sees their art as compromised by their politics, their artistic energies dissipated by their fervent 'associationism' (i.e. a commitment to a variety of political causes). In short, they were not *auteurs*. 'In retrospect,' writes Showalter, 'it looks as if all the feminists had but one story to tell, and exhausted themselves in its narration'.[12]

Thus although Showalter, Cunningham and Stubbs indicate what is missing from what Gerd Bjorhovde describes as the empty space in the history of women's writing between the death of George Eliot in 1880 and the arrival on the literary scene of Virginia Woolf, they do not exactly fill it in.[13] They conclude that the women's writing of the *fin de siècle* is of historical and sociological rather than literary interest; it tells us much about the history of women, but it sheds only indirect light on the history of fiction. The New Woman writing by women, it is suggested, represents either a wrong direction in fiction, or a failed experiment which was perfected by more talented male writers.

It is, I think, by no means 'quite accidentally' (as Stubbs would have it) that the revisionary view of the New Woman fiction should so closely approximate the view of those contemporary critics who first dismissed this writing. Showalter, Cunningham and Stubbs write from a feminist perspective, but it is also a perspective informed by the aesthetic of high modernism which the contemporary response to the New Woman writing itself helped to define. It is becoming increasingly clear that the foundations of the masculinist aesthetic of modernism elaborated by Pound, Eliot and others were being laid in the literary debates of the 1880s and 1890s; not only in the debates around symbolism and the aesthetic inaugurated by Symonds, Wilde and Pater, but also in the controversy over Naturalism, the New Realism, and, most importantly, in the debates about fiction and the feminine.[14]

From the mid 1880s debates about fiction began to display many of the anxieties which were to be key elements in the production of the modernist movement in literature: anxieties about cultural authority, and about the autonomy of the artist and of the domain of Art in a literary world increasingly dominated by markets in which the masses and women played an important part. By the mid 1890s these debates intensified their focus on a perceived feminization of culture, and the need to protect masculine Art from a process of (ef)feminization. 1894, as well as being the year of the New Woman,[15] was also the year of several important pronouncements on the threat to 'Art' posed by the feminization of fiction, most notably Hubert Crackanthorpe and Arthur Waugh's essays on 'Reticence in Literature'.[16] Their theme was taken up in the following year in essays by Hugh Stutfiled and Janet Hogarth.[17] All of these essays attack the New Woman fiction for its degeneracy and 'effeminacy', and state or imply a preference for what was to become the modernist aesthetic of stern impersonality, rigorous abstraction, classical reticence, and transcendence of the merely local and particular. Arthur Waugh, for example, calls for a recognition of the need to separate the man who suffers (or enjoys) from the mind which creates:

> There is all the difference in the world between drawing life as we find it, sternly and relentlessly, surveying it all the while from outside with the calm, unflinching gaze of criticism, and, on the other hand, yielding ourselves to the warmth and colour of its excesses, losing

our judgement in the ecstasies of the joy of life, becoming, in a word, effeminate.[18]

Waugh, like many of his contemporaries, appeared to believe that art and femininity were incompatible, indeed that they were contradictory terms:

> The man lives by ideas; the woman by sensations; and while the man remains an artist so long as he holds true to his view of life, the woman becomes one *as soon as she throws off the habits of her sex,* and learns to rely on her judgement, and not on her senses. It is only when we regard life with the *untrammelled view of the impartial spectator,* when we pierce below the substance of its animating idea, that we approximate the artistic temperament. *It is unmanly, it is effeminate, it is inartistic* to gloat over pleasure, to revel in immoderation, to become passion's slave; and literature demands as much calmness of judgement, as much reticence, as life itself.[19]

Not least among Waugh's fears for the future of a feminized fiction was the fear that the novel would cease to be a literary form, that 'art' would be 'lost in photography', and ideas 'melt into mere report, mere journalistic detail'.[20] Waugh's anxieties about the blurring of the boundaries between fiction and mere journalism and polemic in the New Woman writing were shared by a number of his contemporaries. W.L. Courtney records and reproduces these anxieties in *The Feminine Note in Fiction* (1904):

> Recently complaints have been heard that the novel as a work of art is disappearing and giving place to monographs on given subjects . . . the reason is that more and more in our modern age novels are written by woman for women.[21]

Courtney's rejection of the New Woman writing is based on a masculinist, proto-modernist aesthetic designed to protect English fiction from the destructive incursions of the feminine. Like Waugh, Courtney takes the view that the true artist is masculine – even when she is a woman. The test case (as always) is George Eliot, whose genius 'was essentially . . . masculine . . . in no respect characteristically feminine'; on the contrary, 'characteristically feminine' women, with their unruly passions, and their 'passion for detail', lack the 'proper perspective' for true art. The truly artistic mind is neutral, it does not display 'personality' nor 'take sides'.[22] In other words the true artist, like the male modernist, is aloof, impersonal, paring his finger nails, whereas the New Woman writer is 'self-conscious and didactic', 'she has a particular doctrine or thesis which she desires to expound', and her work is 'strongly tinctured with the elements of her own personality'.[23]

Mona Caird is an interesting case on which to test Courtney's (and others') dismissive characterization of the New Woman writing. Caird is, perhaps, the classic case of the New Woman writer as both campaigning journalist and fictional polemicist. She is the archetypal example of the New Woman writer as a fervent associationist committed to many causes, from the emancipation of women to temperance issues and anti-vivisectionism. From the late 1880s, Caird was a very prominent contributor to the debates about the 'Marriage Question'. Her main contribution was a series of essays collected together under the title *The Morality of Marriage* in 1897.[24] Her first article on the subject was published in the *Westminster Review* in 1888, and her views on marriage attracted some 27,000 letters when the *Daily Telegraph* invited its readers to consider the question 'Is Marriage a Failure?' in the summer of that year. Caird's essays continued to generate widespread debate throughout the early years of the 1890s. Indeed in 1894, on the eve of the publication of her third novel, *The Daughters of Danaus*, she was described by W.T. Stead as better known for 'the famous article [on marriage] in which she scandalised the British household' than for her novels.[25] The aim of Caird's polemic on marriage was:

> [T]o bring evidence from all sides, to prove that the greatest evils of modern society had their origin, thousands of years ago, in the dominant abuse of patriarchal life: the custom of woman purchase. The essays show that this system still persists in the present form of marriage and its traditions, and that these traditions are holding back the race from its best development. It is proved, moreover, that it is a mere popular fallacy to suppose that our present sex relationship is a natural and immutable ordinance.[26]

Commentators on Caird's fiction have tended to see it simply (and fairly literally) as an extension of her contribution to the debates on the Marriage Question and the Woman Question. It has often been suggested that her novels are merely fictionalized versions of her journalistic concerns, rather unsuccessful attempts to propound her views by more popular and palatable means. Thus the entry on Caird in Janet Todd's *Dictionary of British Women Writers* contends that her plots are 'simple and obvious', and that, 'in an effort to focus on the psychological dilemma of the female characters', Caird routinely 'sacrifices characterization and dialogue' producing characters who are 'shallow and verbose' and who 'utter many banalities'.[27] I want to look again at three of Caird's novels in an attempt to see whether there is any way of reading them other than as journalistic polemic. I want to consider whether these novels – *The Wing of Azrael*, *The Daughters of Danaus* and *Pathway of the Gods*[28] – leave us no choice but to reproduce the critical valuations of the 1890s and dismiss them as clumsy generic hybrids marred by inartistic didacticism.

Without wishing to make extravagant claims for the aesthetic achievement of Caird's fiction I would want to argue that *The Wing of Azrael*, *The Daughters of Danaus* and *Pathway of the Gods* are indeed all self-conscious aesthetic artefacts. Their aesthetic self-consciousness is signalled in a variety of ways, not least in their titles with their allusions to classical literature and mythology, and the Bible. It is also signalled in the rhetorical structure and style of the novels. Caird, like many New Woman writers, developed a highly wrought style for representing feminine interiority and for figuring a particular emotional terrain. Certainly Caird was at pains to present her novels to her readers as aesthetic rather than as polemical structures. From the outset of her career as a novelist she attempted to forestall charges of overt didacticism. In the preface to her melodramatic early novel *The Wing of Azrael* she denies that hers is 'a novel with a purpose', claiming that her aim 'is not to *contest* or to *argue* but to *represent*' (WA, p. xi, my emphasis), and that if 'anywhere ... the action is dreamed out of its course in order to serve any opinion of my own ... therein must be recognised my want of skill, not my deliberate intention, – the *failure of my design not its fulfilment* (WA, p. xi, my emphasis). As far as genre is concerned it could be argued that what contemporary commentators (and some more recent critics) saw as generic impurity, might, instead, be seen as generic experimentation. Far from producing monological polemic, Caird, again in common with other New Woman writers, experimented with an interesting range of voices and genres.

One of the most interesting differences between Caird's fiction and her journalistic polemic is the way in which the novels (unlike the journalism) simultaneously engage with contemporary debates on the Woman and Marriage Questions and, both explicitly and implicitly, demonstrate the complex contradictions of the discourses within which those debates were formulated and conducted. Like her essays, Caird's novels bring to the foreground the ideology of female sacrifice and feminine self-sacrifice which the bourgeois family and conventional middle-class marriage produces, and by which it is reproduced. Both *The Wing of Azrael* and *The Daughters of Danaus* dramatize the ways in which daughters are routinely sacrificed on the altar of marriage by the patriarchal family, and they also explore the role of the 'womanly' woman in colluding in that sacrifice. They also examine the ways in which women are taught to, or learn to, internalize an ideology of self-sacrifice as a defining characteristic of femininity.

The Wing of Azrael is the story of the childhood, youth and unhappy marriage of Viola Sedley. Viola, the daughter of an impecunious father – 'a man originally good-hearted', turned into a 'thick headed' and 'brutal' creature by the 'unfailing submissiveness and meek and saint-like endurance' (WA, p. 8) of his wife – marries Philip Dendraith, whom she loathes, in order to save her family from penury. After two volumes of humiliation and suffering at the hands of her husband, Viola stabs him with the ornate paperknife she received as a wedding gift from Harry Lancaster – the man she loves, and with whom she is planning to go away. This melodramatic tale of a woman turned murderous by marital misalliance and the socially sanctioned torment of a powerful man looks back, as does Hardy's *Tess of the D'Urbervilles*, to the sensation novels of the 1860s. It has many of the classic ingredients of the sensation genre: the villainous suitor/husband, the economically, emotionally and psychologically vulnerable heroine, the fallen woman, the violent or murderous woman, and the adultery (or potential adultery) plot.

Like the sensation novel, *The Wing of Azrael* focuses somewhat minutely on the domestic entrapment of women. The comfortable, elegant household, the fantasy goal of the conventional middle-class woman, is represented (as it is in the sensation novel) as a prison to which the wife is confined, and in which she is the object of constant surveillance. In this novel the West Wing of Viola's marital home is represented as both a gothic domain and a region of silence and shadows suggesting ghosts, death, and a history of violence against women (it is associated with the story of an unhappy female ancestor of her husband's). However, the West Wing is also a version of the secret room, that private psychological space that is used in so many New Woman novels to figure the interiority of the central female character. For despite its many points of resemblance with the sensation novel, *The Wing of Azrael* is not simply the repetition of outmoded generic conventions. It is a more psychologized and politicized exploration of women's bitter discontent grown fierce and mad than was the sensation novel, and it modernizes the conventions of sensationalism in order to dramatize the effects of prevailing social institutions on individual lives.

From the outset this novel focuses on female interiority, and the processes by which a child comes to consciousness of herself and learns to be what her society defines as a woman. Viola is portrayed as a sensitive and imaginative child, whose eyes signal 'the nervous temperament, and the yearning look of a sensitive bewildered soul' (*WA*, p. 6). Viola is first glimpsed by the reader in the throes of an existential crisis:

> Was anything real and actual, or was it all a mistake, a shadow, a mist which would presently melt again into the void . . . the child touched herself tentatively. Yes, she was she, she must be real; a separate being called Viola Sedley, – with thoughts of her own, . . . whom nobody in all this big world quite knew (*WA*, p. 3).

She is subsequently represented as yearning for freedom, a yearning figured as oceanic feelings:

if only she could reach the sea she would not be lonely any more. She would throw herself down beside it, and would know everything (*WA*, p. 5).

Viola is a type which recurs throughout Victorian fiction, a character who embodies the contradictions of the contemporary discourse on feminine feeling. Viola's affectivity and sensitivity mark her as the feminine subject who is defined through feeling, while her actions mark her as 'unwomanly'. She is a character whose mode of representation perhaps owes more to George Eliot's Gwendolen Harleth than it does to the sensation heroine proper. Like Gwendolen's, Viola's nervous disposition is used as both a moral and a psychological indicator, as well as a narrative signal. Thus the heroine's hallucinations in Chapter 7, following the incident in which she accidentally pushes her future husband, Philip, through a window (apparently to his death) serve at once to prefigure the climax of the narrative, to represent an aspect of the heroine's psyche to the reader and to figure the heroine's self-conception as 'the same Viola, capable always of the crime that she had this day committed; capable always of – she shrank frantically from the horrible word' (*WA*, p. 120).

The comparison with Gwendolen Harleth is instructive. In *Daniel Deronda* Eliot constructs a plot in which the nervous female is only indirectly responsible for the death of the man, marriage to whom is a daily torment. Gwendolen wills, but does not do the deed, and she is saved from her murderous impulses by the interest of an ultra-sympathetic and sexually unavailable man. Eliot's heroine is, in short, recuperated for and by a life of ennobling renunciation and self-sacrifice. Caird, on the other hand, does what neither Eliot nor the sensationalist novelists dared, and produces a narrative in which the victim-heroine's fear and hatred is converted into a self-assertive act of murder. Caird's rewriting of the script of feminine renunciation and self-sacrifice is significant. Dendraith is slain, but the indeterminate and melodramatic ending of the novel leaves the reader with the feeling that it is the heroine who has been sacrificed. The novel ends, not with the due process of law as in *Tess of the D'Urbervilles*, but with the heroine's disappearance into the mist (a disappearance which presumably leads to death), after she has read her sentence in the flicker of repulsion that crosses the face of the lover who labels her behaviour as madness. In a sense Viola sacrifices herself to save Harry from having to come to terms with the realities of a woman's sufferings and anger.

Like Viola, Hadria Fuller, the central female character in *The Daughters of Danaus*, is a version of the sensation heroine modernized into the New Woman – 'aesthetic' neurotic, fevered, too much moved by music. Like *The Wing of Azrael*, *The Daughters of Danaus* also reworks some of the conventions of the sensation novel, but does so in a way which focuses even more painfully on the ways in which women are sacrificed to and by the family and society. Once more Caird constructs a plot in which a daughter is sacrificed in a loveless marriage for the convenience of her family. This novel, however, also focuses on the way in which its heroine is sacrificed to her mother's ideas about womanhood, marriage and the family. In many respects *The Daughters of Danaus* replays the debates about 'The Revolt of the Daughters' which raged in the pages of the *Nineteenth Century* in 1894.[29] On the whole it takes the daughters' side as it traces the complex network of social and familial forces by which Hadria is locked into the chain of self-sacrifice and renunciation which binds women together across the generations. Hadria's predicament is also used to emphasize women's complicity in their own subjection, and the part they play in enforcing and policing the self-sacrificial subjection of other women. Hadria is pressured into her unsuitable marriage by her mother and misled about her husband by his sister. Her mother and sister-in-law's appeals to conventional views of womanhood and motherhood also play a crucial part in persuading Hadria to give up her attempt at a separate life and career in Paris, and return to the bosom of her family. The intricacies of Caird's plot also develop another chain which links the lives of women, as it connects Hadria to two female suicides: one, the wife of Hadria's mentor, Professor Fortescue, the victim of the struggle between her woman's 'temperament' and her training; the other a teacher who has been seduced and abandoned, and whose daughter Hadria adopts. This last linkage is interestingly complicated by the fact that the seducer and hence father of her adoptive child is Professor Theobald, Hadria's own would-be seducer.

In the early chapters in particular, Hadria is used as a mouthpiece for Caird's views, and her tone is often that of Caird's essays. However, unlike the essays, this novel (in common with Caird's other fiction) focuses minutely on the emotional and psychological effects of a woman's lot, and especially on her *feelings* of frustration, imprisonment and rebellion. *The Daughters of Danaus* attempts to make the reader *feel* the realities of female renunciation and sacrifice, by presenting a complex, feeling woman who desires self-expression, and a fuller, wider experience than that offered by familial confinement. As in *The Wing of Azrael*, the contrast between the restricting actualities of the heroine's life and the expansiveness of her desires is figured in part in her affinity with the vastness of nature. Viola's longing for the sea is replicated in Hadria's longing for the moors which surround her familial home. Hadria's desire for self-expression is also figured in her artistic ambitions: she is an accomplished pianist who has ambitions to compose. Like so many New Woman heroines, Hadria is a portrait of the young woman as a failed or frustrated artist.

One of the most important achievements of *The Wing of Azrael* and *The Daughters of Danaus* is their sympathetic representation of the tormented and fractured female subject produced by the contradictions inherent in the ideology of the domestic, affective, feminine woman, and the tensions between that ideology and the social practices of middle- and upper-middle-class life – 'the peculiar claims that are made, by common consent, on a woman's time and strength' (*DD*, p. 322). The point is put starkly and forcefully in Caird's essay 'A defence of the so-called "Wild Women"', which takes issue with the view that women must submit to circumscribed lives for the good of the race.

> Men are living lives and committing actions day by day which imperil and destroy the well-being of the race; on what principle are women only to be restrained? Why this one-sided sacrifice, this artificial selection of victims for the good of society? The old legends of maidens who were chosen each year and chained to a rock by the shore to propitiate gods . . . seem not in the least out of date. Sacrifices were performed more frankly in those days, and nobody tried to persuade the victims that it was enjoyable and blessed to be devoured.[30]

The old legends of the sacrifice of maidens are elaborately invoked in Caird's strange and mystical novel *Pathway of the Gods* (1898). These legends are also brought into complex relation with contemporary modes of persuading the sacrificial victims that, if not enjoyable, it is at least blessed to be devoured. The central narrative of this novel is a typical New Woman plot. It centres on Anna Carrington, a daughter of the vicarage, cast in the mould of Hardy's Sue Bridehead; 'the woman of the feminist movement – the slight, pale, "bachelor" girl – the intellectualized, emancipated bundle of nerves that modern conditions were producing'.[31]

Anna takes the path of the 'revolting daughter', relinquishes her 'fervent piety' (*PG*, p. 14) for atheism, and leaves the vicarage in search of an independent life, as a journalist, a public speaker, and latterly as a companion-governess. The narrative opens with her renewing her acquaintance with Julian, a man whose attentions she has formerly rejected. She is represented as a brittle, epigrammatic young woman, whose 'big dreams' (*PG*, p. 96) have been disappointed. Like many New Woman heroines she has suffered a nervous collapse after the failure of her ambitions to 'be a speaker, to hold sway over the emotions of men and women . . . to send flying, with winger words, into the heart of my generation' (*PG*, p. 96). The narrative rehearses the history of her abortive relationship with Julian, who is eventually rescued from the 'consuming fire' (*PG*, p. 282) of her love by the actions of a group of womanly women. Anna ends the novel alone and embittered, yet another nineties victim (like Jude, and many more female protagonists) of prematurity:

> We luckless beings of the transition period have to suffer the penalty of being out of line with the old conditions, before the new conditions have been formed with which we could have harmonised (*PG*, p. 316).

Thus summarized, *Pathway of the Gods* seems like countless other *fin de siècle* narratives of defeat and disillusion. However, this novel has another narrative trajectory; one of regeneration and ascent. Anna retires from the fray defeated, her defeat engineered in part by a conspiracy of womanly women who are working for the regeneration of humanity by means of a radical and long-term transformation of relations between the sexes. Anna's impatient egotism is contrasted with (and defeated by) the patient spirituality of another kind of New Woman – represented by the ethereal Clutha Lawrenson and the Swedenborgian, Mrs Charnley – who put their faith in the evolutionary ascent of man. Mrs Charnley, for example, advises Anna to be patient because, 'Man is still a savage and a child' (*PG*, p. 320). Anna, on the other hand, is unwilling to 'wait in captivity and pain, till man had completed his education', and declares that 'when I see the myriads of cages all round me, with their imprisoned souls of women, then I have no philosophy, but only good, sound, able-bodied hatred in my heart' (*PG*, pp. 320–1). In the 'boomerang'[32] narrative that Caird constructs for Anna, this anger proves to be self-immolating.

Pathway of the Gods is the strangest and most self-consciously aesthetic of the three novels under discussion. It has its moments of melodrama, but it is the melodrama of *fin de siècle* mysticism rather than the transmuted sensationalism found in the earlier novels. The narrative is episodic, and is framed by a highly wrought, poeticized, prologue and concluding section. The prologue has echoes of Browning's 'Two in the Campagna' and 'Love among the Ruins', and anticipates D.H. Lawrence's appropriation of the latter poem at the beginning of *Women in Love*. The concluding section depicts a curious rite of spring, a dance in which 'it was as if a dead century had turned in its grave' (*PG*, p. 334), a dance very much in the style of the modern dance theatre of the nineties. At first glance it might appear that the function of this frame is to locate the specific narrative of Anna and Julian in a wider historical perspective. However, it seems to me, that the effect of the frame is, on the contrary, to remove the narrative from material history into the mysterious cycles of time. This move out of history is also effected by means of Julian's strange waking dream, with which the narrative opens. In this dream (which is repeatedly recalled and referred to throughout the narrative) the specific struggles of an historical woman, Anna, are subsumed into the centuries of female martyrdom:

there was a horrible likeness to modern men and women in those eager Romans [in his dream] . . . the same strange, deep-seated cruelty, combined ironically with all the respectable virtues; the same balanced and moderate tone in justifying popular savageries . . . What martyrdom would her fellow men decree for her *this* time? Mere crude lions were not in fashion now (*PG*, pp. 34–7).

The perspective here is that of a confused New Man, but the universalized script of martyrdom and sacrifice with which he works is also the one into which the novel writes its female protagonist.

The triumphalist pagan ceremony with which the novel concludes also has the effect of moving the narrative out of history. It celebrates an alternative script for femininity from that of female sacrifice; the script of feminine *self*-sacrifice. The key figure here is Clutha Lawrenson (and, to a lesser extent Mrs Charnley), a mystical (and mystified) version of the Angel in and out of the House, by means of whom Caird recuperates and modernizes the high Victorian ideal of the spiritualizing feminine influence of the womanly woman. The concluding scene in which – in 'a fantastic ceremony of coronation' – Clutha is crowned 'Queen of the Beautiful Past, and Prophetess of the Beautiful Future' (*PG*, pp. 334–5), welds together the ancient past and the visionary future into a timeless moment. Together, the prologue and concluding scene of this novel make a move which Ann Ardis has noted in the work of other New Woman writers: the move from culture into nature. Ardis suggests that in the work of some New Woman writers (George Egerton, for example) this move results in an exposure of nature 'as culture's vision of what lies below or behind itself in a primitive or archaic cultural formation'.[33] In *Pathway of the Gods* both nature and the long perspectives of history become 'the place where culture's most cherished ideas and ideals can be kept safe from history'.[34] In this novel one of those most cherished ideals, the ideal of feminine self-sacrifice, is both protected and renewed by the move from culture into nature. However, Caird's novel also exposes precisely whose interests are best served by the ideal of feminine self-sacrifice, and what the costs of that ideal are. It is an ideal which nurtures men and destroys those women who cannot, or will not, conform to it: Julian is saved and Anna is painfully sacrificed. *Pathway of the Gods* thus blends formal renovation and innovation with a radical New Woman rhetoric, and what appears to be a kind of feminist conservationism, which preserves sexual difference by insisting on the spiritual and moral superiority of the self-sacrificing, womanly woman.

In her address to the Women Writers' Dinner in 1894 (the *annus mirabilis* of the New Woman) Mary Haweis outlined the project of the modern woman writer: 'Our first duty as women writers', Haweis asserted, 'is to help the cause of women'.[35] In this speech Haweis elaborated a vision of the woman writer's mission as a sacred task. The woman writer of the late nineteenth century, in conformity with the womanly ideal of bourgeois ideology, was charged with the task of embellishing, perfecting, and saving the moral universe. 'In women's hands – in women writers' hands – lies the regeneration of the world. Let us go on with our tongues of fire, consecrated to an entirely holy work, cleansing, repairing, beautifying as we go, the page of the world's history which lies before us now'. Caird took up this call in her polemical essays and in her fiction. Her essays offer a monologic defence of 'the woman's cause', but her novels speak with more than one voice on the woman questions and marriage questions of the day. Caird's novels do not simply transpose into fictional form the polemical rhetoric of her essays, rather they develop what I have described elsewhere as a 'rhetoric of feeling'[36] which simultaneously or by turns represents and explores the complex actualities of women's lives and figures utopian desires. *The Wing of Azrael*, *The Daughters of Danaus* and *Pathway of the Gods* are not simply fictionalized versions of Caird's journalistic campaigns against marriage and on behalf of women. They are self-conscious aesthetic artefacts which situate themselves in relation to the developing aesthetic of the novel of the modern woman, an aesthetic in opposition to which many aspects of literary modernism were defined, but which, nevertheless, was to have considerable influence on the fictional practice of several male writers of the early twentieth century, including D.H. Lawrence and E.M. Forster.

Notes

1. See S. Gilbert and S. Gubar, *No Man's Land: The Place of the Woman Writer in the Twentieth Century* (New Heaven: Yale University Press), i: *The War of the Words* (1988), ii: *Sexchanges* (1989); Bonnie Kime Scott (ed.), *The Gender of Modernism: A Critical Anthology* (Bloomington: Indiana University Press, 1990).
2. W.T. Stead, 'The novel of the Modern Woman', *Review of Reviews*, 10 (1894), pp. 64–73.
3. Ibid., p. 65.
4. Ibid., p. 64.
5. Edmund Gosse, 'The Decay of Literary Taste', *North American Review*, 161 (1895), pp. 109–19, 116.
6. See below, and also Lyn Pykett, *The 'Improper' Feminine* (London: Routledge, 1992).
7. Patricia Stubbs, *Women and Fiction: Feminism and the Novel* (London: Methuen, 1979), p. 120.
8. Ibid., p. 120.
9. Gail Cunningham, *The New Woman and the Victorian Novel* (London: Macmillan, 1978), p. 19.

10. Elaine Showalter, *A Literature of Their Own* (London: Virago, 1978), p. 181.
11. Elaine Showalter, 'Syphilis, Sexuality, and the fiction of the *fin de siècle*' in R.B. Yeazell (ed.), *Sex, Politics and the Nineteenth-Century Novel* (Baltimore: Johns Hopkins University Press, 1986).
12. Showalter, 1978, p. 215.
13. This space has, to some extent, been filled in by Gerd Bjorhovde, *Rebellious Structures: Women Writers and the Crisis of the Novel, 1880–1900* (Oxford: Oxford University Press, 1987); Penny Boumelha, *Thomas Hardy and Women: Sexual Ideology and Narrative Form* (Sussex: Harvester, 1982); Ann Ardis, *New Women, New Novels* (New Brunswick: Rutgers University Press, 1990).
14. See the books by Ardis, Boumelha and Pykett already noted, and Kate Flint, *The Woman Reader 1837–1914* (Oxford: Clarendon Press, 1993).
15. 1894 was a high point in the publication of New Woman fiction. It also saw the publication of two important essays on the New Woman: Sarah Grand, 'A New Aspect of the Woman Question', *North American Review*, 158 (1894), pp. 271–6, and 'Ouida' [Marie Louise de la Ramee], 'The New Aspect of the Woman Question', *North American Review*, 158 (1894), pp. 610–19.
16. Arthur Waugh, 'Reticence in Literature', *The Yellow Book*, 1 (1894), pp. 201–19. Hubert Crackanthorpe, 'Reticence in Literature', *The Yellow Book*, 2 (1894), pp. 259–73.
17. H.M. Stutfield, 'Tommyrotics', *Blackwood's*, 157 (1895), pp. 833–45. Janet Hogarth, 'Literary Degenerates', *Fortnightly Review*, 57 (1895), pp. 586–92.
18. Waugh, op. cit., p. 14.
19. Ibid., p. 210, my emphasis.
20. Ibid., p. 204.
21. W.L. Courtney, *The Feminine Note in Fiction* (London: Chapman and Hall, 1904), p. xii.
22. Ibid., p. xii.
23. Ibid., p. xiii.
24. Mona Caird, *The Morality of Marriage and Other Essays on the Status and Destiny of Woman* (London: George Redway, 1897).
25. Stead, op. cit., p. 66.
26. Caird, 1897, p. 1.
27. Janet Todd (ed.), *Dictionary of British Women Writers* (London: Routledge, 1989), p. 119.
28. Mona Caird, *The Wing of Azrael* (London: Trubner, 1889), *The Daughters of Danaus* (London: Bliss, Sands and Foster, 1894), *Pathway of the Gods* (London: Skeffington and Son, 1898). References in the text use the following abbreviations: *WA*, *DD* and *PG*.
29. See B. Crackanthorpe, 'The Revolt of the Daughters', *Nineteenth Century*, 34 (1894), pp. 23–31, and 'The Revolt of the Daughters (No. I): A Last Word on "The Revolt"', *Nineteenth Century*, 35 (1894), pp. 424–9; M.E. Haweis, 'The Revolt of the Daughters (No. II). Daughters and Mothers', *Nineteenth Century*, 35 (1894), pp. 430–6; A.P. Smith, 'A reply from the Daughters II', *Nineteenth Century*, 35 (1894), pp. 443–50; S.M. Jeune, 'The Revolt of the Daughters', *Fortnightly Review*, 61 (1894), pp. 276–67.
30. Mona Caird, 'A Defence of the so-called "Wild Women"', *Nineteenth Century*, 31 (1892), pp. 811–29, p. 18.

31. Thomas Hardy, 1912 Postscript to *Jude the Obscure* (Oxford: World's Classics, 1985), p. xxxviii.
32. W.T. Stead described Grant Allen's *The Woman Who Did* as having a 'boomerang ending', i.e. one that boomerangs a central female character back into a conventional feminine role. See W.T. Stead, 'The Book of the Month. "The Woman Who Did" by G. Allen', *Review of Reviews*, 11 (1895), pp. 177–90, 187.
33. Ardis, op. cit., p. 100.
34. Ibid., p. 100.
35. Quoted in Elaine Showalter, *A Literature of Their Own*, pp. 182–3.
36. Pykett, op. cit., p. 145.

CHAPTER EIGHT

Gender, Race and Sexuality in Bram Stoker's Other Novels

Jeffrey Richards

Bram Stoker created one of the enduring myth figures of world literature – Count Dracula, the vampire – in a book which has never been out of print since its first appearance in 1897 and which has been reinterpreted and reworked by the theatre and cinema in every generation since. The fascination and the appeal of Dracula are universal. They deal with the eternal mysteries of sex and death. But the context which produced the book was specific. It was the period of crisis of confidence and intellectual turmoil at the end of the nineteenth century, a period when old certainties, boundaries, structures and role models were under threat and in some cases, breaking down. Fears about the future of the Empire and the race, class conflict, the rise of feminism and the campaign for women's rights preoccupied politicians, writers and the mass media. Popular literature mirrored and contributed to these ambivalences and uncertainties and in particular the conflict of ideas and attitudes surrounding sexuality, race and gender.

Stoker is a fascinating case of a popular novelist who while working out his own concerns and preoccupations also plugged into the main currents of anxiety political, theoretical and ideological. *Dracula* has provoked an extensive and ever-growing literature, analysing the novel from religious, psychological, sexual, mythological and ideological standpoints. But the rest of Stoker's books remain for the most part out of print, unread and rarely commented upon. He wrote some 22 works in all: horror novels, society tales, period romances, mystery stories, short stories, fairy tales. So was *Dracula* a one-off? Did it embody themes developed or reworked in other books? Should we be looking at his work as a corpus?

Stoker was at the heart of the cultural world of late Victorian London, where for nearly 30 years he was the business manager of Sir Henry Irving, the acknowledged head of the acting profession and impresario at the Lyceum Theatre of what one journalist called 'a national theatre but without a subsidy'. Stoker rubbed shoulders with the political, social and cultural luminaries of the day, and numbered among his friends such leading writers as Oscar Wilde, Lord Tennyson, Mark Twain, Hall Caine, W.S. Gilbert and Sir Arthur Conan Doyle.

One key to understanding Stoker is that he idolized Irving. In the loving two-volume *Reminiscences* he published after Irving's death, he gives a vivid account of their first meeting in Dublin in 1876. At a private dinner party, Irving recited his tour-de-force party piece *The Dream of Eugene Aram* and Stoker literally had hysterics. Irving was so moved by the effect his acting had had that he inscribed a photograph of himself 'My dear friend Stoker. God bless you!' Stoker writes: 'In those moments of our mutual emotion he too had found a friend and knew it. Soul had looked into soul! From that hour began a friendship as profound, as close, as lasting as can be between two men . . . The sight of his picture before me, with those loving words . . . unmans me once again as I write'.[1]

There are no doubt those who would wish to interpret this feeling as homosexual and some commentators have found elements of homoeroticism in *Dracula*. But this is misguided. Stoker was essentially a hero-worshipper. His hero-worship of Irving superseded a previous heroworship of Walt Whitman. In Irving, he also seems to have found a father figure. It is perhaps significant that Stoker's father died aged 77 in 1876, the year he had his momentous encounter with Irving. Throughout his career Stoker seems to have sought Irving's approval. It was probably also his ambition to write a Lyceum play as a vehicle for Irving. *Dracula* may have been conceived in part for this purpose. But Irving allegedly thought it 'dreadful' and while many of Irving's circle were called upon to provide stage vehicles for him or to adapt old plays for the Lyceum stage (Frank Marshall, Percy Fitzgerald, Hall Caine, Walter H. Pollock, H.D. Traill, Laurence Irving), the call never came for Stoker to provide one.[2] Irving in any case liked to play off the members of his entourage against each other, so that no one person ever got too close to him. In this situation may lie the real explanation of Joseph S. Bierman's interpretation of *Dracula*. Bierman suggests that psychologically Stoker's work can be interpreted as a desire for fratricide.[3] Daniel Farson, Stoker's great-nephew and biographer, rejects this on the basis of the evidence of the known excellent relations between the Stoker brothers.[4] But there may be another interpretation of brothers – Stoker's rivalry with his 'brothers' in the service of the 'father' Irving. Bierman notes that one of Stoker's recurrent preoccupations is the story of Cain and Abel. But in a short story, 'The Coming of Abel Behenna', Stoker gives Abel as surname the maiden name of Irving's mother, suggesting a link with the Irving 'family' circle within which Stoker was nicknamed 'Mama' by Ellen Terry and 'Brother Bram' by Genevieve Ward. It is well known that there was fierce rivalry between Stoker and the other intimates of the Irving circle (Harry Loveday, Austin Brereton, Joseph Hatton, Jo Comyns Carr), and John Martin Harvey, longtime member of the Lyceum company, testifies that Stoker sought to erect barriers to keep 'the Chief' to himself.[5]

It has long been suggested that *Dracula* grew in part out of subconscious resentment of Stoker at his subservience to Irving, and Irving's failure to bestow exclusive affection and approbation on him.[6] This is so far recognized that the new Penguin edition of the novel contains a photograph on the cover of Irving as Mephistopheles, making visually clear the physical inspiration Irving provided for the vampire. The novel itself is steeped in the atmosphere and imagery of the Lyceum. Maurice Richardson sees *Dracula* as an Oedipal fantasy in which the father is slain by a band of brothers.[7] This only makes sense if the father is Irving and not Stoker's natural father. Even more striking is the fact that Dr Van Helsing, the leading vampirehunter and the 'good' father as opposed to the destructive 'evil' father, has Stoker's own father's Christian name, Abraham.

If Stoker was in search of a father, he had no shortage of mother figures. He lived his life under the influence of two strong-willed women. The dominant figure in his family was his mother Charlotte, 20 years younger than her husband and a key influence on her son, especially in those years of his childhood when he was bedridden and housebound with illness. Later her place was taken over by his wife Florence. He married Florence Balcombe, one of the most beautiful women in Dublin, in 1878 shortly before leaving for England to take up his job with Irving. They had one child, christened Irving Noel Thornley Stoker, though known as Noel, born within a year of the marriage. Although she was ten years younger than Bram, she seems to have been as strong-willed as Charlotte and to have functioned perhaps as a mother substitute.

Stoker himself seems to have been preoccupied with issues of gender and sexuality, and this is another important key to understanding him. In 1872 he wrote a passionate fan letter to Walt Whitman whose work he had defended in debates at Dublin. He was then 24 and was entranced by Whitman's 'gospel of comradeship' but clearly also in search of a mentor. He describes himself thus:

> I am twenty-four years old. Have been champion at our athletic sports (Trinity College, Dublin) and have won about a dozen cups. I have also been President of the College Philosophical Society and an art and theatrical critic of a daily paper. I am six feet two inches high and twelve stone weight naked . . . I am ugly but strong and determined . . . I am equal in temper and cool in disposition and have a large amount of self-control and am naturally secretive to the world . . . I have a large number of acquaintances and some five or six friends – all of which latter care much for me . . . How sweet a thing it is for a strong healthy man with a woman's eyes, and a child's wishes to feel that he can speak so to a man who can be if he wishes father, and brother and wife to his soul . . . I thank you for all the love and sympathy you have given me in common with my kind.[8]

Although the 'women's eyes' and 'my kind' might suggest in Freudian terms repressed homosexuality, Stoker's subsequent unselfconscious account of his love for Irving suggests that he saw it as entirely innocent and 'the child's wishes' may indicate a different sensibility, essentially child-like, something reinforced by his writing of fairy stories, his domination by mother figures and his search for a father figure.

Nevertheless the Whitman letter does suggest an element of sexual confusion and implicit concern about his sexual identity. There is further circumstantial evidence about this. In 1910 he published a work of non-fiction, *Famous Imposters*, in which he surveyed the careers of pretenders to the throne, magicians and hoaxers, and stresses that 'he has made no attempt to treat the subject ethically' but rather actually.[9] He was particularly fascinated by cross-dressing. He included a section on women who passed themselves off as men, observing that this form of imposture was so common that 'it seems rooted in a phase of human nature'.[10] He also has a chapter on the Chevalier d'Eon who disguised as a woman in furtherance of his secret service duties. He fiercely defends D'Eon against his enemies' charges that he really was a woman, pointing out that he was 'a very gallant soldier' and had undertaken his imposture out of devotion to the throne of France, and finally that an autopsy on his body confirmed his undoubted masculinity. Stoker's tone suggests that he is anxious to stress that a certain feminine sensitivity in the male nature does not compromise basic masculinity.

Perhaps the most interesting part of the book is the lengthy investigation into the legend of the 'Bisley Boy', a story which, he admitted, fascinated him and which he believed to have substance. It was a longstanding local tradition that Queen Elizabeth I, while still a girl, had died on a visit to Bisley and been replaced by a local boy who grew up to reign as the Queen. He concludes 'the world at that crisis wanted just such a one as Elizabeth. All honour to her whosoever she may have been, boy or girl matters not'.[11]

Much of the detail in Stoker's novels is autobiographical and experiential, and it is reasonable to assume therefore that many of the ideas and dilemmas he is exploring are also personal to him. His heroes are frequently projections of himself, big, burly, athletic manly men who act according to chivalric ideas. Archibald Hunter in *The Mystery of the Sea* is a large, burly, athletic man who had been an invalid as a child but later developed into an athlete. His athletic prowess gave him a position at college 'in which I had to overcome my natural shyness'. He is also a barrister without a practice. This follows Stoker's own career in every particular. He was called to the bar in 1890 but never practised. Rupert Sent Leger, hero of the *Lady of the Shroud*, is Irish, seven feet tall, a much-travelled and bronzed adventurer, devoted to the memory of his dead mother. Harold An Wolf, the titular hero of *The Man*, is deep-chested, broad-shouldered, lean-flanked, long-armed, a man of 'knightly breeding' who had a good academic education and was an expert in most of the manly exercises – riding, shooting, fencing, running, jumping and swimming.

These heroes frequently save someone from drowning, Stoker's regular measure of manhood. Stoker had earned headline praise from the newspapers for trying to save a would-be suicide in the Thames and had been awarded the Bronze Medal of the Royal Humane Society in 1882. Rafe Otwell saves Betty Pole from drowning during Doggett's coat and badge race on the Thames in *Miss Betty*. Harold An Wolf saves a child from drowning when a boy and later when a man saves an American girl, Pearl Stonehouse, receiving the Gold Medal of the Royal Humane Society. In *The Mystery of the Sea* Archie Hunter saves Marjory Anita Drake from drowning. For no particular reason other than to establish his manliness the captain of the *Cryptic* in *Lady Athlyne*, a minor character, is described as holding the Gold Medal of the Royal Humane Society.

The experience of going blind and recovering partial sight, described in *The Man*, is something Stoker himself had undergone following Irving's death in 1905. Stoker regularly uses familiar locales for his tales. Betty Pole lives, like Stoker, in Cheyne Walk. His most regularly used location was the Cruden Bay area of North-East Scotland where he spent his holidays (*Mystery of the Sea, The Watter's Mou, The Man*, the short story 'Crooken Sands'). His vivid descriptions of a blizzard in New York and of transatlantic crossings by ocean liner in *Lady Athlyne* are undoubtedly drawn from his own experience travelling with the Irving company.

But Stoker's individual preoccupations mesh directly with the wider culture. For the 1880s and 1890s were the decades of what Elaine Showalter calls 'sexual anarchy' when the laws governing sexual identity and gender boundaries seemed to be breaking down.[12] For these decades saw on the one hand the rise of feminism and 'The New Woman' and on the other the construction of homosexuality and an obsession with degeneration and demoralization of the race.

'The New Woman' challenged the traditional role of woman as wife and mother, epitomized in Ruskin's essay 'Of Queens Gardens', Tennyson's poem *The Princess* and Coventry Patmore's celebration of *The Angel in the House*. The New Women sought careers, the vote, financial independence, alternatives to marriage, political, social and sexual equality. The phrase 'The New Woman' was coined in 1894 and there was thereafter a spate of 'New Woman' novels and plays. The opponents of the 'New Woman' depicted her as radical, aggressive, over-intellectual and sexually voracious, and as a result undermining the social and sexual order, and denying or rejecting the loving, supportive wife and mother role.

Rebecca Stott has argued convincingly that the *femme fatale*, an old archetype stretching back to Cleopatra, Salome and Helen of Troy and cutting across barriers of race and class, was reconstructed in the late nineteenth century, as a result of imperial insecurity and the rise of feminism.[13] There was clearly a link ideologically between concern over the emergence of the 'New Woman' and concern about degeneration which in its narrow sense meant in the 1890s celebrations of decadence and homosexuality (Wilde, Beardsley, *The Yellow Book*, and so on) and in the broader sense meant a threat to the empire and the race and Britain's world dominance. For the emergence of the 'New Woman' who was liberated and sexually aggressive went hand in hand with the creation of the 'New Man', who was homosexual and effete. They were the polar opposites of what mid-Victorian culture meant by womanly and manly. This focused attention squarely on gender roles.

Stoker's mature novels fall into three categories: the pure horror stories (*Dracula* (1897), *Jewel of Seven Stars* (1903), *Lair of the White Worm* (1911)), the love stories (*The Shoulder of Shasta* (1895), *Miss Betty* (1898), *Lady Athlyne* (1908) and *The Man* (1905)), and romances (*The Snake's Pass* (1890), *The Lady of the Shroud* (1909), *The Mystery of the Sea* (1902)). The horror stories function on the level of the unconscious, as fantasy explorations of his deep sexual concerns. The love stories are realistic psychological studies of young women falling in love and considered meditations on gender difference. The romances mingle the two.

Horror and sexuality

The endless fascination of *Dracula* is that it works on so many levels. The novel can be interpreted as Christian allegory, with religion and science joining forces to destroy the living Satan. It is also an imperial anxiety thriller, part of a genre dubbed by Patrick Brantlinger 'imperial Gothic', arising from concern about the invasion of western civilization by eastern barbarism and fear of individual regression or 'going native'.[14] In this interpretation Dracula, descendant of Attila and his Huns, invades England from Eastern Europe and causes his victims to regress to a state of savagery and unrestrained sexuality. Dracula's first victim is the strangely named Lucy Westenra, whose name suggests a combination of significant elements: Lucy from the Latin word for light, Westen from Western and Ra from the ancient sungod, being eclipsed by Dracula, symbol of the East and of darkness. Dracula is destroyed by a group of

Anglo-Saxon males: one Dutchman, one American, the rest English.

Dracula is explicitly located by Daniel Pick in the debate about degeneration, a key element in nineteenth century thinking, particularly in its last decades. Stoker's references in the text to Nordau and Lombroso, major authorities on the subject of degeneration, confirms his interest in the subject. Pick writes: 'The novel provides a metaphor for current political and sexual discourses on morality and society, representing the price of selfish pursuits and criminal depravity. The family and the nation, it seemed to many, were beleaguered by syphilitics, alcoholics, cretins, the insane, the feebleminded, prostitutes and a perceived "alien invasion" of Jews from the East, who in the view of many alarmists were "feeding off" and "poisoning" the blood of the Londoner'.[15]

Carol Senf sees Dracula as 'Stoker's response to the New Woman', who is slightingly referred to in the text twice.[16] Mina, highly intelligent and accomplished, resists being sexualized by Dracula and helps to destroy him but Lucy, 'liberated' by the Count, becomes sexually voracious and has to be destroyed. But there is more to it than an ideological response, for Clive Leatherdale, in one of the best and most comprehensive explorations of the many meanings of *Dracula*, declares it 'a work stemming from profound sexual repression', whose message is that 'erotically aroused women will annihilate if they are not first destroyed'.[17]

Stoker's work is almost a textbook case for interpretation. It is obsessed with sex. Leatherdale identifies in its pages 'seduction, rape, necrophilia, paedophilia, incest, adultery, oral sex, group sex, menstruation, venereal disease, voyeurism'.[18] But strikingly – and if Stoker were homosexual, there should have been some unconscious echoes of this – 'its sexual framework is rigidly heterosexual'.[19] Dracula preys on women, the female vampires on men.

The powerfully erotic description of Harker's reaction to the approach of the three vampire women sums up the desire for totally unrestrained sex, and at the same time the horror and fear of it. Harker's anguish provides 'a mirror on the suffocating repression which consumed his society'.[20] The counterpart to Harker being threatened with gang-rape by three totally liberated women, is the effective gang-rape by the men of the vampirized Lucy, in which she is penetrated by the phallic stake wielded by her fiancé, Arthur, Lord Godalming, with his prime chivalric Christian name and Home Counties title, thus restoring the balance of the sexes and eliminating threatening sexuality. This can be seen on one level as evidence of a repressed society but on another as evidence of Stoker's own repression, for which there is another piece of Freudian evidence in his self-confessed love of fires, which he raced to and watched until they were put out. He writes: 'It was a standing joke with (Irving) against me that whenever there was a fire within range I was off to it hotfoot'.[21] Fire, the symbol of passion, burns until it is put out and order restored, watched by a fascinated Stoker.

This fear of sex and sexuality runs through all his novels, a surprisingly large number of which contain a positive decision by the hero and heroine to defer the sexual consummation of their relationship. In *Miss Betty* it is deferred for five years while the hero expiates his crimes in military service abroad. In *The Snake's Pass* it is deferred for two years while the heroine completes her education abroad. In *The Mystery of the Sea* Marjory insists that the consummation be deferred until they have known each other well enough to become good comrades. In *The Lady of the Shroud* Teuta insists on deferring consummation until her duty to her country is discharged. It is as if Stoker sees love as better and nobler if unaccompanied by sex.

The horror stories which follow *Dracula*, though less complex in both narrative structure and ideology, are powerful hallucinatory tales, which reinforce and repeat the underlying moral of *Dracula*, but with one instructive difference – the force of evil is no longer male (Dracula) but female. The difference could be that *Dracula* was published in 1897 while Irving was still all-powerful. But by the time of *Jewel* (1903) Irving had lost the Lyceum, was physically declining and approaching retirement, and by the time of *Lair of the White Worm* (1911) he was dead. Stoker, seeking to make a new career for himself as a full-time writer, is free to allow other, perhaps deeper, preoccupations to surface.

Jewel of Seven Stars mingles elements of *Dracula* with *She* and *The Moonstone*. In *Dracula* a group of male friends, mainly professionals, seek to bring about the destruction of Dracula: the solicitor Jonathan Harker, the doctor John Seward, the American traveller and hunter Quincy P. Morris, scientist and philosopher Dr Van Helsing, plus the aristocrat Lord Godalming. In *Jewel* it is barrister Malcolm Ross, physician Dr Winchester, archaeologist Eugene Corbeck and policemen Superintendent Dolan and Sergeant Daws. Corbeck, who holds degrees of Oxford, Cambridge, London, Paris and Berlin is clearly the Van Helsing figure. They seek to combat a mysterious series of nocturnal attacks on comatose archaeologist Abel Trelawney, just as the previous group sought to prevent Dracula getting at Lucy. Trelawney revives from his coma and plans to resurrect the long-dead Egyptian Queen Tera, a woman who was in advance of the attitudes and beliefs of her time. The revival, Trelawney believes, will allow her to become 'a new woman'. Trelawney's daughter Margaret, who is loved by Ross, believes that Tera was seeking love, 'the dream of every woman's life', and that her resurrection would permit this. Ross has grave misgivings, doubting this interpretation on the grounds that Tera had never expressed in her life any interest in love, according to the evidence. But Margaret, who was born at the moment of the discovery of Tera's tomb, begins to change as the experiment nears, from the normal, natural, loving Margaret to a person cold and 'intellectually aloof', a 'new woman' herself. When the great experiment takes place, it fails, Tera's body dissolves and everyone apart from Ross is killed. The message is clear – the attempt to create a 'New Woman' will end in disaster. But the publishers found the ending so stark and disturbing that they persuaded Stoker to rewrite it for editions subsequent to the first and he contributed a happy ending in which both Margaret and Ross survive and are married. But the first ending clearly mirrors Stoker's real mood, a mood which became even bleaker and more savage in his final horror novel, *Lair of the White Worm*.

The Lair of the White Worm centres on the legend of an ancient and terrible giant serpent, rumoured to survive in the caves of Derbyshire. In this novel, the snake is able to take human form, as Lady Arabella March, owner of Diana's Grove, 'the lair of the White Worm'. She has a sinuous body and sibilant voice, and is cold, ruthless and domineering. There are constant references to her coldbloodedness. She has an ally, the Dracula figure, landowner and castle-dweller Edgar Caswall, hard, selfish, dominating, descendant of a family as old as the Roman occupation, and possessed of hypnotic powers.

Arabella seeks to aid Caswall in his pursuit of Lilla Watford. The two Watford girls, grand-daughters of a tenant farmer, are Lilla, who is fair, and Mimi, who has some occult powers from a Burmese ancestor; Mimi battles with Caswall for hypnotic possession of Lilla. Lilla, however, dies from the attempt to resist Caswall's power, and Caswall goes mad, his 'decadence' exaggerating his self-importance into egomania.

Meanwhile Arabella is pursuing the hero, Adam Salton, an Australian, who falls in love with Mimi and is aided in his struggles by wise old man, Sir Nathaniel de Salis, president of the Mercian Archeological Society. She tries several times to dispose of Mimi but fails. Eventually Adam and Nathaniel plant dynamite at Diana's Grove and when the lair is struck by lightning, it blows up, destroying the serpent.

The story is set within the context of a battle between good and evil, symbolized by the Watfords' Mercy Farm, on the site of a celebrated Saxon monastery, and Diana's Grove, the site of a pagan temple. But much more central than religious motif is the horror of sex that pervades the book. Adam and Nathaniel see the 'Worm' one night, a huge great white snake, like a giant phallus towering over the countryside. Adam, confronted by the well-hole in the basement of Diana's Grove is appalled by the noxious stench that almost makes him sick. 'He compared it with all the noxious experiences he had ever had – the drainage of war hospitals, of slaughterhouses, the refuse of dissecting rooms. None of these was like it, though it had something of them all, with, added the sourness of chemical waste and the poisonous effluvium of the bilge of a water-logged ship, whereon a multitude of rats had been drowned'.[22] At the end when the worm, its hole and Lady Arabella are all blown up, the 'nauseous' and 'sickening' remains, rapidly corrupt and are covered with 'insects, worms, and vermin of all kinds. The sight was horrible enough, but, with the awful smell added, was simply unbearable. The Worm's hole appeared to breathe forth death in its most repulsive forms.'[23]

The symbolism is clear. The well-hole as the vagina, Diana's Grove as the pubic bush, the snake as phallus, all inspire horror and loathing. Added to this is the fact that Arabella becomes the phallic snake. The predatory 'New Woman' takes on a fundamental masculine form, upsetting the order of nature. But she remains a woman and is all the more dangerous for all that. Sir Nathaniel explicitly casting the contest in terms of a gender battle, says: 'I never thought this fighting an antediluvian monster would be such a complicated job. This one is a woman, with all a woman's wit, combined with the heartlessness of a cocotte. She has the reserved strength and impregnability of a diplodocus. We may be sure that in the fight that is before us there will be no semblance of fair play . . . but being of feminine species, she will probably over-reach herself. Now Adam, it strikes me that as we have to protect ourselves and others against feminine nature, our strong game will be to play our masculine against her feminine.'[24] So once again Stoker's personal preoccupations potently intermesh with his ideological position.

It has been suggested that the peculiar horror of sexuality manifested in this 1911 novel is associated with his approaching death, attributed by his biographer Daniel Farson to tertiary syphilis, which he believes Stoker may have originally contracted around the time of *Dracula* in 1897.[25] But the horror of snakes manifested itself in Stoker's first novel, *The Snake's Pass* (1890), the only one to be set in his native Ireland. It reveals preoccupations and imagery fully formed.

The story interweaves two themes. One is the search for a lost treasure, which according to legend is hidden in the bog on the Hill of Knockcalltecrore and the Snake's Pass. It is either the golden crown of the King of the Snakes, driven out of Ireland by St Patrick, or a treasure chest of gold lost by an invading French army during the Napoleonic Wars. But interwoven is the romantic story of the contest for the hand of Norah Joyce, beautiful daughter of a peasant farmer Phelim Joyce, which is played out according to Stoker's idea of gender roles. Norah has 'a heart of gold, a sweet pure nature and a rare intelligence'. She is loved by the hero, wealthy gentleman traveller Arthur Severn, who when he first sees her exclaims like Sir Geraint in Tennyson's *Idylls of the King*: 'Here, by God's rood, is the one maid for me.' His love for her, as befits his name, is pure and chivalric. She is loved by the evil gombeen man (moneylender), Murtagh 'Black' Murdoch, who is also seeking the treasure, and by Dick Sutherland, burly, bearded geologist, old school friend of Arthur, brought in by Murdoch to drain the bog.

When Arthur reveals that he too loves Norah and she him, Dick resigns her, sobbing on Arthur's shoulder. But their friendship is reinforced. 'Thank God for loyal and royal manhood. Thank God for the heart of a friend that can suffer and remain true', writes Stoker, commenting later that Dick displayed: 'a noble manliness . . . which was beyond description'.[26] This is a characteristically Victorian celebration of that male love, the love of David and Jonathan, that passes the love of women in its spirituality and strength.[27]

Phelim agrees to Arthur marrying Norah once the treasure is found. Norah, wishing to be worthy of him before marrying, insists on spending two years in Paris, Dresden and London to gain an education. She is willing to marry him before she sets out but insists that the consummation be deferred until she returns. Arthur's admiration for her increases and he agrees to defer the marriage.

Yet Arthur dreams constantly of snakes and of the King of Snakes, which sometimes has the head of his rival Murdoch.[28] The snake has long been recognized as a symbol of sexuality, not only phallic in shape but a reminder of the serpent who tempted Eve in the Garden of Eden to Original Sin, the discovery of sexuality.

The climax of the story takes place in the swamp. Norah is lured there by Murdoch in a storm and attacked. She is rescued by Arthur. She then herself rescues Arthur, the swamp swallows Murdoch and his house, and then disappears through the Snake's Pass into the sea. The cleansing rain completes the action of the storm in eliminating what remains, and both the chest and the crown are discovered.

In Freudian terms, the snake is male sexuality, which threatens Norah in the form of Murdoch. The Snake's Pass is the vagina, the swamp the womb. But the swamp is characterized, like the snake's hole in *Lair*, as a noxious bog of ooze and slime and decayed vegetable fibre. Arthur falling and almost being sucked into it but being rescued by the pure Norah indicates a feeling that sex is dirty and that the hero can be rescued from it to continue a celibacy arrangement which will end after two years with marriage. The rescue of the gold and the treasure from the swamp is symbolic of the retrieval of integrity and perfect inner wholeness from the taint of corruption. It is another drama of sexual repression and the endorsement of gender roles, with true men chivalric and manly and true women pure and devoted but spirited and intelligent.

Gender, love and sexuality

The dominant male code in Stoker's world is chivalry. Chivalry had been deliberately revived in the nineteenth century as a programme for life. Mark Girouard defines it precisely:

> A chivalrous gentleman was brave, straightforward and honourable, loyal to his monarch, country and friends, unfailingly true to his word, ready to take issue with anyone he saw ill-treating a woman, a child or an animal. He was a natural leader of men, and others unhesitatingly followed his lead. He was fearless in war and on the hunting field, and excelled in all manly sports; but however tough with the tough, he was invariably gentle to the weak; above all he was always tender, respectful and courteous to women, regardless of their rank. He put the needs of others before his own.[29]

Word for word, this could be a description of all of Stoker's heroes.

The emergence of the chivalric gentleman was no accident. The concept was deliberately promoted by key figures of the nineteenth century, like Thomas Carlyle, Charles Kingsley, Edward Fitzgerald and Robert Baden-Powell, as a code of behaviour for the ruling elite. But it also filtered down through the rest of society by the agency of popular culture. It was not deemed to be class specific. Samuel Smiles argued: 'Riches and rank have no necessary connection with genuine and gentlemanly qualities. The poor man may be a true gentleman in spirit and daily life. He may be honest, truthful, upright, polite, temperate, courageous, self-respecting and self-helping – that is be a true gentleman'.[30] The concept was promoted to mitigate fears about mass democracy, the worship of money in society as a concomitant of industrialization and the placing of expediency before principle in politics. Chivalry was equally advanced at the end of the century, particularly in the genre of romance, to affirm traditional manliness and counter the rise of feminism and homosexuality.

The mutually agreed code of chivalry is one of the links that binds Britain and America and is stressed throughout Stoker's work. In *Lady Athlyne*, Colonel Lucius Ogilvie of Kentucky is the embodiment of chivalry ('Honour is the first thing in all the world. What men should live for; what men should die for. To a gentleman there is nothing is so holy').[31] Ogilvie and the English Captain of the *Cryptic* become friends on the basis of this shared code, as do Lord Athlyne and the American Lt Flinders Breckenridge. At the end, when the Colonel, finding Athlyne with his daughter in compromising circumstances, challenges him to a duel, Athlyne explains what happened but will accept the duel. However, being unwilling to shoot his sweetheart's father, he will expect to die. 'Instinctively Colonel Ogilvie bowed. His action was simply a spontaneous recognition of the chivalry of another and his appreciation of it.'[32]

The loves of Stoker's heroes are always depicted in chivalric terms. Both Athlyne on seeing Joy and Arthur Severn on seeing Norah exclaim 'Here by God's rood is the one maid for me', echoing Sir Geraint in Tennysons's *Idylls of the King*. The loves of Archie Hunter for Marjory Drake and of Harold An Wolf for Stephen Norman are consistently developed in chivalric terms.

Chivalry too lay at the heart of Stoker's attitude to women. John Martin Harvey confirms this when he noted 'the conspicuous courtesy with which he always treated my wife, even when she was merely a very obscure little member of the company'.[33] Stoker himself underlines this view in an anecdote he tells in the *Reminiscences*. When Irving was playing *Hamlet* at the Star Theatre, New York, a fire broke out and one man in the audience dashed up the aisle in panic. Stoker grabbed him, threw him to the ground and dragged him back to his seat, to prevent a general panic, saying: 'It is cowards like you who cause death to helpless women'.[34] This encapsulates his view of man as protector and woman as object of devotion.

Stoker liked women. Most of the novels are dedicated to women: *Miss Betty* to his wife, *The Lady of the Shroud* to actress Genevieve Ward, *The Lair of the White Worm* to Bertha Nicholl, *Jewel of Seven Stars* to Eleanor and Constance Hoyt, *The Man* to Gwladys Burrell, and *Lady Athlyne* to 'Lady Athlyne', suggesting that the eponymous heroine was inspired by a real person. But he particularly like women of intelligence and spirit, who nevertheless accepted their traditional role in society. His heroines, Stephen Norman, Teuta Vissarion, Joy Ogilvie, Betty Pole, Marjory Anita Drake, Norah Joyce are invariably cast in this mould. The link between men and women is love. Love makes them whole, two halves of a single spiritual being.

Stoker was clearly preoccupied with love. As he writes in *The Man*: 'Love is in fact the most serious thing that comes to man: when it exists all else seems as phantoms, or at best as actualities of lesser degree'.[35] He wrote two novellas (*Miss Betty* and *The Shoulder of Shasta*) and two full-length novels (*Lady Athlyne* and *The Man*) about love and the process of falling in love. Intriguingly all four works are written from the point of view of their female protagonists, explore in pulsating detail the agonies and ecstasies of falling in love, and examine gender roles and gender relations.

The actual stories are usually quite flimsy but the discussion of gender and sexuality are lengthy and dominant. *Miss Betty* is a romance set in early eighteenth-century England. Intelligent, attractive and spirited Betty Pole is courted by poor but dashing gentleman Rafe Otwell. He proposes marriage and she accepts. Rafe is pressed by Prime Minister Sir Robert Walpole to marry a rich aristocrat heiress but refuses, insisting on holding to his engagement. But his poverty leads him to become a high-wayman in order to support his position as a gentleman. Betty, her suspicions aroused, deliberately sets out to unmask him and when she does so, he is overcome with remorse. She sends him abroad to redeem his honour in the armed forces, and after five years, he returns, purged and ennobled, and they are reunited.

Stoker stresses the spirituality of their love. 'The first kiss is a holy thing. It should be the symbol of spiritual marriage – of the union of two souls.'[36] But throughout, their encounters are punctuated by Stoker's statements about what he considers the innate and desirable characteristics of manliness and womanliness and the relationship of the sexes.

Rafe has 'a certain masculine dominance in his manner but to this she did not object – what woman ever did object to such a quality in her lover?' When he is unmasked, he experiences 'genuine manly shame' and offers to renounce his engagement as a penalty. But she refuses. 'When the conviction began to dawn upon him that he had not lost Betty's love, the supremacy of the man over the woman began unconsciously to assert itself.' When she tells him she set out to unmask him, he is 'speechless with indignation ... this outcome of jealousy and love and vanity which was so thoroughly masculine in its nature as to be beyond feminine comprehension'. But when she cries, he falls on his knees in remorse: 'All the man in him rising to the heights of his humility'.[37]

By contrast, she has qualities that are distinctively feminine. 'Truly the intuition of a woman is a divine thing, and complete with the calm perfection of things beyond the earth'; and 'There is an adaptability in woman's nature, intellectual as well as physical and moral, which always answers when called upon.'[38] In the end, it is clear that while physically and by the order of nature, he remains superior, she is emotionally and intellectually the moving force. He, soldier, highwayman, man of action, is redeemed by her love, feeling and example.

The Shoulder of Shasta is another analysis of a young woman's feelings, in particular hero-worship. Esse Elstree is an intelligent, well-bred, brave, imaginative heroine, who is on a mountain trip in the USA and is saved from a grizzly bear by tall, handsome, longhaired trapper and mountaineer Grizzly Dick. Back in San Francisco, she romanticizes him and their adventure together. Then when her portrait is painted by a charming and refined young English painter Reginald Hampden, she forgets Dick and falls for Reginald. Her feelings for Dick were 'school girl romanticism'; her feelings for Reginald real love. She tells him all about Dick. But Dick turns up, overdressed, overfamiliar and out of place, on the day of her engagement party, intending to propose. He is encouraged by Esse's sophisticated friends to propose to her in front of everyone and they mock him for his clumsiness. But the situation is calmed by Reginald who welcomes Dick as a friend, shames the sophisticates and exchanges hunting knives with Dick. So while Dick is 'a generous and chivalrous soul' who treated Esse with 'grave courtesy that seemed like a knightly act by a natural man', he is not a gentleman and is from a different world to which he must return. The hero-worship of Dick by Esse is part of her emergence as a true woman finding real love with Reginald.

The Shoulder of Shasta is almost a preliminary sketch for Lady Athlyne, which develops much more fully the idea of hero-worship turning to love. American Joy Ogilvie, daughter of a fiery Kentucky colonel, hero-worships the gallant British Boer War hero, the Earl of Athlyne, and becomes jokingly known as 'Lady Athlyne'. When the Earl hears that someone in America is posing as his wife, he goes there incognito to investigate. He saves Joy's life from a runaway horse, falls in love with her, follows her to England where she is holidaying in the Lake District and there courts her. Due to a train of coincidental circumstances, they are caught together at an inn in the Scottish borders in a compromising situation, but their predicament is resolved by a quirk of Scottish law, and they are married.

It is first and foremost an exploration of hero-worship, something Stoker knows all about at first hand. But he also mounts a full explanation of love, gender and gender difference. When the Earl saves Joy's life, it is love at first sight for both of them, as it is for most of Stoker's other heroes and heroines. The Earl is to her a 'Prince Charming'. He is 'all that she had ever longed for. He was tall and strong and handsome and brave. He was a gentleman with all a gentleman's refined ways. He had taste and daintiness, though they were expressed in masculine ways. He too had love and passion.'[39] 'His breeding and the kindliness of his nature' check him from pushing ahead too far, despite his longing to hold her in his arms and kiss her.

Everything begins with love at first sight, which is profound and all-consuming and the attainment of the Platonic idea of ultimate spiritual beauty:

> This is the true heart's content. It is the rapture of hearts, the communion of souls. Passion may later burn rapture into fixed belief; but in that first moment of eyes looking into answering eyes is the dawn of love – the coming together of these twin halves of a perfect soul which was at once the conception and, realization of Platonic belief.[40]

He sees love as existing in the perfect harmony of soul, mind and body:

> In physical life when flesh touches flesh the whole body responds, provided that the two are opposite yet sympathetic. When ideas are exchanged, mind comes forth to mind till each understands with a common force. When soul meets soul some finer means of expres-

sion comes into play. Something so fine and of condition so rare that other senses can neither realise nor conceive. But in the lover all the voices speak simultaneously; the soul and the mind and the body all call, each to its new-found mate. What we call 'heart' gives the note for that wonderful song of love; that song of songs whose music is as necessary in a living world as light or air, and which is more potent in the end than the forces of winds or seas.[41]

Lady Athlyne is full of page after page of rhapsodic pulsating descriptions of Joy's state of mind. Every flush of the cheek, every tremble of the voice, every beat of the heart, every racing of the pulse, every fluttering of the eyelids, is lovingly recorded. At the end of it, 'she had accepted him as Her Master; and that acceptance on a woman's part remains a sacred duty of obedience so long as love lasts. This is one of the mysteries of love. Like all other mysteries, easy of acceptance to those who believe an acceptance which needs no doubting investigation, no proof, no consideration of any kind whatever. She had faith in him and where faith reigns patience ceases to be a virtue.'[42]

Stoker, drawing on the Lake District's association with Wordsworth and Nature, links the love of Joy and Athlyne to love of God and Nature:

For happiness is not merely to be at rest. It is to be with God, to carry out to the full His wish that His children should appreciate and enjoy the powers and good things given them by His hands. And when that happiness is based on love – and there is no true happiness on aught that is not high – the love itself is of the soul and quivers with flapping of its wings. Then indeed can we realize that marvellous promise of the words of the Master: 'Blessed are the pure in heart for they shall see God'. Wordsworth and those who held with him saw God and worshipped Him in those myriad beauties of the lake they loved; and as the beauty and its immortal truth soothed and purified their souls, so was the spirit of the love-sick girl cleansed of all dross.[43]

Yet for all his stress on purity, Stoker acknowledges the physical side of love:

It is a mistake to suppose . . . that the love of a man and a woman for each other is, even at its very highest, devoid of physical emotion. The original Creator did not manifestly so intend . . . The world of flesh is the real world . . . into this world has been placed Man to live and rule. To this end his body is fixed with various powers and complications and endurances; with weaknesses and impulses and yieldings; with passions to animate, with desires to attract, and animosities to repel. And as the final crowning of this wondrous work, the last and final touch of the Creator's hand, Sex for the eternal renewing of established forces. How can souls be drawn to souls when such are centred in bodies which mutually repel? No! If physical attraction be not somewhere, naught can develop . . . Athlyne loved Joy in all ways, so that the best of his nature regulated the standard of his thoughts.[44]

So Stoker conceded the existence of the sex urge but crucially saw it as balanced and controlled by strength of character.

As their love surges up, Athlyne and Joy go for a drive from Ambleside where she is staying through the Lakes to the Scottish Borders in a powerful new Delaunay-Belville car. They drive slowly at first, then faster and faster, and her blood is soon racing. The drive becomes a metaphor for the sex act, culminating in orgasm. 'The rushing speed stirred her blood. She was silent, save at ecstatic moments, when she was quite unable to control herself.' When they arrive, he is hungry, and they set out a picnic and kiss and embrace, expressing their love for each other. But real physical consummation will be deferred until after they are safely married. Stoker also clearly outlines in the novel his understanding of gender:

> That deep-thinking young madman who committed suicide at twenty-three, Otto Weininger, was probably right in that wonderful guess of his as to the probable solution of the problem of sex. All men and all women, according to him, have in themselves the cells of both sexes; and the accredited masculinity or femininity of the individual is determined by the multiplication and development of these cells. Thus the ideal man is entirely or almost entirely masculine, and the ideal woman is entirely or almost entirely feminine. Each individual must have a preponderance, be it ever so little, of the cells of its own sex; and the attraction of each individual to the other sex depends upon its place in the scale between the highest and the lowest grade of sex. The most masculine man draws the most feminine woman, and *vice versa*; and so down the scale till close to the border line is the great mass of persons who, having only development of a few of the qualities of sex, are easily satisfied to mate with any one. This is the true principle of selection which is one of the most important of Nature's laws; one which holds in the lower as well as the higher orders of life, zoological and botanical as well as human. It accounts for the way in which a vast number of persons are content to make marriages and even liaisons, which others, higher strung, are actually unable to understand.[45]

Weininger's *Sex and Character*, published in Vienna in 1903, had appeared in English translation in 1906, two years before Stoker published *Lady Athlyne*. In it Stoker had evidently found the solution to the feeling that he had something feminine in his nature. He summarizes Weininger's argument accurately. But it is worth noting that Weininger advanced this explanation in the framework of a belief in fixed and eternal masculine and feminine values, with the masculine absolutely superior to the feminine. Men were by nature clear-thinking, alert, articulate, moral, strong-willed; women sentimental, unintellectual, amoral, illogical and vain. He believed that women were only interested in sex and that virginity was imposed on them by men and they complied in this because of their essential passivity. Love he saw as Platonic idealization; sex as bestial and disgusting.[46] There are echoes of all these ideas throughout Stoker's work.

In *Dracula* Mina comments sarcastically about the 'New Woman' that in future she would probably want to do the proposing. This idea and its catastrophic consequences are explored in depth in *The Man*, which is Stoker's fullest exploration of gender roles. It is the story of Stephen Norman, a girl who grows up to assume a masculine role in society and to attempt to implement sexual equality.

Stephen is born the only child of Squire Stephen Norman of Normanstand and his wife, who dies in childbirth. The girl is christened with her father's name and raised by her father to have 'a man's knowledge and a man's courage' because she will have a man's responsibilities running the estates. But this is in conflict with her instincts from the start. She is indisputably female and grows up thoroughly feminine, though wilful, domineering and inclined to get her way. But she resolves to subdue her feminine sensibility to her masculine duty as squire. She insists on exploring the darker side of life by visiting the petty sessions and a university mission house in the East End of London. This enables her to develop a greater sense of the tolerance, justice and reason which Stoker argues are essentially male qualities.

She begins to insist on female equality and in particular she advocates proposing to a man, to the horror of her aunt Laetitia:

> Surely if a woman is to be the equal and lifelong companion of a man, the closest to him – nay, the only one really close to him: the mother of his children – she should be free at the very outset to show her inclination to him just as he would to her.[47]

But the rest of the book demonstrates the folly of this position, the misery and tragedy it induces and gives the answer to the question why – because that is the way things are.

Squire Norman is killed in an accident and Stephen takes over and devotes herself to her duties to her tenants. Feeling lonely and being attracted to handsome Leonard Everard, she proposes and is brutally rejected: 'You're too much of a boss for me'. The whole central section of the book – the build up, the proposal, the rejection – are powerfully and evocatively described by Stoker who enters fully into the mind and feelings of his heroine. At the end, 'the punishment of her arrogant unwomanliness had, she felt, indeed begun'.

Harold An Wolf, who has loved her since childhood, self-sacrificingly proposes to her to allow her to reject him. She pours out on him all her hatred and he leaves for America. Later she realizes his nobility and confides tearfully to Aunt Laetitia that he had acted 'in the most noble and knightly way in which any man could act'. Later inheriting a title and estate, Stephen goes to the North-East and plunges herself into good works. There by these good works which reaffirm her womanliness and by confession of her error she purges her fault and is eventually reunited with Harold when he swims ashore from a sinking ship and she nurses him back to health. The traditional gender roles are restored and all ends happily.

Romance, race and gender

From the 1880s onwards, the 'historical romance' was in vogue, developed by Rider Haggard and Robert Louis Stevenson and enthusiastically taken up by Stanley J. Weyman, Arthur Conan Doyle, A.E.W. Mason and Baroness Orczy. Romance, whether set in Africa, India or the South Seas during the present or in colourful and exciting episodes of the past like the French Revolution and the English Civil War, has a definite social function. As P.J. Keating puts it, it was 'to sustain the mood of adventurous exploration that was necessary for the expansion and maintenance of the British Empire' and 'to nurture the qualities of courage, justice and fairplay that had made, and would keep Britain great, and be willing to die for those ideals'.[48] The writers of romance were writing with the grain of the dominant ideology – imperialism and gentlemanliness.

The medieval chivalric romance (imprisoned king, beautiful princess, treacherous nobles, knight errant) was brought up to date with a contemporary setting, involving modern firearms, travel by train and political intrigue in Central Europe, to create a new literary genre – Ruritanian romance. It was launched by the worldwide success of Anthony Hope's *The Prisoner of Zenda* (1894). The *Zenda* phenomenon inspired a host of imitations and the map of Europe began to burst at the seams with imaginary kingdoms – Kravonia, Novodnia, Carpathia, Pannonia, Flavonia – in all of which gentleman heroes sought to preserve the throne and win the hand of beautiful ladies. It was the latest literary manifestation of the gentlemanly ethic, here in the service of monarchy, chivalry and empire.

Stoker's romances are set firmly in a context of belief in and support for the British Empire and the Anglo-Saxon race. Stoker was a Protestant Irishman, proud of his Irishness, but equally a devoted admirer of the British Empire. In his *Reminiscences of Henry Irving*, he talks of 'the great book of England's wise kindliness in the civilization of the savage' and in describing rapturously the Coronation reception Irving held in 1902 for the Indian princes and colonial premiers, he says: 'Everywhere a sense of the unity and the glory of Empire. Dominating it all, as though it was floating on light and sound and form and colour, the thrilling sense that there, in all its bewildering myriad beauty, was the spirit mastering the heart-beat of that great Empire on which the sun never sets'.[49]

He makes two of his heroes, Lord Athlyne and Rupert Sent Leger, Irish but sets them firmly in the context of the Empire, in a sense in which Britishness transcends the nationalities which make it up. Rupert Sent Leger, hero of *The Lady of the Shroud*, is a 'man to whom no adventure is too wild or too daring. His reckless bravery is a byword amongst many savage people and amongst many others not savages, whose fears are not of material things, but of the world of mysteries in and beyond the grave. He dares not only wild animals and savage men; but has tackled African magic and Indian mysticism . . . He is in the very prime of life, of almost giant stature, and strength trained to the use of all arms of all countries, inured to every kind of hardship, subtle-minded and resourceful, understanding human nature from its elemental form up'.[50] But there is a racial basis to his qualities – he has the 'fighting instincts of his Viking fore-bears' – and he is valued in chivalric terms. He is a 'paladin' and his achievements are 'worthy of a hero of old romance'. He is acknowledged as superior even to the Balkan mountain men by the Voivode of the Blue Mountains.

Rupert is steeped in empire on both sides of his family. His father, Captain Sent Leger, a dashing Irishman, won the Victoria Cross at the battle of Amoaful in the Ashantee campaign and his paternal uncle, a subaltern, was killed at the battle of Maiwand, where Dr John H. Watson also sustained his injury from a jezail bullet. His mother, Patience Melton, was of an English gentry family. One of her brothers was killed in the Indian Mutiny and another made his fortune as a merchant prince in the Eastern trade. Since his mother died, when he was 12, Rupert was raised by his maiden aunt Janet McKelpie, a Scotswoman with second sight, sister-in-law of Rupert's uncle, Major General Sir Colin McKelpie Baronet VC, a highland laird, honoured for his distinction on the Indian frontier wars. McKelpie later brings a hundred of his clan to help Rupert liberate the Land of the Blue Mountains. So Rupert has Irish, English and Scottish roots and an imperial service context.

Lord Athlyne is equally carefully constructed to stress his British identity. Calinus Patrick Richard Westerna (that name again) Hardy Mowbray Fitzgerald is 2nd Earl of Athlyne in the peerage of the United Kingdom, 2nd Viscount Roscommon in the peerage of Ireland and 30th Baron Ceann-da-Shail in the peerage of Scotland. Educated at Eton and the University of Dublin, he is a JP in Wiltshire, Ross and Roscommon and has houses in Ross-shire, Roscommon, Cornwall, Gloucestershire and London. He had served in the Irish Hussars with distinction during the Boer War.[51]

To make it clear to anyone who has missed the obvious implication, Stoker has Mrs O'Brien, Athlyne's wetnurse who loves him like her own child, and declares her pride in his Irishness, stress that he is not only Irish but also English, Scottish and Welsh, in other words British and Imperial. She compares him to the Duke of Fife, who married Queen Victoria's grand-daughter, an Irish and Scottish earl who became a British duke.[52]

Stoker's clear and regularly expressed devotion to America was based on a common racial heritage and code of beliefs. He wrote in his essay *A Glimpse of America*:

> We have not, all the world through, so strong an ally, so close a friend. America has got over her childhood. There is every reason we can think of why the English on both sides of the Atlantic should hold together as one. Our history is their history – our fame is their pride – their progress is our glory. They are bound to us and we to them, by every tie of love and sympathy . . . We are bound each to each by the instinct of a common race, which makes brotherhood and the love of brothers a natural law.[53]

He admired the American standard of living, standard of justice, clubbability and above all sense of chivalry:

> One of the most marked characteristics of American life is the high regard in which woman is held. It seems, now and then, as if a page of an old book of chivalry had been taken as the text of social law. Everywhere there is the greatest deference, everywhere a protective spirit.[54]

Marriages between Britons and Americans, then, are essentially family affairs, as when Joy Ogilvie, daughter of a Kentucky colonel, marries Lord Athlyne, and Marjory Anita Drake marries Archie Hunter.

In *The Lady of the Shroud* (1909), Stoker sought to create a generic hybrid – blending the Transylvanian vampire tale which he had so triumphantly mastered with the Ruritanian romance so much in vogue. The latter undoubtedly appealed to his own very real sense of chivalry, patriotism and monarchism and to his Liberal political instincts. In so doing, he created his own Ruritania, the Land of the Blue Mountains in *The Lady of the Shroud*.

In the book Stoker performs a literary *trompe d'oeil*, since he seems initially to be embarked on a vampire tale. The title, the structure (letters, journal entries, newspaper reports) and the powerfully atmospheric passages steeped in supernatural atmosphere in which the British hero Rupert Sent Leger visits a remote Balkan castle, encounters a strange woman in a shroud at night and later discovers her in a glass coffin in a lonely chapel, evoke strong memories of *Dracula*. But there is a rational explanation for it all and one which transforms the story into Ruritanian romance. The woman is the Voivodin Teuta, daughter of the leading chieftain of the land, whose death has been faked to fool the Turks who are threatening the independence of the country. Stories of vampirism prevent closer investigation of the imposture. So in fact *Dracula* becomes *Zenda* as the Voivodin and her father are kidnapped, rescued by the hillmen under Rupert's leadership and Rupert is crowned king of the newly liberated country. The ruling council of the Blue Mountains adopts British-style constitutional monarchy and Rupert creates an airforce and a fleet to protect his new kingdom's liberty and arranges for a Balkan Federation, brokered by Edward VII 'King of the greatest nation on earth', whose state visit inaugurates an era of peace and security, guaranteed by 'British fleets . . . and British bayonets'.

This theme of the book fulfils Keating's interpretation of the romance. But there is another theme intertwined. The striking central episode of the book has a beautiful dark mysterious woman, Teuta, turning up at the castle, freezing cold, and asking to be made warm. Rupert is a much-travelled man and a man of passions but is concerned about the conventions and her reputation. He is immediately attracted to her, but 'even a man of passions and experiences can, when he respects a woman, be shocked – even prudish – where his own opinion of her is concerned. Such must bring to her guarding any generosity which he has, and any self-restraint also. Even should she place herself in a doubtful position, her honour calls to his honour. This is a call which may not be – must not be – unanswered. Even passion must pause for at least a while at sound of such a trumpet-call'. So his natural desire must be tempered by his respect. 'This woman I did respect – much respect. Her youth and beauty; her manifest ignorance of evil; her superb disdain of convention, which could only come through hereditary dignity; her terrible fear and suffering . . . would all demand respect, even if one did not hasten to yield it.'[55] In all his visits, he continues to guard and respect her, even though he comes to believe her a vampire. He falls deeply in love with her; 'So entirely and sweetly womanly did she appear . . . the veritable perfect woman of the dreams of a man, be he young or old. To have such a woman sit by his hearth and hold her holy of holies in his heart might well be rapture to any man'.[56] She tells him 'You are a true gentleman and my friend'. Eventually they marry. This episode and its consequence contrast markedly with another novel of the same period, to which Stoker's can be seen as a direct rebuttal.

Lady of the Shroud was published the year after Stoker had published an almost hysterical article in *The Nineteenth Century* calling for the censorship of fiction. In the article, he calls 'reticence' – 'the highest quality of art . . . its chief and crowning glory', and the greatest possible evils of the imagination 'the evil effect produced on the senses'. 'The only emotions which in the long run harm are those arising from the sex impulses'. He says:

> Fiction is perhaps the most powerful form of teaching available. It can be most potent for good; and if we are to allow it to work for evil we shall surely have to pay in time for the consequent evil effects . . . Within a couple of years past quite a number of novels have been published in England that would be a disgrace in any country even less civilized than our own. The class of works to which I allude are meant by both authors and publishers to bring to the winning of commercial success the forces of inherent evil in man. The word man here stands for woman as well as man; indeed women are the worst offenders in this form of breach of moral law. As to the alleged men who follow this loathsome calling, what term of opprobrium is sufficient, what punishment could be too great . . . They in their selfish greed tried to deprave where others had striven to elevate . . . such works . . . deal with vices so flagitious, so opposed even to the decencies of nature in its crudest and lowest forms, that the poignancy of moral disgust is lost in horror.

Since 'press criticism . . . is sadly deficient', 'self restraint and reticence . . . has not . . . been exercised by the few who seek money and achieve notoriety through base means', then censorship is the only answer.[57]

Stoker's perception of a trend in contemporary fiction is supported by a modern commentator. P.J. Keating points out 'throughout 1907 and 1908 the sex-novel consolidated its position'.[58] It came in a variety of forms, among them the 'sensationally erotic' and here he cites Elinor Glyn's *Three Weeks* and H. De Vere Stacpoole's *The Blue Lagoon*.

Three Weeks (1907) by Elinor Glyn, partly inspired by the murder in 1903 of Queen Draga of Serbia, looks like the novel to which Stoker was consciously providing an antidote. Its hero, Paul Verdayne, (Eton, Oxford and the hunting field), handsome, athletic gentleman and sportsman is on the Continent to escape an unfortunate romantic entanglement. In Lucerne he meets and falls passionately in love with a mysterious lady, white-faced, green-eyed, dark-haired, exotic and foreign. They make love on a tiger rug before the fire and begin a passionate three-week romance in Lucerne and Venice, in which Madame Glyn luxuriates in heavily perfumed sensuous prose, ornate and extravagant.

When the three weeks is over, she leaves him and Paul collapses with brain fever. He has never known who she was but has called her 'My Lady'. He discovers that she is a Balkan Queen who has returned to her duties and given birth to a son, Paul. He arranges to meet her in her Bosporus Villa, sails there in a steam yacht only to find that she has been murdered by her dissolute husband the King, who has himself been strangled by her faithful servant Vassili. Paul travels for five years to forget and then attends the fifth birthday of his son, now King Paul, 'a fair, rosy-cheeked, golden-haired English child'. The sight of him 'melted forever the iceberg of grief and pain' in Paul's heart.

The book was denounced by newspaper critics for its uninhibited celebration of an extra-marital affair. But it was a huge success in Britain and the United States, selling two million copies in its first nine years. The censor banned a proposed stage version – though it eventually reached the stage, much altered, in 1917 and then the screen in 1922. A judge called it: 'nothing more nor less than an sensual adulterous intrigue . . . a grossly immoral work which . . . advocates free love and justifies adultery where the marriage tie has become merely irksome.'[59] Elinor Glyn claimed in the preface to the 1916 edition that the story was highly moral because the Lady died, 'the inevitable result of the breaking of any law, whether of God or of Man'.[60] Given Stoker's known opposition to sex in literature, *The Lady of the Shroud* can be seen as a robust response to *Three Weeks*, operating as it does in the same territory of the Balkans and royal politics, featuring a heroine whom the hero calls 'My Lady', just as Paul Verdayne does his mistress, but centrally featuring a romance in which the protagonists do not succumb to their passion, even after marriage.

Rupert and Teuta profess their love, they marry but without consummating the marriage. Teuta makes an impassioned speech explaining that prior duties and obligations prevent them living together for the moment. He says he will wait as patiently as he can: 'I was moved by pity so great that all possible selfishness was merged in its depths. I bowed my head before her – my lady and my wife'.[61]

Teuta is no wilting violet. She is brave, noble, resolute and strong-willed. She insists on participating in the rescue of her father and is described as having 'the fighting blood of her race'. The Voivode praises her in chivalric terms: 'This brave woman has won knightly spurs as well as any paladin of old'.[62] She , however, insists on her subordination, in a speech to the National Council:

> We women of Vissarion, in all the history of centuries, have never put ourselves forward in rivalry to our lords . . . I am a wife of the Blue Mountains . . . and it would ill become me, whom my husband honours . . . to take part in changing the ancient custom which has been held in honour for all the thousand years, which is the glory of Blue Mountain womanhood. What an example such would be in an age when self-seeking women of other nations seek to forget their womanhood in the struggle to vie in equality with men! Men of the Blue Mountains, I speak for our women when I say that we hold of greatest price the glory of our men. To be their companions is our happiness; to be their wives is the completion of our lives; to be mothers of their children is our share of the glory that is theirs.[63]

Teuta thus resoundingly affirms traditional gender roles.

Linked to the maintenance of gender roles is the maintenance of the race. Stoker subscribes to the racial ideas dominant in his period, in particular the superiority of the Nordic races to all others. This is most explicit in the case of Harold An Wolf, titular hero of *The Man*. He is consistently described in the language and imagery of chivalry but with the learned code of chivalry goes a racial inheritance. By blood Harold is 'Gothic through the Dutch'. He had studied the sagas and been taught by his father the philosophy and racial qualities of the Viking. 'For a parson, Dr An Wolf held particularly militant ideas' notes Stoker. They were:

> There never was, my boy, such philosophy making for victory as that held by our Vikings. It taught that whoever was never wounded was never happy. It was not enough to be victorious. The fighter should contend against such odds that complete immunity was impossible. Look at the result! A handful of them from the bays and creeks of the far northern seas would conquer cities and whole lines of coast. Why, their strength, and endurance, and resolution, perfected by their life of constant hardihood and stress, became so ingrained in their race, that to this day, a thousand years after they themselves have passed away, their descendants have some of their fine qualities. Go where you will throughout this country, or any seaboard of Europe, and you will find that where the old type remains they dominate their fellows. Ay, even where the passing of centuries has diluted their blood with that of weaker races. Fight, my boy, fight! Look at that hecatomb of skulls in the crypt at Hythe and see the wounds all in front; better still, see the cicatrices of the old wounds . . . You will get some idea there of the strength and endurance and resolution of this mighty race. Let your cause be ever a just one; and you need never lack such whilst sin and crime and wickedness and shame are in the world. Then fight, fight against any odds! If you go down, you go down in truth and honour! And the battle of truth and honour is God's battle.[64]

Stoker seems to have been haunted by his church at Hythe, since for no very good reason other than to emphasize their Nordic links he has Arthur Severn and Norah Joyce married there in *The Snake's Pass*. Other Stoker heroes are given Nordic pedigrees. Lord Godalming, staking the sexually aroused Lucy in *Dracula*, is compared to the Norse god Thor. Even his heroines have racial inheritances. Stephen Norman has the qualities of Saxon, Viking and Norman – 'pride, self-reliance, dominance and masterdom'. The Normans had come over with the Conqueror and the family had fought in the Crusades, at Crecy and Poiters and Agincourt, and against the Armada. Stephen has a racial courage: 'She had no use for fear. This element of human composition had long ago in her race been forgotten, lost in the wild surges of the northern seas or amid the reek of the burning cities on the seaports of the south'.[65]

By contrast with the white Nordic race, the black races are primitive and inferior. In *Lair of The White Worm* Caswall has a black servant

Oolanga, an Obi man, a practitioner of voodoo, of whom De Salis says: 'Monsters such as he is belong to an earlier and more rudimentary stage of barbarism'. He is described as 'a debased specimen of one of the most debased races of the earth, and of an ugliness which was simply devilish.'[66] There are recurrent references to his ugliness, savagery and grotesqueness. He lusts after Lady Arabella and proposes marriage. Stoker writes: 'No man or woman of the white race could have checked the laughter which rose spontaneously to her lips. The circumstances were too grotesque'.[67] She objects to him on racial, class and aesthetic grounds ('You – a savage – a slave – the basest thing in the world of vermin'). When he persists, she drags him down the well-hole to his death.

It is in *The Mystery of the Sea* that race and gender are most explicitly linked. Archie Hunter rescues from drowning Marjory Anita Drake, 'the richest heiress in America' and a descendant of Sir Francis Drake, thus of prime Anglo-Saxon stock. One theme is the now familiar Stoker preoccupation tracing the process of their falling in love. They marry but she insists on non-consummation until they have become true comrades. 'What could a man say to this? It seemed like the very essence of married love and was doubly dear to me on that account'.[68] Their relationship is described in explicitly chivalric terms, as he refers to her as his Queen and she knights him. His devotion and subordination are stressed.

But the other main theme is racially based. Marjory is bitterly anti-Spanish due to the Spanish–American War. She and Archie discover a treasure in a cave beneath his house. It is a Spanish treasure entrusted by the Pope to Bernardino de Escoban at the time of the Armada to help overthrow the Protestant regime in England. They decipher Bernardino's coded papers and learn that the treasure has a racial mission: 'The treasure was collected by enemies of England for the purpose of destroying England's liberty, and so the liberty of the whole human race for which it is made'. That racial mission continues. For even though England is not now at war with Spain, America is and if the treasure is returned to Spain it could be used to fight America:

> This great treasure, piled up by the Latin for the conquering of the Anglo-Saxon, and rescued from its burial of three centuries, would come in the nick of time to fulfill its racial mission; though that mission might be against a new branch of the ancient foe of Spain, whose roots had been laid when the great Armada swept out in all its pride and glory on its conquering essay.[69]

A descendant of Bernardino, also called Bernardino, is searching for the treasure. But when Marjory is kidnapped by a criminal gang and held for ransom, he joins Archie in rescuing her, though he is drowned in the process.

It is made clear from the outset that Marjory hates the Spaniards

('Nasty, cruel, treacherous wretches! Look at the way they are treating Cuba! Look at the *Maine*!'). She has helped finance American military efforts against Spain during the Spanish–American War. She and Don Bernardino are explicitly contrasted in racial terms:

> They stood facing each other; types of the two races whose deadly contest was then the interest of the world . . . It would have been hard to get a better representative of either, of the Latin as well as the Anglo-Saxon. Don Bernardino, with his high aquiline nose and black eyes of eagle keenness, his proud bearing and the very swarthiness which told of Moorish descent, was, despite his modern clothes, just such a picture as Velasquez would have loved to paint . . . And Marjory! She looked like the spirit of her free race, incarnate. The boldness of her pose; her free bearing; her manifest courage and self-belief; the absence of either prudery or self-consciousness; her picturesque, noble beauty, as with set white face and flashing eyes she faced the enemy of her country, made a vision never to be forgotten. Even her racial enemy had unconsciously to fall into admiration; and through it the dominance of his masculine nature spoke.[70]

Stoker insists on the non-European element in Bernardino's racial makeup.

> The cruelty which lay behind his strength became manifest at once. Somehow at that moment the racial instinct manifested itself. Spain was once the possession of the Moors, and the noblest of the old families had some black blood in them. In Spain, such was not, as in the West, a taint. The old diabolism whence sprung fantee and hoodoo seemed to gleam out on the grim smile of incarnate rebellious purpose.[71]

But in the end Bernardino recognizes a fellow gentleman in Archie and his learned code of chivalry overcomes the innate racial heritage. He helps save Marjory, earning the accolade: 'He is a noble fellow and has behaved like a knight of old'.

The chivalry which counterbalances race in Bernardino does not operate in the kidnap gang, which is described as including a half-breed Spanish 'dago', a Dutchman, an American gangster and a 'buck nigger from New Orleans' who is described in hysterically racist terms:

> He was callous to everything, and there was such a wicked, devilish purpose in his look that my heart hardened grimly in the antagonism of man to man. Nay more, it was not a man that I loathed; I would have killed this beast with less compunction than I would kill a rat or a snake. Never in my life did I behold such a wicked face. In feature and expression there was every trace and potentiality of evil; and these superimposed on a racial brutality which made my gorge rise.[72]

Conclusion

It is clear then that we should regard Stoker's work as a coherent corpus. There is a consistency of theme and subject running through the books, of whatever genre. On one level Stoker is working out a deeply personal preoccupation with his own sexual nature and anxieties and on another he is tackling head on some of the principal ideological issues of the day, in particular those of gender and race. They are truly both a mirror of the man and of the age.

Notes

1. Bram Stoker, *Personal Reminiscences of Henry Irving* (London, 1907), p. 21.
2. Daniel Farson, *The Man Who Wrote Dracula* (London, 1975), p. 164.
3. Joseph Bierman, 'Dracula, Prolonged Childhood Illness, and the Oral Triad', *American Imago*, 29 (1972), pp. 186–98.
4. Farson, *The Man Who Wrote Dracula*, pp. 155–6.
5. John Martin Harvey, *The Autobiography* (London, n.d.), p. 64.
6. See for instance Christopher Frayling, *Vampyres* (London, 1991), pp. 75–6, and Jeffrey Richards, *Sir Henry Irving and Victorian Culture* (Lancaster, 1992), pp. 16–17.
7. Maurice Richardson, 'The Psychoanalysis of Ghost Stories', *Twentieth Century*, 166 (1959), pp. 419–31.
8. Horace Traubel, *Walt Whitman in Camden*, iv (Philadelphia, 1953), p. 183.
9. Bram Stoker, *Famous Imposters* (London, 1910), p. v.
10. Ibid., p. v.
11. Ibid., p. 345.
12. Elaine Showalter, *Sexual Anarchy* (London, 1991).
13. Rebecca Stott, *The Fabrication of the Late Victorian Femme Fatale* (London, 1992).
14. Patrick Brantlinger, *Rule of Darkness: British Literature and Imperialism 1830–1914* (Ithaca and London, 1988), pp. 227–53.
15. Daniel Pick, *Faces of Degeneration* (Cambridge, 1993), p. 173.
16. Carol A. Senf, 'Dracula: Stoker's Response to the New Woman', *Victorian Studies*, 26 (1982), pp. 33–49.
17. Clive Leatherdale, *Dracula: the Novel and the Legend* (Wellingborough, 1985), pp. 159, 157.
18. Ibid., p. 146.
19. Ibid., p. 156.
20. Ibid., p. 148.
21. Stoker, *Personal Reminiscences*, pp. 408–9.
22. Bram Stoker, *Lair of the White Worm* (London, 1911), p. 172.
23. Ibid., p. 323.
24. Ibid., p. 206.
25. Farson, *The Man Who Wrote Dracula*, p. 234.
26. Bram Stoker, *The Snake's Pass* (Dingle, County Kerry, 1990) pp. 136–7.
27. Jeffrey Richards, 'Passing the Love of Women', in J.A. Mangan and James Walvin (eds), *Manliness and Morality* (Manchester, 1987), pp. 92–122.

28. Stoker, *The Snake's Pass*, pp. 181, 205, 218.
29. Mark Girouard, *The Return to Camelot: Chivalry and the English Gentleman* (New Haven and London, 1981), p. 260.
30. Samuel Smiles, *Self-Help* (London, 1911), p. 470.
31. Bram Stoker, *Lady Athlyne*, (London, 1908), p. 8.
32. Ibid., p. 269.
33. John Martin Harvey, *Autobiography*, p. 64.
34. Stoker, *Personal Reminiscences*, p. 410.
35. Bram Stoker, *The Man* (London, 1905), p. 414.
36. Bram Stoker, *Miss Betty* (London, 1898), p. 53.
37. Ibid., pp. 94, 148, 149, 152, 153.
38. Ibid., pp. 124, 147.
39. Stoker, *Lady Athlyne*, pp. 83–4.
40. Ibid., pp. 72–3.
41. Ibid., pp. 112–13.
42. Ibid., p. 127.
43. Ibid., p. 150.
44. Ibid., p. 169–70.
45. Ibid., p. 82.
46. On Weininger's ideas, see Viola Klein, *The Feminine Character* (London, 1971), pp. 61–5.
47. Stoker, *The Man*, p. 93.
48. P.J. Keating, *The Haunted Study; a Social History of the English Novel 1875–1914* (London, 1989), pp. 354–5.
49. Stoker, *Personal Reminiscences*, p. 234.
50. Bram Stoker, *The Lady of the Shroud* (London, 1909), p. 54.
51. Stoker, *Lady Athlyne*, pp. 17–19.
52. Ibid., p. 13.
53. Farson, *The Man Who Wrote Dracula*, p. 78.
54. Ibid., p. 76.
55. Stoker, *Lady of the Shroud*, p. 92.
56. Ibid., p. 130.
57. Stoker, 'The Censorship of Fiction', *The Nineteenth Century*, 64 (September 1908), pp. 479–87.
58. Keating, *The Haunted Study*, pp. 209–10.
59. Anthony Glyn, *Elinor Glyn* (London, 1955), pp. 126, 128–9.
60. Elinor Glyn, *Three Weeks* (London, 1974 reprint), pp. xxiii–iv.
61. Stoker, *Lady of the Shroud*, p. 170.
62. Ibid., p. 237.
63. Ibid., p. 237.
64. Stoker, *The Man*, pp. 52–3.
65. Ibid., p. 71.
66. Stoker, *Lair of the White Worm*, p. 126–7.
67. Ibid., p. 126.
68. Bram Stoker, *The Mystery of the Sea* (London, 1902), p. 203.
69. Ibid., p. 335–6.
70. Ibid., p. 269.
71. Ibid., p. 328.
72. Ibid., p. 438.

CHAPTER NINE

'Women who Dids, and all that kind of thing . . .' Male Perceptions of 'Wholesome' Literature

Fiona Montgomery

In the late nineteenth and early twentieth centuries, literature was the main medium for conveying both accepted views of gender relations (social assumptions about femininity and masculinity) and those wishing to challenge stereotypes. Novelists themselves were anxious to emphasize this belief, thus the father in H.G. Wells's *Ann Veronica* (1909) was in no doubt who to blame for his daughter's desires for independence: 'It's these damned novels. All this torrent of misleading, spurious stuff that pours from the press. These sham ideals and advanced notions. Women who Dids, and all that kind of thing . . .'[1] Kate Flint in a study of the *Woman Reader* comments, 'The reading of those who were involved in the Women's movement, and more specifically within the Suffrage campaign of the early twentieth century, makes a particularly significant study'.[2] Of even greater significance perhaps, is the attitude of male suffragists, since relatively little has been written on them. One such organization was the Manchester Men's League for Women's Suffrage (MMLWS) founded in 1908 to campaign for women's enfranchisement.[3] The members were well aware of the value of the printed word, and in 1916 with the formation of a Girls' Club in Manchester, gifted a collection of literature, 'designed to present to young women entering industrial and professional life the views of advanced writers (especially women) on the part that women might play in the reconstruction of Society and the more effectual treatment of life's many problems after the war'.[4] Their choice of fiction and non-fiction and their general comments on contemporary literature provides valuable insight into *male* perceptions of gender roles, free love, the double standard, the place of women in society, and of what was considered 'wholesome' literature for women.

The MMLWS always had no doubts of its own importance:

> . . . if any organisation of men can claim on widely representative grounds to voice public opinion, the Men's League for Women's Suffrage, both in London and the provinces, is in that position. The Manchester centre contains among its members Unionists, Liberals,

Labour men and Socialists; Anglicans, Catholics, Nonconformists, Jews, and members of other religious bodies; clergymen, medical men, University professors and students (over twenty per cent of our members are University graduates), schoolmasters, journalists, lawyers and other professional men, businessmen, working men, and tradesmen.'[5]

As such its attitudes reflected those of the professional upper classes. It prided itself on the level of education of its members, among whom were such eminent men as the noted medievalist, T.F. Tout, the physicist, Sir Ernest Rutherford, and the future Labour politician, Fenner Brockway.

They certainly had quite well-developed perceptions of gender roles, which at times showed evidence of advanced thinking. On 20 April 1914, John Beanland as secretary of the MMLWS wrote to the editor of the *Manchester Guardian* in support of Charlotte Gilman's opposition to the 'cult of the doll as a girl's plaything only, and of the foolish coupling of the idea of maternity with it in their case and in their hearing'. He was fully agreed with Gilman's views as outlined in *Women and Economics*:

> When our infant daughter . . . wails in maternal agony because her brother has broken her doll, whose sawdust remains she nurses with piteous care, we say proudly that 'she is a perfect little mother already'. What business has a little girl with the instincts of maternity? No more than the little boy should have with the instincts of paternity. They are sex instincts and should not appear till the period of adolescence. The most normal girl is . . . the young creature who is human through and through, not feminine till it is time to be. The most normal boy has calmness and gentleness as well as vigour and courage. He is a human creature as well as a male creature, and not aggressively masculine till it is time to be. Childhood is not the period for those marked manifestations of sex.[6]

It is interesting that both believed that there was a time when men and women must assume recognized gender roles, nevertheless such a repudiation by men of accepted gender differences was, by contemporary standards, forward thinking. The MMLWS also had very definite ideas of what constituted 'suitable' fiction. *Ann Veronica* had both 'good and bad' in it. 'Her chafing at the repressive somnolence and emptiness of her home life', and 'her gradual assertion of her own personality' was praised. But it was doubted whether she would have been willing to consider marrying her fiancé 'after he had shown his hand in the restaurant incident . . . that she finally discovered him to be unendurable is a satisfactory outcome'. Furthermore Ann Veronica's 'infatuation for that student beast', could not be countenanced because they considered that a woman would always choose 'the higher rather than the lower as a mate'. Here attitudes were both sexist (in favour of women) and racist: 'many white men in tropical countries marry (really marry, I do not mean simply cohabit with) black women, but you seldom see a white woman marry a black man – if she does it is generally through the processes of economic hardship and the lure of the opposite as represented by the marriage'. *Ann Veronica* was a dangerous book to let loose on the unsuspecting public. 'To anyone who can think for himself, it offers food for thought; but the average man and woman don't think, and unfortunately they don't *want* to think. They want their opinion ready made, and the only teaching they can assimilate is something didactic. The book may not do harm, but I doubt whether it will do much good'.[7] Here again was the element of condescension and patronizing attitude. A much better writer was Upton Sinclair, especially his *The Jungle* (1906) which depicted 'far lower depths, graver evils, and even meaner vices', but with strength, power, generosity and decency.[8]

Given these attitudes, the list of books chosen for the Girls' Club was interesting and did reflect their commitment to female writers (nearly 70 per cent were by women):

C.P. Gilman, *The 'Forerunner' for 1915*
———— , *What Diantha Did* (1910)
———— , *The Crux* (1910)
————, *Women and Economics* (1898)
O. Schreiner, *Women and Labour* (1911)
———— , *Dreams* (1890)
E. Robins, *Where Are You Going To?* (1913)
———— , *The Open Question* (1899)
C. Hamilton, *Marriage as a Trade* (1909)
N. Angell, *The Foundations of International Polity* (1912)
————, *Peace Treaties and the Balkan War* (1912)
————, *The Great Illusion* (1910)
————, *Problems of the War and the Peace* (1915)
W. James, *Letters to My Son* (1913)
————, *More Letters to My Son* (1915)
C.C. Stopes, *The British Freewoman* (1894)
J. Sutter, *Britain's Next Campaign* (1903)
Lady Lytton, *Prisons and Prisoners* (1914)
S.B. Rowntree, *Poverty* (1909)
E. Sharp, *Rebel Women* (1910)
E. Holmes, *What is and What Might Be* (1911)
J.S. Mill, *The Subjection of Women* (1869)
Baroness von Suttner, *Lay Down Your Arms* (1894)
H.N. Brailsford, *War of Steel and Gold* (1916)
H. Keller, *My Life* (1902)
Suffrage Leaflets

Indeed some authors like Schreiner, Lytton, Gilman and Mill figure on many a modern Women's Studies course, and on the whole they reflected the level of education of the MMLWS and an awareness of 'advanced' literature. As might be expected they included a proportion by members of the Women Writers Suffrage League (Elizabeth Robins, Cecily Hamilton, Evelyn Sharp). Schreiner's *Women and Labour* was described as the 'Bible of the women's movement'. The secretary, John Beanland, correctly considered that it was better 'to choose such as are in the form of fiction rather than something solid, since the former are pretty sure to get read the most', and for this reason if he had to dispense with one of Mrs Gilman's, it would be *Women and Economics* ('though it is undoubtedly the best and most illuminating of the four'). Anything 'pronouncedly militant' or controversial was to be omitted. This included Christabel Pankhurst's *Great Scourge,* and material on the White Slave Trade. Where venereal disease was concerned, it was to be the soft sell: 'Mrs. Gilman's The Crux though worded and restrained, is unmistakedly clear on these matters, and "gets there" just as effectively'. Books on peace and war were to be ethical or philosophical rather than political.[9] To appreciate this list fully however, would require a high degree of education and commitment, and it reflects what Kate Flint has correctly identified as the importance given by suffrage campaigners to 'serious reading'.[10]

The MMLWS was endorsing ideas inviting women to question accepted views of marriage and the family. The non-fiction works in the list affirmed the beliefs that marriage was legalized prostitution, that women were economically and emotionally dependent on men and that this oppression equalled sexual politics. Women's oppression and consequent suffering was caused by society's sexism. Women and men were interdependent, and if society was to progress, then both must be allowed to develop equally. In the past, men and women had had equal tasks, but men had constantly eroded women's position so that now they were either working-class drudges or middle-class dolls. Unlike men, who would starve if they did not work in modern society, women had the alternative of becoming sex parasites. Women, therefore, needed to be able to do all the intellectual and administrative jobs that there were in the modern world to save them from this fate. Men had to be taught that freedoms could not be bought at the expense of enslaving women. Schreiner was at pains to point out that the male desire to limit women to a child-bearing role, however ennobling that might be supposed to be, was only used to prevent women from undertaking the professions (such as medicine or law). Thus she concludes that men objected to women receiving an appropriate reward for their labour.[11]

Marriage as practised was a trade (not the institution as such). Women married because they had no alternative but to do so to earn a living. Marriage therefore was a woman's most viable economic option. Given the appalling conditions that they endured in marriage, it was obvious that it must be a last resort. Marriage benefited men because, within it, women would do all the jobs that men did not want and did not even get paid for doing them. This proved that men considered women inferior; their liberty is stolen by men and women only exist in relation to them.[12]

In a chapter of this length, it is of course impossible to deal in any meaningful way with all of these books. It is proposed therefore to concentrate on Schreiner's *Dreams,* and three novels, Gilman, *What Diantha Did,* Suttner, *Lay Down Your Arms,* and Sarah Grand, *The Heavenly Twins,* although not in the original list considered by the MMLWS to be 'an education'.[13]

At first sight, *Dreams* might seem a rather odd choice. After all *The Story of an African Farm* (1883) deals with the question of the suffragettes. *Dreams* does include much impressive language and there is an overwhelming feeling of being ground down. It is difficult however, to imagine teenage girls identifying with an author for whom heroes or heroines are never named and the first dream, 'The Last Joy', appears particularly abstruse. For all its popularity, there is no doubt that others thought similarly: Constance Lytton in *Prisons and Prisoners* (also in the list) told how she had read them often 'but their meaning had evidently not penetrated to me'.[14] And Schreiner delighted that her mother could not understand 'The Sunlight Lay Across My Bed': '. . . my mother says that she doesn't know *what* it's about. That's rather encouraging! . . .'[15] It is only fair to mention however that Schreiner had a very particular audience in mind for *Dreams:* 'Dreams is not published by me with the special intention of reaching the poor. I would prefer the rich to have it. If I dedicated it to the public, I should dedicate it "To all Capitalists, Millionaires and Middlemen in England and America and all high and mighty persons".'[16]

Some idea of the power of *Dreams,* however, is conveyed in Constance Lytton's description of a meeting of Women's Freedom League prisoners in Holloway Prison, at which Mrs Pethwick Lawrence recited 'Three Dreams in a Desert'. The allegory is fully brought to life. 'The words hit out a bare literal description of the pilgrimage of women . . . "How am I to get there [the Land of Freedom]?" The old man, Reason, answers, "There is one way and one only. Down the banks of Labour, through the water of suffering. There is no other" . . . Is there a track to show where the best fording is? . . . It has to be made . . . And she threw from her gladly the mantle of ancient-received opinions she wore, for it was worn full of holes . . . And he said, "Take the shoes of dependence off your feet".'[17] The woman wonders how she will get to the land of freedom, since she feels totally alone. Then she hears the sound of feet, and is told that they will cross in the way that locusts cross a stream by forming a bridge with their bodies. 'And in the last dream she sees in that land of

Freedom where Love is no longer a child but has grown to a man. "On the hills walked brave women and brave men, hand in hand. And they looked into each other's eyes, and they were not afraid".'[18]

The message of *Dreams*, then, is that liberty cannot be achieved for one woman only, and that women also oppress each other. Thus 'I Thought I Stood' tells of one woman who, on her first trip to heaven, had not noticed that she had trampled on other women on the way. But the second time comes with her 'sister' and tells God, 'She was upon the ground in the street, and they passed over her; I lay down by her, and she put her arms around my neck, and so I lifted her, and we two rose together.'[19] Feminism therefore must not victimize others. What is required is a collective advance for *all* women. Once a start has been made, then it will be so much easier to make progress. The important step is to make a start, to try to change. It is made quite clear, however, that it is up to women to help themselves, as the companion of the woman ground down by continuous child-bearing to a position of dependency tells the narrator in 'Three Dreams in a Desert', 'He cannot help her, *she must help herself*. Let her struggle till she is strong.'[20] In 'The Sunlight Lay Across My Bed' where Schreiner deals with the downfall of capitalism in the guise of a palace, the exploiters repent when they are faced with the condition of their exploited slaves.[21]

In none of the novels on the list is the storyline particularly strong, and *Lay Down Your Arms* is no exception. It is easy to be highly critical of it: 'The prevailing tone of the novel is melodramatic sentimentality, despite the fact that much of the book consists of war scenes described in lurid detail. The characters are shallow representations of various points of view, and the dialogue is declamatory and tedious'.[22] However, as Chickering points out, it was written as a 'polemic' and by this criterion 'the novel was one of the most successful and effective pieces of antiwar literature ever written'.[23] It is also very important for its portrayal of gender roles. Its setting is the mid-century Austrian Wars, and it begins by vividly describing the frustrations inherent in a woman's position. The heroine, Martha, an Austrian countess, wants to be able to do the same things as a man. Initially, in particular, she wishes to be able to go to war. She makes the point that girls are educated from the same books as their brothers, but then are denied the same opportunities. Such desires, however, do not unsex her, for she is shown to be an attractive woman who falls in love. She also takes issue with the idea of a woman's place being in the home. When she remonstrates with her husband because he is excitedly going off to war and leaving her, he replies,

> Your place is here, by the cradle of the little one, who is also to become a defender of his country when he is grown up. Your place is at our household hearth. It is to protect this, and guard it from any

> hostile attack, to preserve peace for our homes and our wives, that
> we men have to go to battle.[24]

To which she thinks that these were mere 'phrases'; it was 'ambition'
which was driving him on: 'his delight in the march out, which promised
change and adventure – his seeking for distinction and promotion'.[25]

Martha therefore is a strong woman who wants to, and does, develop
her mind. She reads the great inspirations of progress, Thomas Buckle's
History of Civilisation in England, and Darwin. After reading Buckle,
she felt

> like a man who had dwelt all his life in the bottom of a narrow val-
> ley, and then, for the first time, had been taken up to one of the
> mountain tops around, from which a long stretch of country was to
> be seen, covered with buildings and gardens and ending in the
> boundless ocean.[26]

Despite this, she loses none of her womanly features. After the death
in battle of her first husband, Arno, many men pay court to her. She,
however, is aware that she now has little in common with her contemporaries. She laments the fact that she cannot have a serious conversation:

> . . . even if I had squeezed into such a company the conversations
> that might have been just begun about the economy of nations,
> about Byron's poetry, about the theories of Strauss and Renan,
> would have been hushed, [*sic*] and the talk would have been: 'Ah,
> Countess Dotzky, how charming you looked yesterday at the ladies'
> pic-nic; and are you going to-morrow to the reception at the Russian
> embassy?'[27]

She falls in love again with another soldier, Freidrich von Tilling. This is
a marriage of both mind and body. They are portrayed as equals, they
develop their intellects together and both share a profound dislike of the
futility of war. Martha suffers many disasters in her life, but still emerges
at the end of the novel as a strong woman and a great inspiration to all.

The Heavenly Twins, in its 679 pages, deals with three interwoven
stories, those of Angelica and Diavola (the 'heavenly twins' of the title),
Evadne, and Edith. The plots concern gender roles (and conditioning), a
woman's right to independence and the menace of venereal disease
wrought on unsuspecting women by men with colourful pasts. It was a
great success and sold 20,000 copies in its first year.

Angelica and Diavolo's names are carefully chosen to convey the
impression of the angelic little girl and the naughty 'devilish' little boy. In
contrast to the usual image conjured up by 'angelic little girl', Angelica is
given black hair and Diavolo, fair.[28] Angelica is also portrayed as the
livelier, stronger, more intelligent of the two. It is she who always

originates the many amusing pranks, and she who wishes to learn: 'Men are always jeering at women in books for not being able to reason, and I'm going to learn . . .'[29] Throughout their childhood, they are depicted as equals. Angelica is very much a tomboy, and the contents of her pocket illustrate this graphically:

> . . . two pocket-handkerchiefs of fine texture and exceedingly dirty, as if they had been there for months (the one she used she carried in the bosom of her dress or up her sleeve), a ball of string, a catapult and some swan shot, a silver pen, a pencil holder, part of an old song book, a pocket book, some tin tacks, a knife with several blades and scissors etc.; also a silver fruit knife, two coloured pencils, indiarubber, and a scrap of dirty paper wrapped round a piece of almond toffee.[30]

She also thought nothing of physically attacking her brother. But the differences in their expected roles become evident in adolescence. Angelica aimed to teach Diavolo to respect women:

> When he didn't respect them she beat him; . . .
> 'You wouldn't strike me if you didn't know that I can't strike you back because you're a girl,' he remonstrated.
> 'What do you mean by this nonsense?' she demanded.
> 'We always *have* fought everything out ever since we were born.'
> 'Yes,' he said regretfully, 'and you used to be as hard as nails. When I got a good hit at you it made my knuckles tingle. But now you're getting all boggy everywhere. Just look at your arms.!'[31]

Angelica has mixed feelings about wearing her first grown-up dress. She chaffs under the restrictions of womanhood, and enters an early marriage with a much older respectable man whom she calls 'Daddy'. 'Daddy' allows her almost unlimited freedom; indeed this was one of the conditions that she made prior to marriage, but will not allow her to earn money by playing her violin in public.

To relieve her boredom, she begins a rather flirtatious relationship with 'The Tenor'. To overcome the restrictions on a woman's role, she adopts a male persona, dressing as a boy and stealing out at night to meet 'The Tenor' in secret. 'The Tenor' is unaware of her true sex and the relationship is essentially platonic. 'The Tenor' does seem to be attracted to her as a boy, though basically he is in love with the image that he has of Angelica. When the deception is discovered, after he has to save her from drowning, as part of her explanation as to why she acted as she did, the restrictions on and frustrations of a woman's position are clearly detailed. Because she was a girl, this ruled out the possibility of individuality: 'I found a big groove ready waiting for me when I grew up, and in that I was expected to live whether it suited me or not. It did not suit me. It was deep and narrow, and gave me no room to move.' She wanted to

make music. 'I wanted to *do* as well as to *be* . . .' But her friends, 'armed
. . . with the whole social system', opposed her. They tried to domesticate
her and she attempted to both conform and be true to herself. 'I had the
ability to be something more than a young lady, fiddling away her time on
useless trifles, but I was not allowed to apply it systematically, and ability
is like steam – a great power when properly applied, a great danger otherwise . . . I had the feeling . . . that if I broke down conventional obstacles –
broke the hampering laws of society, I should have a chance . . . '.[32]

She sees her sex as a great disadvantage: 'As a woman, I could not
expect to be treated by men with as much respect as they show to each
other'.[33] If only she had been allowed 'to support a charity hospital with
my violin – or something; made to feel responsible.' The uselessness of
her life is stressed:

> you often hear it said of a girl that she should have been a boy, which
> being interpreted means that she has superior abilities; but because
> she is a woman it is not thought necessary to give her a chance of
> making a career for herself. I hope to live, however to see it allowed
> that a woman has no more right to bury her talents than a man has;
> in which days the man without brains will be taught to cook and
> clean, while the clever woman will be doing the work of the world
> well which is now being so shamefully scamped.[34]

After a lot of heart-searching, Angelica realizes how lucky she is in her
husband and settles down to helping him in his career as an MP, while he
in turn utilizes some of her talents by delivering speeches which she has
helped to write.

To what extent is gender stereotyping evident? Women are certainly
depicted as having particular characteristics. Thus no matter how 'new'
she may be, Grand is eager to point out that she will always be maternal:
'Whatever defects of character the new women may eventually acquire,
lack of maternal affection will not be one of them';[35] curiosity is 'woman-
ish';[36] women can be described by their fathers as 'cow-like';[37] precision
of thought is 'masculine'.[38] Lady Clan was 'a cheery old lady, masculine
in appearance, but with a great kind, womanly heart, full of sympathetic
insight'.[39] Nevertheless, there is an attempt to deal with the concept of
'womanliness' as this speech by Mr Price demonstrates:

> womanliness is a matter of sex, not of circumstances, occupation, or
> clothing; . . . That little incident of Jane Austen, hiding away the pre-
> cious manuscript she was engaged upon, under her plain sewing,
> when visitors arrived, ashamed to be caught at the 'unwomanly'
> occupation of writing romances, and shrinking with positive pain
> from the remarks which such poor foolish people as those she feared
> would have made about her . . . has saved me from braying with the
> rest of the world upon this subject.[40]

Gender stereotyping, however, is used to point contrasts. Thus while innocence is prized by Evadne's mother ('. . . she is perfectly innocent, and I am indeed thankful to think that at eighteen she knows nothing of the world and its wickedness, and is therefore eminently qualified to make somebody an excellent wife'[41]), the novel is at pains to point out that the real issue is that of innocence abused. Innocence is a device which victimizes women rather than protects them. This has disastrous consequences as far as Evadne and Edith are concerned.

Evadne is shown as a sensitive young woman who is oppressed by conventional desires to such an extent that she loses her ability to make any meaningful contribution to life. She begins as a self-educated, very bright girl who easily outwits her intellectually lumbering father. She sees woman's position of inferiority as a social construct. Beginning with the question 'Why are women such inferior beings?', she quickly passes to 'Are women such inferior beings?' and concludes that 'women had originally no congenital defect of inferiority', and although they have a long way to go, it was up to women to do something about this situation.[42] Furthermore, 'Withholding education from women was the original sin of man'.[43] Evadne falls in love with the dashing Major (later Colonel) Colquhoun. But on learning of his past excesses, she decides not to consummate the marriage and gives her husband the slip at the start of her honeymoon. This causes great consternation to her parents. In response, Evadne points out the double standard being shown in her parents' behaviour: 'You would not counsel a son of yours to marry a society woman of the same character as Major Colquhoun, and neither more nor less degraded, for the purpose of reforming her, would you, mother?' Evadne suggests that it is the clergy's role to reform such men: '. . . although reforming reprobates may be a very noble calling, I do not, at nineteen, feel that I have any vocation for it . . .' and that her mother, in fact would be a better person to do so.[44] She wants a 'Christ-like' man as a husband.

> For . . . there is no romance in marrying a man old already in every emotion, between whom and me the recollection of some other woman would be for ever intruding. My whole soul sickens at the possibility, and I think that it must have been women old in emotion themselves who first tolerated the staleness of such lovers.[45]

The novel gives life to the unhappy existence produced by the prevailing ideology of the feminine woman. Daughters are expected to fufil their parents' expectations. Thus Evadne's mother complains that she should be willing to abide by her father's wishes: 'I repeat that your father is the proper person to judge for you. You know nothing of the world, and even if you did, you are not old enough to think for yourself.'[46] The dire consequences of such an act, not just for Evadne but for the entire family, are graphically spelt out: 'He [her father] says he shall be obliged to put you in a lunatic asylum if you do not give in at once, and consent to live with your husband. And there is the law, too, which your husband can invoke. And think of your five sisters. Will anybody marry them after such a business with you? Their prospects will be ruined by your heartless selfishness. No girl in my young days would have acted so outrageously. It is not decent. It is positively immodest.'[47]

In a rather improbable compromise, however, Evadne agrees to live with Colquhoun providing that they do not share a bed. This is a frustrating experience since she still finds him physically attractive and is shown eyeing him up in exactly the way that the reprobate Monteith was accused of: 'The outside aspect of the man still pleased her . . . he was a fine specimen of his species, a splendid animal to look at'.[48] The difference is that Evadne can never forget his past, 'the kind of past, too, which can never be over and done with! A returned convict is always a returned convict, and a vicious man reformed is repaired by the process. The stigma is in his blood.'[49]

Evadne, though appearing to make the best of her life, is horrified to learn that her friend Edith, daughter of a bishop, is to marry a man of whom even Colquhoun has reservations. Edith embodies conventional feminine qualities taken to extremes. She is the Victorian ideal of selfless, patient, self-sacrificing womanhood with 'her simple unaffected manners . . . She had been fitted by education to move in the society of saints and angels only, and so rendered as unsuited as she was unprepared to cope with the world . . .'[50] It is only a matter of time, however, before Edith succumbs to the ravages of venereal disease and dies a horrible death having given birth to a deformed child. Throughout the novel, the words 'venereal disease' are never mentioned, and there must have been many a young girl for whom the meaning was not clear.[51]

Here Grand is attacking the idea of the angel in the house whose moral superiority is accepted by the selfish man as the means to keep him on the straight and narrow:

> The first thing they do when they begin to know anything is to turn round upon us, and say we aren't good enough. And, by Jove! if we aren't isn't it their fault? Isn't it their business to keep us right? When a fellow's had too good a time in his youth and suffered for it, what's to become of him if he can't find some innocent girl to believe in him and marry him? But soon there won't be any innocent girls.[52]

Having begun as a character of great intellect, then, Evadne now withdraws from cerebral activity even to the point of not wanting to be able to think. She promises Colquhoun that she will not become involved in women's issues. When he dies of a heart attack and she is therefore freed to make a second match, this time with the sensitive Dr Galbraith, she still does not achieve a happy ending. She tries to commit suicide on the eve of the birth of her first child because she is convinced that it will be a girl and she does not want her to suffer as Edith has done. The child is a boy and is followed by a sister. Though Evadne derives great pleasure from her children and her marriage, she still cannot stand any thought of the world's suffering, and still worries that her children will come to harm. The moral of the book therefore is that she has suffered irreparable harm through being sacrificed to a sexless marriage by the rigidities of the conventional Victorian family.

Other novelists also took the view that the patriarchal family is an instrument which smothers creativity. Thus Gilman makes it clear in *What Diantha Did* that the family restricts both men and women but particularly women. Diantha's parents expect her to realize that her place is in their home; her mother, despite having accountancy abilities (of which she is aware) is not allowed to play a part in the family concern; while Diantha's fiancé, Ross, accepts that it is his responsibility to look after his mother and four sisters even though they are obviously well able to look after themselves. Diantha, however, determines to take charge of her own destiny and after surprising her father by showing that he actually owes *her* for all the housework that she has done, sees this as a means of making a living by undertaking paid housework. This is an attempt to show the value that should be placed on housework, since Diantha is a trained teacher, but prefers paid housework to teaching. This brought a horrified response from her sister: 'A girl with a good home to live in and another to look forward to – and able to earn money *respectably*! to go out and work like a common Irish girl!'[53]

Diantha's first position is with Mrs Porne, who is finding the experience of keeping house stultifying, and not at all what she had expected from marriage:

> 'Do you love me?' they ask, and, 'I will make you happy!' they say: and you get married – and after that it's Housework! They don't say, 'Will you be my Cook?' 'Will you be my Chambermaid?' 'Will you give up a good, clean well-paid business that you love – that has big hope and power and beauty in it – and come and keep house for me?'
>
> 'Love him? I'd be in Paris this minute if I didn't! What has "love" to do with dust and grease and flies?'[54]

She made the point that while marriage had brought a great change in life-style for her, it had had no similar effects on her husband, 'He hasn't had to change his business'.[55] And, '... if I'd had any idea of what housework was like I'd never have given up architecture to try it.'[56] Diantha changes all this, and with her help in the house Mrs Porne is able to resume her career, though it is worth noting that her husband thought it was suitable because '. . . architecture – that's a business a woman could carry on at home . . .'[57] Furthermore, Diantha does more than merely survive, she succeeds. With the help of her wealthy patrons, she fully organizes housework in the area, giving the girls who work for her a sense of their own dignity and worth, runs a commercial catering business, utilizing her mother's business skills, and eventually a hotel complex. The only dark spot is the fact that Ross wants her to give up her work to marry him: 'No man – that is a man – would marry a woman and let her run a business.'[58] She eventually marries Ross even though he still does not approve of her work, and after two years has a baby son. 'She loved it, nursed it, and ran her business at long range for six months.' It is interesting that Gilman refers to the baby as 'it', and it perhaps reflects what has often been considered to be a lack of genuine maternal feeling on her part.[59] After six months, she moved her baby and nurse to the hotel complex, 'but always in the background was the current of Ross's unspoken disapproval'.[60] For Gilman then, male approval was obviously still seen as valuable. This point is made repeatedly: 'I want him to *approve* of me – not just put up with it, and bear it!'[61] And in the last two pages Ross sees at last the value of what she has been doing:

> . . . what brave, strong, valuable work you have been doing for the world. Doing it scientifically, too. Your figures are quoted, your records studied, your example followed. You have established certain truths in the business of living which are of importance to the race. As a student I recognise and appreciate your work. As man to man I'm proud of you – tremendously proud of you. As your husband! Ah! my love! I am coming back to you . . . coming with my whole heart, yours![62]

These novels, then, illustrate attitudes to role expectation. Angelica does not wish to be restricted by a woman's conventional role, so much so that she resorts to transvestism. Evadne refuses to submit to her parent's wishes and consummate her marriage, though in the process she loses her spiritedness and conforms to convention in that outwardly at least she devotes herself to being a model wife. Diantha rejects the role that she must wait for her future husband to provide for her, but sets off to forge a career for herself through the scientific application of housework. Martha renounces the conventions of her class by working for peace. Fathers in general are shown to be stupid; neither Evadne's, Diantha's nor Martha's are shown to be any matches for their daughters intellectually. The novels are not anti-man, however; it is a certain type of man that they are trying to eradicate. Thus each has at least one example of a sensitive caring, intelligent man. Martha's husband, shares her concerns and hatred of war; Mr Price makes a spirited defence of women in general and Evadne in particular,[63] and Diavolo is imbued with qualities designed to mark him out as a new man; while Ross by the end of the book sees the need for women to have both a career and marriage.

There is also concern to show that women could still be attractive:

> Beauty is a great power, and it may be used for good as well as for evil. Beauty is beneficent as well as malign. Angels are always allowed to be beautiful, and our highest ideal of manhood is associated with physical as well as moral perfection ... Be sure that beauty is a legitimate means of grace; and you who have it should use it as such ... True beauty, I mean of course, ... not the fashionable travesty of it.[64]

If any girls had the stamina to complete the MMLWS's list, then, they would have been presented with all the frustrations and restrictions imposed on Victorian middle-class girls: the denial of education, the lack of intellectual stimulation and personal freedom, the difficulties encountered in trying to enter the world of independent work. They would have been given the idea that the family was an institution which upheld patriarchal authority, an institution through which men exploited women and became their economic masters. Men expected to rule, and women were to submit, whereas individuals should be able to develop their interests and talents in whatever direction these might lie. They should now also be aware of the danger of seeing marriage as their only future, and be in a position, should they wish to do so to reject the ideal of self-sacrifice. The many references in these works to other literature should also have encouraged them to read more widely. The fact that a man's group should have been encouraging young women to read such material says much for their liberal feminist stance.

Notes

1. H.G. Wells, *Ann Veronica* (T. Fisher Unwin, 1909), p. 21.
2. Kate Flint, *The Woman Reader 1837–1914* (Oxford: Clarendon, 1993), p. 234.
3. For a full discussion of the MMLWS see F. Montgomery, 'Gender and Suffrage: The Manchester Men's League for Women's Suffrage, 1908–1918' in *Bulletin of the John Rylands University Library of Manchester* (Spring, 1995), forthcoming.
4. Beanland to Prof. and Mrs Merrick, 28/5/1916, MMLWS Correspondence Files. Material on the Manchester Men's League for Women's Suffrage is to be found in the Manchester Men's League for Women's Suffrage Collection, located in John Rylands University Library of Manchester.
5. Letter sent to *Manchester Guardian*, 22 April 1913, MMLWS Correspondence Files, 1913–1914.
6. MMLWS quoting from C.P. Gilman, *Women and Economics* (New York: Torchbook, 1966; 1st edn 1898), p. 56.
7. Beanland to Miss Heyes, 27 Feb. 1915, MMLWS Correspondence Files.

8. Ibid.
9. Ibid.
10. Flint, op. cit., p. 234.
11. Olive Schreiner, *Women and Labour* (T. Fisher Unwin, 1911); see also Gilman, *Women and Economics*.
12. C. Hamilton, *Marriage as a Trade* (The Women's Press, 1981; 1st edn 1909).
13. Beanland to Miss Heyes, 27 Feb. 1915, MMLWS Correspondence Files.
14. C. Lytton, *Prisons and Prisoners* (Virago, 1988; 1st edn Heinemann, London, 1914), p. 157.
15. Letter to Havelock Ellis, 12 May 1890, in Cherry Clayton (ed) *Olive Schreiner* Johannesburg: McGraw Hill, 1983), pp. 114–15.
16. Letter to T. Fisher Unwin, 26 Sept. 1892, in Clayton (ed.) *Olive Schreiner*, pp. 114–15.
17. Lytton, *Prisons and Prisoners*, p. 157.
18. Ibid., p. 158; see also O. Schreiner, *Dreams* (T. Fisher Unwin, 1890), pp. 55–74.
19. Schreiner, *Dreams*, p. 107.
20. Ibid., p. 62.
21. Ibid., pp 109–60.
22. Roger Chickering, *Imperial Germany and a World without War. The Peace Movement and German Society, 1592–1914* (Princeton: Princeton UP, 1975), p. 89.
23. Ibid.
24. B. von Suttner, *Lay Down Your Arms* (London: Longmans, 1894), p. 12.
25. Ibid.
26. Ibid., p. 47.
27. Ibid., p. 52.
28. Sarah Grand, *The Heavenly Twins* (London: Heinemann, 1894), p. 7.
29. Ibid., p. 125.
30. Ibid. Gilman thought that the tomboy state was much more natural for girls; see *Women and Economics*, p. 56.
31. Grand, *The Heavenly Twins*, 255.
32. Ibid., p. 450.
33. Ibid., p. 451.
34. Ibid., p. 453.
35. Ibid., p. 288.
36. Ibid., p. 408.
37. Ibid., p. 254.
38. Ibid., p. 5.
39. Ibid., p. 332.
40. Ibid., pp. 196–7.
41. Ibid., p. 39.
42. Ibid., p. 13.
43. Ibid., p. 24.
44. Ibid., p. 89.
45. Ibid., p. 90.
46. Ibid., pp. 90–1.
47. Ibid., p. 90.
48. Ibid., p. 226.
49. Ibid., p. 226.

50. Ibid., p. 159.
51. This was in marked contrast to C.P. Gilman, *The Crux* (1911) where Dr Jane Bellair makes it quite plan why Vivian should not marry Morton Elder relating her own story in support.
52. Grand, *The Heavenly Twins*, p. 327.
53. C.P. Gilman, *What Diantha Did* (1910), p. 86.
54. Ibid., pp. 74–5.
55. Ibid., p. 74.
56. Ibid., p. 98.
57. Ibid., p. 107.
58. Ibid., p. 230.
59. For a good study of Gilman, see M.A. Hill, *Charlotte Perkins Gilman: The Making of a Radical Feminist, 1860–1896* (1980).
60. Gilman, *What Diantha Did*, p. 256.
61. Ibid., p. 259.
62. Ibid., pp. 261–2.
63. Grand, *The Heavenly Twins*, p. 219.
64. Ibid., pp. 197–8.

Index